John Leifchild

Remarkable Facts

Illustrative and Confirmatory of Different Portions of Holy Scripture

John Leifchild

Remarkable Facts
Illustrative and Confirmatory of Different Portions of Holy Scripture

ISBN/EAN: 9783337107093

Printed in Europe, USA, Canada, Australia, Japan

Cover: Foto ©Lupo / pixelio.de

More available books at **www.hansebooks.com**

REMARKABLE FACTS:

Illustrative and Confirmatory of Different Portions of Holy Scripture.

BY THE LATE
REV. J. LEIFCHILD, D.D.

WITH A PREFACE BY HIS SON.

FIFTH EDITION.

London:
HODDER & STOUGHTON.
27, PATERNOSTER ROW.
MDCCCLXXV.

PREFACE.

THE present volume may be regarded as now first published; for although it was actually printed in 1860, yet the edition was very small, and was limited to a circle of subscribers, amongst the author's private friends, and even these did not receive all the copies which they had requested. The immediate testimonies to the value and usefulness of the work which Dr. Leifchild received were very gratifying to him, insomuch that this last product of his pen, and this latest mental effort of his life, appeared to obtain a readier and heartier reception than the more elaborate publications of his active years. To the writer of this preface it was peculiarly interesting to observe the intense delight with which the aged minister received each additional letter or personal communication, indicating the pleasure that had been felt in reading this work. No one expected a great literary effort from the octogenarian author, and yet perhaps no one of his subscribers was prepared for so well-sustained an exercise of the author's faculties, for such clear details, and such graphic representations of the circumstances connected with each incident and narrative as this book displays. In truth, this last literary project occupied all his thoughts and feeling that it would be really his last work on earth, he busied himself about it during all his remaining days of tolerable health.

His own preface, which follows, will show his precise purpose—to elucidate Scripture by the facts of human experience. This indeed was not only the purpose of the present volume, but also that of the author's entire public ministrations. His love for Scripture was the animating principle of his preaching, the passion of his life, and even the ruling passion at his death. I have elsewhere* recorded one of his expressions during his last illness,—"O this blessed Bible! I should like to die with it in my arms!" Assuredly he did die with it in his heart.

If there be occasionally some lack of vigour in the style of this book, it must be regarded as the work of an octogenarian, and perhaps most readers will think, such lack of vigour in style is replaced and compensated by richness of experience and breadth of observation. A sentence which Dr. Leifchild penned in a blank page, in 1859, may here be quoted as apposite to our remark: "The setting of the jewels

* Memoir of Dr. Leifchild, p. 324.

of Scripture in the right light and proper order, so as to attract every beholder, requires a knowledge of their nature and value, to be learnt only in the school of experience, and at the feet of the Divine Teacher."

From readers in Holland and in France, as well as in various parts of his own country, the venerable author heard with gratification how much pleasure and instruction his book had afforded. The few copies printed seem to have been sent and lent in many and diverse directions, so that, since the author's decease, expressions of a like character have been conveyed even from Australia. So frequent and so urgent were the requests made for copies to Dr. Leifchild, that he proposed to publish the work, but his illness and decease prevented the accomplishment of that purpose.

His son, however, has always intended to execute his father's design. As this book derived none of its acceptance from temporary circumstances, and as the author himself observed, "The Bible will never be out of date, or cease to be supremely useful, if seriously and judiciously applied," it is thought that the publication of this volume exactly as it was at first printed, will prove acceptable and beneficial to a large class of readers. To have added to its pages might have been no difficult task, but there is an individuality about the book which would be marred by miscellaneous additions; and moreover it is now invested with a simple sanctity which places it beyond attempts at improvement, and which seems to forbid the touch of other hands.

Numerous letters which Dr. Leifchild received showed that the readers of this volume regarded it as the result of his long and matured experience, and in this lies the charm and special character of the book. The writer of these lines, therefore, feels confident that he ought to content himself with this preface, and, as he concludes it, presents one out of many of the letters alluded to, as an illustration of the manner in which the volume was received by the original subscribers.

"BEDWELL PARK, HATFIELD,
"*January*, 1861.

"MY DEAR DR. LEIFCHILD,

"I have been reading with great interest your volume of anecdotes connected with passages of the Bible, and I cannot tell you how interested I am in it.

"I don't know when anything has struck me as more calculated to do good. I thought, as I felt it, you would permit me to say so to you.

"I hope you are as vigorous in body as you can hope to be, and as joyful in spirit as you can wish to be.

*　　　*　　　*　　　*　　　*

"Most truly yours,
"C. E. EARDLEY.

"REV. DR. LEIFCHILD."

Sir Culling Eardley, Bart., had been much associated with Dr. Leifchild during the formation of the Evangelical Alliance and had attended the first meeting held to establish it, at Craven Chapel, of which Dr. Leifchild was at that time the minister. They never met again on earth after the above letter was written.

Other communications to the author testify to a similar pleasure in perusing this volume, and it is now hoped that a widely extended interest in it will be promoted by its publication.

J. R. LEIFCHILD.

AUTHOR'S PREFACE.

THE explanation and application of the principles of Holy Scripture form the great purpose of a Christian minister's life. The public ministrations of the pulpit are the principal means for its accomplishment; but there are other and auxiliary methods which he does not fail to employ for the same object. By conversation, he seeks to instil the sentiments of Scripture into the minds of those who listen to him; by the pen, he endeavours to teach those who are not within reach of his voice; and by the pen, also, he hopes to be a silent teacher of the same truths which his living voice once proclaimed, when that voice shall no longer be heard upon the earth.

In the prosecution of his high purpose, he possesses advantages that are peculiar to his sacred calling; for it may be said, without presumption, that in the daily exercise of its more private duties, he acquires a deeper insight into human nature, and a profounder knowledge of the operations of providence and grace, than are common to men in general.

Such advantages the author of the present volume has received, and gratefully acknowledges. In the course of a ministry protracted for a considerable period, he met with numerous instances of providential and gracious interposition, which he recorded at the time for his own use, and by which he was directed, encouraged, and animated in his work. A selection from these, with some other of a kindred nature that were brought under his notice, he has embodied in the ensuing pages, in the hope that they may prove alike useful to others. They are arranged under appropriate passages of Scripture, which, after BRIEF EXPOSITIONS of their primary import, they serve still further to elucidate, confirm, and seal upon the heart.

The habit of elucidating Scripture by the facts of human experience is in several ways productive of benefit. It invests the facts themselves with significance and interest, as illustrating the principles of Holy Writ and renewing their impression. It recalls by their occurrence the Scripture to mind, as one thing always suggests another with which it has been associated. The text is thus before us, and the commentary that unfolds and applies its truth. For the want of such a habit, the most instructive providences may be passed by unheeded, the most salutary warnings be disregarded, and portions of Scripture be left out of sight, whose presence, for guidance, comfort, and solace, would prove an inestimable blessing. Should these pages contribute to promote and extend the formation of such a habit, the design of their author will be answered and his labour be abundantly recompensed.

The Bible, it should be remembered, will never be out of date, or cease to be supremely useful, if seriously and judiciously applied for the purposes that have been mentioned.

Its principles are universally applicable, its counsels salutary, and its discoveries ever new and interesting. No discoveries by human intelligence can supersede those of Divine revelation for the welfare, happiness, and dignity of the human race. The progressive history of the world will serve at every stage to develop more clearly the infinite wisdom, justice, goodness, and mercy displayed in the pages of inspiration; and upon the employment of any method that can be devised for bringing them to answer their designed ends, the benediction of their adorable Author may be confidently anticipated. To Him be glory !

J. L.

4, Fitzroy Terrace,
   Primrose Hill.

CONTENTS.

	PAGE
The Self-sowing Seed. (Gen. i. 11.)	1
The Awfulness of the Deluge Illustrated. (Gen. vi. 13.)	7
The Hardening of the Heart. (Exod. ix. 12.)	17
Sin brought to Remembrance. (Num. xxxii. 23.)	23
Maternal Piety rewarded. (1 Sam i. 27, 28.)	32
Perfect Resignation. (Job i. 21.)	39
The Preciousness of Life. (Job ii. 4.)	45
The Recompense of Uprightness. (Job v. 26.)	53
Remarkable Dreams. (Job xxxiii. 14, 15.)	67
Divine Teaching. (Job xxxvi. 22.)	78
The Susceptibility of the Young. (Ps. xxxiv. 11.)	95
Avarice and Bountifulness. (Ps. xxxix. 6.)	105
Seasonable Succour. (Ps. xlvi. 1.)	118
Extremes of Trial. (Ps. lxvi. 12.)	128
The Marvels of Grace. (Ps. lxxi. 7.)	134
Remembered Preservations, etc. (Ps. ciii. 2-4.)	142
Light in Darkness. (Ps. cxix. 130.)	154
The Backslider Restored. (Prov. xiv. 14.)	162
Successful Reproofs. (Prov. xxviii. 23.)	171
The Vanity of Human Pursuits. (Eccles. ii. 17.)	182
Sowing and Finding. (Eccles. xi. 1.)	189
The Soul's Mirror. (Eccles. xii. 14.)	193
Premonitions. (Isa. xxx. 21.)	201

	PAGE
Marvellous Issues. (Isa. xxviii. 29.)	210
The Soul's Triumph over the Body. (Isa. xl. 29–31.)	215
Special Answers to Prayer. (Ezek. xxxvi. 37.).	228
Youthful Disciples. (Luke x. 21.).	239
Christian Boldness. (Acts v. 20.)	252
The Converted Persecutor. (Acts ix. 6.).	257
A Word in Season. (2 Cor. iv. 2.).	264
Life in Death. (2 Cor. iv. 16.)	269
Providence and Grace conjoined. (2 Cor. xi. 25.).	285
Filial Piety honoured. (Eph. vi. 2, 3.)	296
The Spiritual Rest. (Heb. iv. 3.)	302
The Faithful Promiser. (Heb. x. 23.).	307
Ennobling Examples. (Heb. xiii. 7, 8.)	310

Brief Expositions of Scripture

ILLUSTRATED.

GENESIS.

The Self-sowing Seed.

"And God said, Let the earth bring forth grass, the herb yielding seed, and the fruit tree yielding fruit after his kind, whose seed is in itself: and it was so."—GEN. i. 11.

THE self-propagating power of herbs and plants, by means of their seeds, is an admirable provision of the Creator for the perpetuation of their species. They thus continue of themselves from generation to generation, and would so continue, independently of man, for the future. He may aid, indeed, in their cultivation and propagation; but if there were not a man upon the earth, they would still clothe it with verdure and adorn it with beauty.

Naturalists have been struck with the proofs of infinite wisdom and goodness in these minute objects of creation, not less, if not even more, than in the vast and stupendous bodies in the firmament above and on the earth beneath. In the herb, "whose seed is in itself, and yieldeth after its kind," may be seen a world of wonders. For not only is the seed produced in itself, but sown by itself, also. In countless ways, and in a diversity of operations, it is its own sower. Sometimes it is found on the summit of elastic spires, to be agitated by the winds, which, when it is fully prepared, carry it forth in currents of air even to other regions. Sometimes birds of the air and beasts of the field convey it in their systems to different places by a mysterious process, which prevents it, while administering to their nourishment, from being injured, and even helps to its being quickened in its vegetative powers. It even floats upon the water as well as the air, in which case it is provided with a covering which is insoluble, and operates not *till* it strikes against a hard substance and is broken, when it lets forth its contents, which adhere to the substance; and by this means the dry coral rocks are clothed with verdure, and the island rises above the surface of the ocean adorned with a living green. These facts, with numerous others of a like nature, are open to the most careless observer; but he who enters into them will discover the proofs of a power which baffles all calculation, added to the most consummate art, proclaiming a divine Author, whom if he refuses to acknowledge, he may cease to study his works, for creation teaches him in vain.

> "To study God, God's student, man, was made,
> To read him, as in nature's text conveyed;
> Not as in Heaven, but as He did descend
> To earth, his easier book; where to suspend
> And save his miracles, each little flower,
> And lesser stem, shows his familiar power."

A testimony to the benefit of such study was borne by one who was well known to me, and who communicated to me the particulars of his life. He had at an early period given way to a sceptical turn of mind, which led him into avowed and practical Atheism. In this state of mind, he was a wanderer in Australia, which was then far from being known to our countrymen as it has now been for some time. Having discarded the idea of a Deity from his mind, he sought to occupy his attention and divert his thoughts by the novel scenes and objects that presented themselves to his notice in his wanderings. After a long time spent in this desultory way, his mind took a more deeply reflective and meditative turn, and by a series of incidents, instructive and monitory, and some of them remarkably suited to the awakening of his mind, he became a devout Theist, and eventually a genuine disciple and diligent teacher of Divine Revelation, in which capacity I was acquainted with him. I give the account of one of these incidents at some length, in his own words.

"The several particulars of the belief of the being of God obtaining its first thorough and settled hold of my mind were as follows :—I had, in the course of my occupation, to take a journey of several days across a very barren and thinly inhabited tract of country. I set out on the morning of a day as close and sultry as can well be imagined. As the day advanced, it fulfilled to the utmost its early promise. Long before noon, I was so thirsty that, although I could see, by the sandiness of the soil and formation of the country, that there was but little hope of success in meeting with either a running stream or lodgment of water, I could not refrain from every now and then tracing down the flats and the beds of creeks, in search of relief. Noon came, and still every fresh experiment ended only in a further disappointment. On I toiled over the sterile and stony ranges and across lower tracts of deep, hot sand ; for the most part, too, through a country where the timber was so stunted as to cast no serviceable shade. The sky was cloudless, the sun like a ball of fire, the earth and atmosphere glowing with heat, and not a breath of air stirring.

"At length I cast myself down beneath the most shady tree I could find, unable to hold out any longer, and determined to await the cool of the evening. As I lay thus, after some time, I saw the seed stem of a little plant, close before me, move in the slightest degree several times, each time accompanying the motion with a single low, sharp sound, like the tick of a watch. Interested to discover the connection of the motion and the sound, I leaned over and examined it. It was a small plant with a short and more than proportionally thick flower-stem, having a single seed-pod at the extremity. The seed-pod was an oblate spheroid, not much larger than a garden pea; but it was composed of a number of sections, which, shrinking as it ripened, separated themselves from one another; and, finally, each section detached itself at the bottom of the stalk, which ran right through to the upper side, and sprang out, nearly straightening itself, so that eventually, when all the sections had extended themselves, it would be something like an open umbrella. But to the extremity of each of these sections, before it sprung out, on the inside, was attached a single small round seed, which was cast, by the spring of the section to which it belonged, to a considerable distance. I struck the stem lightly, and thus artificially expedited the process of disjunction, and found that the seeds were thrown out upwards of two feet. On paying close attention to the plant itself, I observed that its stem was so stiff that the wind could have no power to sway it to and fro and thus scatter the seed; so low, likewise, that amid the surrounding grass the wind would scarcely ever reach it in force sufficient to carry the seed away; and, lastly, that it was placed in the midst of leaves all spreading upwards and outwards in a funnel form from the root, so that if the seed were not cast beyond them, they would catch and carry it back again to the bosom of the plant itself. The disadvantage thus was threefold, and so complete in the whole as to bar this little fraction of nature from the performance of one of its grand generic offices, that of properly depositing its seeds. Nothing could relieve it but some mechanical contrivance. And here was that mechanical contrivance; and not only was it a contrivance in itself, but there was design and adaptation in fixing the very juncture of its operations. The seed should not be thrown off till it was ripe; and till it was so ripe that its very reservoir began to separate into fragments, this mechanical contrivance could not act. The completion of the ripening process was the condition on which the contrivance for scattering the seed depended for coming into action. It was an instance of design and contrivance so indubitable that there was no leaving it to be accounted for in any way but by the agency of a God.

"The effect on me at the time was highly gratifying and cheering. I immediately bethought myself that *He* who thus carefully anticipated, and sagaciously and faithfully provided for, the exigencies of a lonely plant in the wilderness, whose only use seemed to be to blossom and perfume for a few short days the breath of the vagrant air, or perhaps add the tenth of a mouthful to the provender of some stray forager of an unreclaimed land—that *He* could by no means be ignorant of, or forget or despise, the wants of his human creatures.

"But I thought, that is only a partial view of the case—that little plant has done something more. It has answered a much loftier end. It has acted this very hour upon my mind. It has had the ear of the soul, and determined one of its most important decisions. Can it be a true thing that it has told me? Let me know this before I conclude any further. What *it* tells me all nature tells me too. I never looked closely at the question as I now do for the first time; but I knew before these same marks of contrivance discernible in all things. I am full of them myself. The human frame alone is a work of many volumes, all indicating an origin from design and wisdom and benevolence as their ultimate proposition. Reason, impartially applied, never swerves from this declaration for an instant. Can then the most universally-testified truth of all truths that could be picked out, be unworthy of credit? There is not a bird, not a tree, not a rock in the bowels of the earth, but has its peculiar task assigned to it, with functions fit for its task in the material system. But besides the peculiar duty of each in its relative physical position, all concur in their one great office of *attesting* to MAN a CREATOR. There must be a Creator."

He travelled nearly a hundred miles in search of the volume of inspiration, which he at length obtained, purchased, and pursued with great eagerness. It was as a delicious spring to a newly-awakened thirst. And now the desire arose in his soul to return home, which was excited by a passage in the history of the cure of the lunatic by Christ, who on wishing to remain with him, was directed first to go home and inform his friends and the members of his own household of the change that had been wrought. This he had done when he was introduced to my knowledge, and received into our communion. His zeal was such as led him at once to engage as a visitor in a society for the instruction of the ignorant around, which he attended to with great assiduity. I was delighted with his strong sense and decision of character, and assisted him in obtaining encouragement as an author. About this time a young man of great literary attainments, and a constant writer in one of our best periodicals, fell ill with over-exertion, and was obliged for a while to desist. He had imbibed infidel sentiments; but on one Sabbath morning in his wanderings, he heard a sermon which struck him forcibly, and he applied to me, through his sister, for some information respecting the preacher. On learning his state, both mentally and physically, I spoke to our friend from Australia to be his visitor and instructor. He attended him for several months diligently. Their conversation was close on the most serious points, and by slow degrees the scepticism of the inquiring sufferer yielded to the cheering and life-giving influence of the truths of the glorious Gospel. From that time he began a "Diary," reporting the gradual transition of his mind from doubt to certainty, in which the most subtle objections were stated and refuted. This diary, which was presented to me after his decease, I have still by me, and it may one day see the light. Our friend was thus the instrument of converting one who had gone astray like himself, from the error of his way, and of bringing him into the path that leadeth to everlasting life.

---o---

The Awfulness of the Deluge Illustrated.

"And God said unto Noah . . . Behold, I, even I, do bring a flood of waters upon the earth, to destroy all flesh, wherein is the breath of life, from under heaven; and everything that is in the earth shall die. But with thee will I establish my covenant; and thou shalt come into the ark, thou, and thy sons, and thy wife, and thy sons' wives with thee."—GEN. vi. 13, 17, 18.

THIS account of the most stupendous calamity that has transpired on our globe should inspire us with emotions of reverence and awe at the Divine judgments, and yet with adoring wonder at God's condescension and mercy. And this it would almost invariably accomplish, were the Scripture narrative simply credited. But, unhappily, such questions have been suggested on reading it, and such different solutions of them proposed as to the extent of the Deluge, the time of its duration, and its immediate causes, as to embarrass the mind, and to prevent its making a due impression.

The best remedy perhaps against this would be to peruse the account of some more recent calamity of the same nature, on a limited scale, graphically depicted, and to transfer the impressions thus derived to the Flood of Noah, as brought before us in the sacred page.

Such a catastrophe was the great flood at St. Petersburgh in Russia, in the year 1824—of which we have a minute account from actual witnesses, republished in this country, and confirmed, and still more particularised, as it has been to myself, by some friends who were resident on the spot at the awful juncture, and were powerfully affected by its devastations.

"In the previous autumn," says the narrative, "the weather had been unusually tempestuous through the whole of Europe. The wind, which set in from the west, blew with resistless force from that quarter, so that the waves of the Atlantic were driven into the bosom of the North Sea, thus mightily swelling the waters of that vast expanse, and these in their turn poured their surcharge into the Baltic, and from thence into the gulf of Finland, close to St. Petersburgh."

"On the morning of the 19th of November," writes Dr. Patterson, who, with Dr. Henderson, was residing there as a principal agent of the Bible Society in that city, under the patronage of the Emperor Alexander, "the wind became a perfect hurricane. The water of the canal before the Bible House rose very fast, and I soon perceived it to be up to the street, which lay higher than most parts of the city. All the men on the premises, nearly one hundred, were ordered to remove the thousands of bound Scriptures, ready for dispersion, to the highest part of the building; the gates were shut, and secured with planks and earth; the common sewers stopped up, and every means resorted to that could be thought of to keep out the enemy. For two hours we succeeded, but the water then rose to about four feet in the streets, undermined our garden wall, and rushed with violence against the door of the building where the men were at work, shutting them all in, so that they were obliged to escape through the window, up to the waist in water, to gain the second floor. What a scene now presented itself! —a wide-spread sea of water, stretching out itself on every side, with the houses just appearing above it. The hurricane tore up the fairest and finest trees, and rolled up the iron roof of our building like a sheet of paper, carrying it away in the air. Fear was on every side at the devastation which was now being made. We saw one of the sentry-boxes on the other side of the canal swimming down the stream, and another, with the policeman himself inside, fairly carried off along the side of the street, where, passing a poor fellow wading up to the neck in water, he took hold of him and saved his life. The kitchen and lodging apartments had several feet of water in them, and in some up to the very roof. The large, heavy barks in the river were lifted high, and thrown down upon the shore. All the horses that were kept in the stables were drowned; those that were let loose swam for their lives and were saved. The soldiers on sentry, not being relieved, nor daring to stir, stood till the waves flowed over them, and buried them in the midst. Boats were got out, but it was impossible for them to live, except in the shelter of the few neighbouring houses, and hundreds perished by overcrowding into them. Many log houses on the island were lifted from their foundations and carried into the stream, with their inhabitants on their roofs, where several of them met with a watery grave. Whole villages, with houses, people, and animals were swept away. The prisoners in the fortress were drowned. Churchyards near the river were torn open, and the remains of the dead either swept into the river, or deposited with their coffins in the streets. One I saw, of a poor Englishman, who had been buried but a few days before, lying in the street, with his name and age fresh upon it. The coffin of a newly buried and dearly loved child came swimming in at the windows of the still weeping parents, and dismay and terror were depicted on every countenance.

"But much as St. Petersburgh suffered, Cronstadt, from its lying lower, suffered still more. The hills were covered with the waves, which threatened to submerge the whole island. Ships of war were driven from their moorings, and set down high and dry upon the land. One of them of a hundred guns was never got off. Stacks of corn were borne to a great distance, and cattle buffeting the torrent were mingled with the corpses of persons drowned or at their last gasp. The Emperor, in a shattered state of health, beheld the tumultuous scene with the greatest consternation. Wringing his hands, he cried, It has come upon us for our sins; and lifting them up to heaven, he implored the Almighty to let his anger fall on his devoted head, but to spare his people.

"The day wore away towards the afternoon, and still the waters continued rising. What, had they continued rising during the following night and day, would have been seen but a universal wreck? But about four o'clock, P.M., just as the greatest consternation was prevailing—just when deliverance was most needed to prevent the entire destruction of the city,—at that moment, the bow of promise appeared. One of the most beautiful rainbows was seen stretched across the sky. It was as a voice from heaven testifying to the mercy and faithfulness of that God who declared to Noah that the waters should never again overflow the earth. Encouraged by this token of peace, every one looked up, and lo! the rising of the water was stayed! Hope was kindled in many an anxious breast, and they who feared the Lord gave thanks to his name, saying, 'He retaineth not his anger for ever, because he delighteth in mercy.'

"Great were the depredations occasioned in these few hours. Houses thrown down, or rendered unfit for habitation; bridges broken, and roads strewed with ruins everywhere met the view. Dead corpses and pallid living sufferers in all parts made their appearance. In Cronstadt, five hundred persons perished, and in St. Petersburgh, one thousand; besides many others who were disabled and maimed for life. It was reported that the Emperor publicly avowed it as a judgment for their sin in having not long before refused to assist the Greek Christians at Constantinople in a dire and overwhelming persecution of them by the Turks. 'Righteous art thou, O Lord, in thy judgments, and in the desolations thou hast made on the earth.'"

Yet many were the instances in which mercy rejoiced against judgment. The following touching one is recorded by my esteemed friend, Mrs. Henderson, an eye and ear-witness of the transactions she relates. "Early in the morning, before the wind had risen so high as to give any indication of the coming catastrophe, a poor German mechanic and his wife, who resided in a low part of the city, were obliged to go out on business. They were pious and industrious, and much respected by the religious community to which they belonged. The wife had risen betimes, dressed her two little children, given them their breakfast, and was prepared to leave them at home for as short a time as possible, at most for two or three hours. The children, a little boy five years of age, and his sister a year younger, were the joy of their fond parents' hearts; and when the mother turned the key of the door to depart with her husband, she inwardly commended her beloved ones to the care of her Heavenly Father.

"They took their way, confident of his love and care, to that part of the city to which their business called them, and which was known by the name of the Nevesky, a street running in a direct line from the Admiralty, and familiar to all who have viewed the beautiful metropolis of the Russian Empire. On reaching the house to which they were journeying, they proceeded to transact the business that required their attention, and were so engrossed by it, as not to observe the gentle but rapid encroachment of the unwonted tide. On opening the door they beheld, to their surprise and consternation, the flood as it covered the ground rising higher and higher, and threatening destruction to man and beast. The first impulse of the father was to wade through the water, then knee-deep, to the rescue of his children; but the idea seemed hopeless, for the room in which he had left them was so situated partly below the level of the ground, and in a low quarter of the town, that the water must have entered it and done its fatal work. And then his dear wife; if he were to leave her, what must be the event? No one could tell how far the waters might prevail, and should he abandon his beloved partner, she might be drowned in his absence, and have none to deliver her. On her part she durst not urge her husband to venture, lest his life should be sacrificed in the attempt. They looked at each other in perplexity and disquietude, and then turned their eyes upwards in silent prayer to Him whose arm is not shortened that it cannot save, nor his ear heavy that it cannot hear.

"In their distress they hastened to make known to those dwelling on the premises where they were staying the alarming condition of their children, inquiring of them if they could suggest anything to be done, if not too late, to save their lives. Alas! the families to whom they applied, though they pitied them, were unable to help them, being intent on saving their own relatives, their merchandize, books, property, and whatever would be damaged by contact with water. Convinced by experience how vain is the help of man, they felt that their only resource was in prayer, not for the life of their children, for that they could not hope for, but that themselves might be prepared to resign them, and to say with the bereaved Patriarch, 'The Lord gave, and the Lord hath taken away, blessed be the name of the Lord.' Thus watching, praying, and searching the Scriptures for some word of comfort, and endeavouring to console one another, they passed the weary hours, waiting with anxious longing for the waters to subside. At four o'clock in the afternoon, as we have seen, the tempest abated, and the waters began sensibly and rapidly to decrease. The flood had risen, indeed, within a single step of the apartment occupied by the writer of this narrative, and the whole family felt how seasonable was *their* deliverance. Mournfully tempered, however, were the joyful feelings of the agonized parents, whose gratitude for their personal preservation was mingled with the bitter prospect of finding their darling children lying pale and cold and lifeless in a watery tomb.

Three painful hours elapsed before it was safe for them to venture through the water yet in the streets, to the humble dwelling that contained all they held dear on earth. They reached the door, and as it moved heavily on its hinges, the mother's heart fainted and almost died within her. They looked in and saw the bodies of their dear ones, stretched out upon a small round table, motionless and locked in each other's arms. No water covered them, but on looking up it was evident from the state of the room that the flood had reached far above the height of the table, and that the rest of the furniture had been completely under water. The fatal consequences seemed inevitable. The father approached the table; he looked at his children—they breathed; he laid his hand upon them—they were warm; they were in a sweet sleep. 'Miracle of mercy!' he exclaimed. 'The God of love,' said the mother, in a transport of joy, 'be praised!' Yet how can it be? Surely their senses have deceived them, and they are in an illusion! Then by an instinct they were prompted at all hazards to dispel it, and roused the lovely little sleepers from their tranquil slumber. On opening their eyes and recognising their parents, they clung to them with fond delight, interrupting, however, the caresses bestowed upon them by complaints of hunger and urgent cries for food. Some remains of biscuit from the mother's pocket were instantly shared between them, and after a short while they sought to solve the mystery of their preservation, by asking them what they had been doing, and what had happened to them during their absence.

"'When you and father,' said the boy, 'were gone, we played about the room. The water began to come in under the door, and I got some chips of wood, and sissy and I played at ships, and the ships sailed along *so prettily*. Then the water came over our shoes, and we got up on that chair, and when it came up a little more we got frightened, and so we got up on the table, where it could not hurt us, and played on the table; and when we were very hungry we laid ourselves down and went to sleep, till you and father came home.' From this recital, and from the fact of the surface of the table being dry, it was apparent that when the water had risen to its height it had lifted it up, like a little raft, bearing up its precious burden, while in its subsidence it was let gently down, and the slumbering babes were unconsciously and wonderfully preserved, to be restored to the arms of their praying parents. They were joined by their neighbours in the adoring exclamation, 'What hath God wrought!'" Thus ends the narrative.

It will surely not be difficult after this to form a lively conception of the consternation of the inhabitants of the world at the time of the Great Deluge. We may see their terror-stricken countenances as they found at last all their hopes of the waters subsiding, or, at least, ceasing to increase, failing them, and their worst fears being realized. All efforts are directed to find some means of escape from the encroaching enemy, or of braving its fury. One lofty precipice after another is scaled; the summits of the mountains are swarming with terrified mortals. Escape is sought by some in the topmost boughs of the loftiest trees, but in vain do they look for help from any quarter, and their mutual inability to afford any relief or succour heightens their agony. Refuge fails them, and they sink in all directions the victims of despair. A picture in the Louvre, some years ago, struck every spectator on entering, as it did me, with a feeling of terror. It was of the Deluge rising to its height. Among the vain fugitives from the pursuing waves, spent, overcome, and exhausted, appeared in the topmost bough of a lofty but solitary tree, the aged father of a family, whose household were climbing after him and clinging about him; the bough, which had sustained them all, was seen to be breaking at that moment, by their weight and the agitation of the tempest, and the gulf beneath yawned to receive them.

But while thus realizing the awful spectacle of a perishing world, let us not lose sight of the display of the mercifulness and faithfulness of God in the preservation of Noah and his family in the ark, with the different species of living creatures, for the future repeopling of the earth. They ride securely on the surface of the overflowing waters, looking courageously out at the windows of their new habitation, assured of Divine protection and support, while, as we may well imagine, their adoring anthems of praise and thanksgiving are interspersed with the roaring of the tempest and their sighs for a lost world.

Happy they who, imitating Noah, believe in both the threatenings and promises of the Almighty, being moved with fear by the one, and with hope by the other, to flee unto the refuge which he has provided in the person and mediation of his Son, and are in covenant with God through him! In all times of trouble and calamity they will be lifted up above fear and alarm by the assurance of Divine protection and support, and the hope of arriving at a state of repose and blessedness that will last for ever. Well may they sing, with Luther and his companions, when the world, as he said, was splitting into pieces: "God is our refuge and strength, a very present help in trouble; therefore will not we fear, though the earth be removed, and though the mountains be carried into the midst of the sea: though the waters thereof roar and be troubled, though the mountains shake with the swelling thereof.—The Lord of hosts is with us, the God of Jacob is our refuge. Selah."

EXODUS.

The Hardening of the Heart.

"And the Lord hardened the heart of Pharaoh, and he hearkened not unto them; as the Lord had spoken unto Moses."—EXOD. ix. 12.

"For the Scripture saith unto Pharaoh, Even for this same purpose have I raised thee up, that I might show my power in thee, and that my name might be declared throughout all the earth."—ROM. ix. 17.

THE hardening of Pharaoh's heart which is here in the book of Exodus ascribed to God, is so according to the customary style of speaking in Scripture, which excludes nothing from his sovereign agency, and speaks of what he *permits* to be done, as caused by him. The *history* of Pharaoh makes it evident that the hardening of his heart was owing to the continual return of his cruelty (after all his relentings and promises of compliance with the Divine will), as soon as ever he was "*raised up*" from the judgments that subdued him. The end therefore having been answered, of the display of the power and forbearance of God, he was permitted to remain without any further visitation, and was confirmed in his wickedness.

It is clear from various parts of Scripture that a period may arrive in a man's life, when all warnings have proved fruitless to his amendment, and all calls and overtures of mercy having been trampled upon and rejected, a sentence goes forth for the suspension and cessation of all further influence of that nature; so that his heart settles into a state of callousness, and his character becomes adamant.

The voice of righteous judgment has said, "He that is filthy let him be filthy still."

The possibility of a surrender to such a state in this life is apparent from these declarations of Scripture—"My Spirit shall not always strive with man." "To-day if ye will hear his voice, harden not your hearts." "Lest I swear in my wrath, they shall not enter into my rest." "If thou hadst known, even thou, in this thy day, the things which belong unto thy peace! but *now*, they are hid from thine eyes." Was not the rebellion of the Jews against the Gospel, *after* the pouring out of the Holy Spirit, and the full display of his power and grace, a case of this permitted judicial hardening, so that their impenitence and infatuation remained till the overwhelming destruction of their city and temple? Does not the Apostle afterwards warn the *professing disciples of Christ* among them of such a dangerous state, as the consequence of *Apostasy?* when "it would be impossible to renew them again to repentance!"

Persisting in sin against convictions, warnings, and scriptural knowledge and impressions, may entail upon the individual the withdrawment for ever of all softening influences. Men in such a case are given over to a reprobate mind and an unconquerable induration of heart. Let every trifler with the Word of God be aware of the possibility of such a consequence of procrastination and continuance in impenitence, when a death-like apathy shall steal over his soul to all spiritual things, while he continues alive to all things else. He is like a blighted and withered tree, which retains its form and partial foliage, but death has struck its roots, and its vital sap has ceased to flow.

Many years since, such an instance fell under the observation of the writer. It related to a Mr. K., an individual who had moved in fashionable society, and was related to persons of rank, but who had lived a dissipated life, and had committed forgery to a great extent. He was tried and convicted at the Old Bailey, and sentenced to be hung. One who had known him formerly, and was anxious about his fate, called upon the writer, with whom he was acquainted, and besought him to visit the culprit in the condemned cells of Newgate, with a view of leading him to the important duty of repentance and faith in Christ for pardon. It was thought necessary to dispossess him of a confident hope which he entertained, from the interest made for him by his friends, of a remission of his sentence; since, till that was effected, it was not likely that he would pay a proper attention to the expostulations about to be addressed to him. The Recorder was seen, and it was learnt from him that the Prince Regent, to whom application had been made on his behalf, had *determined*, from the notoriety of his case, to refuse the exercise of the prerogative of mercy.

I found him in the condemned cell, heavily ironed. He was one of the finest men I ever beheld—tall, well dressed in mourning, and having the air of a perfect gentleman. On informing him of the name of his former acquaintance, at whose request and by whose aid I had obtained admission to him, he allowed me to converse with him; but on learning my object, he at once apprised me that it would be in vain, as he could not give his mind to such a subject, till the endeavours making for his release had succeeded, of which he had every reason, from the representations made to him, to be perfectly confident.

Feeling that nothing could be done with him in this state, I cautiously apprised him of our visit to the Recorder, and the result. He turned pale. He saw that he had been deceived, and that his life was indeed in jeopardy. I availed myself of the opportunity to set before him the nature of that much more awful tribunal before which he was to appear, and the tremendously fearful sentence that awaited him there, unless his future Judge should, by his now sincere repentance, faith, and prayer, become his Saviour and Friend. I spoke of his mercifulness and compassion, as evinced in his death upon the cross for sinners, and conjured him at once to betake himself to him for forgiveness and salvation.

He listened to this impatiently, and at length said—" Sir, I appreciate your motive. I am not ignorant of the truths you have been stating. You may be aware, from my name, of my connection with men who have been in high station. I was in my youth the companion of some dignitaries of the Church, and their example had no good effect upon me. You speak of multitudes of sins, but I perceive from your manner that you are little acquainted with iniquity. I could," said he, "unfold to you *depths of iniquity* which would make you stand aghast. But I am not now about to become the pusillanimous creature that calls for pity and mercy, when I know it cannot be shown me. I *cannot* feel; and I *will not* pray. You see that stone," he added, pointing to the pavement on which he stood; "it is an image of the insensibility of my heart to all the impressions you are striving to make."

I thought it best to leave him, but asked permission to see him again. "I am loth," he replied, "to refuse your kindness by a denial; but tell your friend, and assure yourself, it will be all in vain."

When I next saw him, he had learnt the truth of my statement, and received me, I thought, more respectfully. Again I renewed my representations, warnings, and expostulations. At this moment his wife and daughter were introduced to him, and for the first time I saw him shed tears.

They, however, were far less moved; for it appeared that he had for some time abandoned and plundered them. He had robbed his wife of all her jewellery and finery, and had driven past her residence with a female who was dressed in *her* apparel, and calling her to the window to mock her with the spectacle. When they were gone I returned again to my task; but I had not the consolation of perceiving that though he heard me patiently, there was the least glimpse of one soft emotion or feeling. "I told you," he said, when I had done, "it would be all in vain; I am"—looking at me in a most determined manner—" PAST FEELING."

On the evening previous to his execution, I visited him again, and found him in no better state of mind, but considerably agitated with the thought of his approaching doom. "Good God!" said he, taking out his watch and examining the time, "I have but so many hours to live, and then ——!!" I asked if he would allow me to remain with him all night, and attend him in the morning? "If you wish it," said he, "you may, but upon condition that you do not interrupt me for a moment in the last sleep I am ever likely to have!" I was too much overcome myself to press the point, and left him. He remained in the same hardened state in the morning, and so departed out of the world. On the following Sabbath, I preached from the text, "No man can come to me, except the Father which hath sent me draw him;" enforcing, from what I had seen, the danger of sinning away all drawing influence, by which alone the soul can be attracted to Jesus.

Cases of this description are among the most difficult

and painful which ministers of the Gospel are ever called upon to treat. All their efforts to produce impression are met by an inward resistance that chills their zeal and paralyses their spiritual strength. Although it is their duty to persevere and retain hope in God's mercy and grace to the last extremity, yet it is only by special communications of ardent love and strong faith that they can be kept from abandoning such characters in hopeless despair of their salvation. But let the servants of God be strong in his might, for as long as life lasts, even those who seem to be left of God are still to be followed, and the utmost effort made to pluck them as brands from the everlasting burning. The patience and perseverance, accompanied by fervent prayer, which have occasionally been manifested by ministers in these circumstances, have, through the Divine blessing, triumphed, and brought the hardened sinner to the feet of Jesus, weeping and "in his right mind."

NUMBERS.
Sin brought to Remembrance.

"Behold, ye have sinned against the Lord : and *be sure your sin will find you out.*"—NUM. xxxii. 23.

SINS committed secretly, to escape the notice of man, and thought but slightly of on that account, are such a practical denial of the Divine Omniscience as to provoke the Almighty to vindicate that attribute by the employment of unusual means for bringing them to light and making them manifest.

Sometimes it is by a direct excitement of the conscience, when it brings sins to remembrance that had scarcely been thought to be such at the time of their commission, or had hardly ever since recurred to the thoughts in that light. But now they are seen by the mind's eye under that aspect, in all their turpitude and folly, and with all the aggravations of the preceding, attending, and subsequent circumstances, as vividly as though they had been a transaction of yesterday. Nor can the mind get rid of their presence, or of the self-reproach and pain inflicted by it. Though there should be no outward observers or accusers, yet, from the intensity of the recollection, they are ready to suppose there may be in some they meet with, a kindred consciousness of the transaction. Hence a pointed remark in a discourse, or sentence in a book, or the discovery of the same sin in others, will have the effect of exciting the remembrance anew, and of inflicting a fresh sting of remorse.

When the sin has been one of injury to others, the burden of condemnation can sometimes be thrown off only by making confession, and, as far as possible, restitution. Especially do the sins of blood-guiltiness, the only possible witness to which has been removed out of the way, call for this discovering work of Divine Providence, so as to produce a conviction of its immediate agency in the breast of the perpetrator and of others, that has the force of a thousand arguments. When the utmost ingenuity of contrivance has been exerted to secure concealment and to baffle inquiry, and the culprit has preserved a hardened insensibility to his crime, some trivial circumstance has led to a series of connecting links, producing a chain of evidence against him amounting to all but demonstration. So much so is this the case that, on the discovery of the last link completing the chain of evidence, the guilty one has sometimes been constrained to confess the secret that he had kept locked np in his own breast, but which he could no longer retain.

Instances of this kind are so numerous and well known that it is unnecessary to adduce more than one or two, with which the readers of these pages are not likely to be familiar. The reflection naturally arising from them will refer to the infatuation of the human mind, and the power of the great seducer and tempter, who can lead any one to repeat the same actions with the flattering hope of covering them with a veil that shall defy the power of all human penetration; not listening to the warning voice which Moses addressed to the children of Reuben and Gad, "Be sure your sin will find you out;" or to the denunciation of the prophet, "Woe unto them that seek deep to hide their counsel from the Lord, and their works are in the dark, and they say, Who seeth us? and who knoweth us?"

The reflections of the reader will, also, naturally turn on the power of conscience, as thus made manifest. What need of an outward accuser when a man can be made, in the absence of all other witnesses, to accuse himself, and to divulge, sometimes unintentionally, either in sleep, or in some unguarded hour, or only to relieve the mind of painful emotions struggling for vent, crimes that could be told by no other tongue? Blind and insensible indeed must he be who can meditate on these things and not see the proofs they afford of man's moral responsibility, and the preparation making for the decision of a final judgment. Happy, indeed, are they who, by timely confession, repentance, and faith, have obtained a *Divine* forgiveness for the past, and a gracious cleansing for the future. Yet let such ever pray with David, after his repentance and recovery,—"Who can understand his errors? cleanse thou me from secret faults. Keep back thy servant also from presumptuous sins; let them not have dominion over me: then shall I be upright, and I shall be innocent from the great transgression."

A late respectable minister gives the following account, which was published in a periodical of limited circulation:— " I was once applied to by a stranger, in a place where I was labouring for a few Sabbaths only, for the sight of a letter which I had received, calumniating his character. I looked at the man and pitied him, and coolly replied, it would be a breach of the common principles of society to show confidential letters, written to us for the purpose of doing people good. He retorted in an angry tone,—' I demand a sight of it, sir, as an act of justice due to an injured man. I replied, ' How did you know that I had received a letter concerning you?' 'Know,' said he, 'it was impossible not to know it; your language and manner were so pointed, that it was impossible I should be deceived.' I rejoined, 'Do not be too positive : you have been deceived before now, I suppose: you may be so again.' 'It is not possible,' said he. 'You described the sin of which I am accused in the clearest language, and looking me in the face and pointing towards me, you said, "Sinner, be sure your sin will find you out." I therefore expect from you, sir, as a gentleman and a Christian minister, that you will give me a sight of the letter, that I may know its contents and repel its charges.' I observed, 'I do not know your name ; to my knowledge, I never saw you before: and as you have not told me in what part of the sermon I was so pointed, if I show you any letter, I may show you the wrong one; I shall, therefore, certainly not exhibit any of my letters to you, nor satisfy you, till you describe the case alluded to.' He hesitated, but afterwards described the sin of which he was accused. When he had finished, looking him full in the face, and assuming a solemnity of manner and tone of voice, I said, 'Can you look me in the face, as you must do your Judge at the great day, and declare that *you are innocent* of the sin laid to your charge?' He trembled, turned pale, and his voice faltered; guilt and anger struggled in his breast, and summoning up his remaining courage, he answered, 'I am not bound to make any man my confessor, and if I were guilty, no man has a right to hold me up to public observation as you have done.' I then assumed a benignity of countenance, and softened my tones, saying, 'Do you believe the passage I have cited, " Be sure your sin will find you out," is the word of God?' He answered, 'It may be so.' 'Surely it is, said I ; '"He that planted the ear, shall he not hear? he that formed the eye, shall he not see?" Can he have any difficulty in bringing your sin to light? Now, I will tell you honestly, that I never received any letter or any information about you, but I am persuaded *your* sin *has* found you out: the preaching of the word is one method by which God makes a man's sins thus manifest to him. Let me entreat you seriously to consider your state and character: who can tell? God may have intended this sermon for your good; he may mean to have mercy upon you: this may be the means of saving your body from the gallows, and your soul from hell; and let me remind you that you are not there yet, there still is hope.' He held down his head, clenched his hands one into the other, and bursting into tears, said, 'I have never met with anything like this. I certainly am obliged to you for your friendship. I am guilty, and hope this conversation will be of essential advantage to me.'"

I recollect on one occasion particularly, after having preached a sermon on the power of conscience to bring forgotten or covered sins to a vivid and terrifying remembrance, and after calling upon the conscience of any such one present to perform its office—receiving a letter on the following morning from a young naval officer, complaining of my unmanliness in exposing some parts of his life to a public congregation, and, forgetting the sacredness of my office, threatening me with a challenge for the insult, unless I made an apology. His relative whom he accompanied to the place of worship was acquainted with me, and he concluded that she had made me aware of some peculiarities in his career, which then occurred to him in a more painful light than they had ever done before. It was not without difficulty that in the presence of his relative, who averred that she had never spoken to me on the subject, and my own positive declaration of the most entire ignorance of his character, he became convinced of the power of the Word of God to reveal men to themselves, that they might be brought to confess and forsake their sins, and turn unto the Lord who will have mercy upon them, and to our God, who will abundantly pardon.

One Sabbath evening I was preaching at Kensington on behalf of a society for visiting and relieving the sick poor at their own habitations. I selected for my text a passage in the book of Ecclesiastes,—"In the day of prosperity be joyful, but in the day of adversity consider : God also hath set the one over against the other, to the end that man should find nothing after him." My reflections were directed to the illustration of the twofold method of Divine Providence employed in leading sinners to repentance,— first, by forbearance and mercy, drawing them to obedience with "cords of a man, with bands of love." In illustration of this principle, it was shown that in a great many cases God showers upon men the blessings of prosperity and earthly happiness, making their cup overflow with benefits, that he may allure them to love and serve him ; but that too often even his goodness fails to lead them to repentance, and is rather abused by them to the increase of their guilt and condemnation. The second illustration of the text which I employed was derived from the Divine chastisements and judgments inflicted in various ways, providential, physical, or mental, but all designed to awaken the conscience, humble the heart, and constrain the offender to implore the exercise of the Divine mercy. I observed that, in too many instances, both these methods seem to fail of working any salutary change in the hearts of men. They were neither affected by God's goodness nor awed into penitence by his corrections. They "knew not the rod, or who had appointed it," but pursued their own course, forgetful of the past and heedless of the future. It was added, that God did not even then give up sinners, or leave them as being utterly hopeless, but sometimes employed the very trumpet of judgment to rouse their torpid consciences and to summon them to behold the inevitable consequences of final impenitence.

At this point of the discourse, I said, "Both the wooing and the warning voice may have been unheeded hitherto by some present, and, for aught you can tell, the next voice that addresses you may be that of the commissioned angel, saying, 'Come to judgment!'" At these words, a soldier, who was seated in the midst of the congregration, suddenly started up, and exclaimed with great vehemence, "O sir, say not so—say not so—oh, stop!" The assembly was confused, but upon my motioning to him and them to be still, became composed. I then observed that it is the great privilege and happiness of a Christian minister to be authorized to assure all who are pained with a sense of guilt and with apprehensions of impending judgment, and all who are tremblingly anxious to know what they must do to be saved, that, whatever their guilt, there is free pardon for them in Jesus Christ, if they will repent and accept his grace.

After proceeding for some time in this strain, I said, "But to return"—— "Oh, pray, sir," exclaimed the soldier, who had been standing all the while in evident consternation, "do not return!" I then found it necessary to address him more seriously. I told him he was disturbing a religious assembly and rendering himself amenable to the law; that he must, therefore, either remain quiet and allow me to finish my discourse, or leave the place, as he could not be permitted to renew the disturbance. He then sat down : the service was closed somewhat abruptly, and the collection for the charity was made. I was soon informed that the soldier, on leaving, had put his watch into the plate as a contribution. I requested that he should be called back. Presently, he stood before me, and proved to be an intelligent, well-behaved young Scotchman. As soon as I recognised the latter circumstance, I remarked, that I was surprised, considering the manner in which, as a Scotchman, he must have been brought up, that he should have behaved in so inconsiderate a manner during the period of God's worship, as he might have had an opportunity of making known his feelings to me afterwards in private. His eyes appeared red and swollen, as if he had wept much, and, with great emotion, he replied,—"Sir, you would have done the same had you been in my situation." I appeared surprised, and he added, with increased emotion,—"I had a dear mother, who trained me up religiously and tenderly. I fear that the bad habits I had contracted in mixing with depraved soldiers and dissolute persons hastened her death. She said to me, with her dying breath "—— and here his sobs and tears prevented his utterance for awhile. When he had regained his self-possession, he proceeded,—"She said to me, 'Promise me you will never be a soldier, and that you will forsake all evil company.' I took her clay-cold hand in mine, and made the promise, which seemed to relieve her. Oh, if I had but kept it! but I have broken my word, and for some time now have been leading a sad and strange life! But lately I have thought a good deal on my ways, and hearing that there was to be a service here this evening, such as I used to attend in my native country, I came to listen. As you proceeded, sir, my sins came to my remembrance, and when you spoke so solemnly of a voice of a different nature that would succeed yours, I felt as if some hindrance had fallen from my ears, and in one of them my mother was crying, 'Don't be a soldier;' and in the other your words were again sounding loudly, 'Come to judgment!' If the world had been given me to sit still, I could not have done it." "But what," I remarked, "made you put your watch into the plate?" He replied, "Didn't we sing at the last, that 'we should give him all,' and I had nothing else to give." His watch, of course, was restored, and I dismissed him with some friendly and affectionate counsel, inviting him to call upon me on the morrow. It appeared, however, that he belonged to a recruiting party which had been staying in the town, and had been ordered to depart ere he could comply with my invitation. I afterwards made all possible inquiries concerning him, but the utmost information I could obtain was, that he became an altered man and had procured his discharge from the army.

In the foregoing narrative we have an instance of the fidelity of conscience, the power of memory, and the irresistible energy of the Divine Word to quicken both into action, and constrain their guilty subject to cry for mercy. But what disclosures await the last day, when sentence must be pronounced on every soul of man! and all consciences which have not been cleansed from their defilement and deprived of their tormenting power by the precious blood of Christ, must present their fearful accounts and assert their avenging right to punish those who through life have despised God's vicegerent in the human soul!

I. SAMUEL.

Maternal Piety Rewarded.

"For this child I prayed; and the Lord hath given me my petition which I asked of him; therefore also I have lent him to the Lord; as long as he liveth he shall be lent to the Lord."—1 SAM. i. 27, 28.

THE tender bonds that unite parents and children are mysteriously appointed, and overruled by God for the welfare of the human family, and to sustain a moral influence that may be exerted to draw men to the paths of virtue and holy obedience.

The *maternal* power over the infant mind for good or evil is proverbial, and has been recognised in all ages of the world. The tender care, loving solicitude, and unwearied devotedness of a mother attract the fond affections of her child, even if she be devoid of that superior influence which the pious parent gains over her children by the power of prayer, a holy example, and the principles of gospel truth.

The solemn warnings, wise counsels, and prayerful solicitude of a *mother* who herself exhibits the evidence of true godliness in her daily life and conversation, constitute a moral influence brought to bear upon the character which cannot be surpassed. The recollection of these flowing back upon the heart of a wanderer, after years of vice and reckless living, has often been instrumental, even sometimes apart from other means, in bringing him to repentance. Many a mother's neglected words and disregarded warnings will embitter the portion of those who to the last stop their ears and steel their hearts against the tenderest and wisest of earthly counsellors.

Doubtless, most religious parents constantly pray for the conversion and salvation of their children. Some, perhaps, occasionally feel discouraged on finding all their prayers apparently abortive, and their sons and daughters wandering farther and farther from Christ, and more and more engrossed with worldly pleasures and friendships; but let none such despond, for it is written, "Men ought always to pray and not to faint;" and though the blessing tarry long, they must hopefully "wait for it." Their duty, as well as their privilege, is to continue pressing their suit, and confidently to trust in the power and grace of God. Their perseverance may be severely tested, but if they pray in faith and according to the will of God, they shall, like the Syro-Phœnician woman, prevail, though the blessing may come after they have entered into their eternal rest.

The biographies of many eminent characters in the Church of Christ abundantly testify to the happy results of maternal instruction and tenderness; and, for the encouragement of pious mothers, it is of great importance to recall cases of success and answers granted to prayers, even long after anxious parents had been separated from the objects of their solicitude.

The following is a brief account of an instance of this kind. It has obtained some degree of publicity already, but as the author of this volume has had private means of assuring himself of its verity, he can with confidence place it among the indubitable facts which he here offers to the consideration of the Christian reader

A youth, the son of highly respectable parents, in one of our provincial towns, had been brought up piously, and had been the especial care of his devoted mother. She was accustomed not only to pray *for* him but *with* him, particularly while, yet in tender years, he submitted implicity to her directions. But as he grew in years she saw, to her deep sorrow, no fruit of all her anxiety and prayers. His disposition was amiable, but he was marked by much frivolity and a world-loving spirit. When the hope so long delayed began to make her heart faint, his mother formed a new purpose with the one end in view—his conversion to God. She fitted up a chamber for her son's sole use, and bestowed on it all the care and taste she could employ to render it conducive to his comfort and suitable for a place of study. She furnished it with books of an instructive and lively description, as well as with some of a decidedly religious character. On his taking possession of this apartment as his own, she begged him to kneel down by her side, and there, with strong emotion, she poured forth a most fervent prayer for his best and truest welfare. He was not, however, overcome even with this singular exhibition of maternal love, and only one part of her remarkable and touching prayer at all arrested his attention: it was, that, *in this very room*, he might seek and find the God of his parents, and give up himself entirely to his service. . . . Years passed away in total disregard of his affectionate mother's concern for his salvation, and all recollection of her special and earnest prayer for him seemed to have faded from his mind, and he remained a devotee to the world. During this lapse of time, his mother had been taken to her heavenly home, and thus her personal influence over him had ceased.

His father's professional engagements increasing, it became necessary to take a larger house in the town. On the day of removal, after superintending the transfer of the goods, the young man felt a strong desire to take a last look at the rooms so full of the associations of a lifetime, but now to be for ever forsaken. He placed himself, in imagination, once more in the chair where he had sat with his father and mother, at the table by the fireside, enjoying one another's society. He almost fancied his mother was looking at him from the spot where her portrait had hung, and her voice once more sounded in his ears with accents of tenderness. He visited every room, and silently took a long farewell of his mother's chamber, where so many pleadings for his soul had been sent up to the God of all grace. He, then, for the last time, entered that room so closely associated with his departed mother's love and pious care. Here vivid recollections of the past, and his first entrance on the possession of that chamber, crowded upon his mind. He felt inclined to rush from a spot that brought such convictions of wilful sin into his conscience. But his heart smote him as he was about to say farewell, and he stayed to live over again those scenes which memory held so tenaciously. On that very spot his sainted mother had wept and prayed with him and for him, that, in the apartment from that time dedicated to his own use, he might *seek and find the God of his parents and give himself entirely to his service.* " Ah, mother, dear ! " he inwardly exclaimed; "is it possible you can know how I have lived in forgetfulness of all this ? O God, let that prayer *now* be fulfilled ! Be thou my God ! Make *me* thy servant, thy child, ' the son of thine handmaid ! ' "

After this season of deep emotion and earnest petition, it may easily be believed that he commenced his residence in the new house with new feelings and an altogether changed disposition. Gradually the transition from darkness to light developed itself, and its evidences became unmistakable. His mother's prayers were at last answered, in his becoming, not only a convert to the truth, but a zealous minister of Christ (of the Episcopal Church), and he is now, I believe, labouring to bring souls to seek and find the same salvation.

Another case of a similar nature, coming under my own personal observation, may fitly be added to the foregoing narration.

While exercising my ministry in the metropolis, a youth, who was the son of pious parents and of an eminently pious mother, left the parental roof for a residence in the great city. He had given some indications of religious feeling, and left home with the advantage of having been brought up in the nurture and admonition of the Lord. But, as the result of evil associations and bad example, he soon became reckless and his habits disorderly, to the evident injury of his health and the discomfort of his mother in her last days.

The mode of his conversion manifested such a marked interposition of the Divine and Gracious Spirit as to constrain him to pronounce it an act of as great sovereignty as that which saved the penitent malefactor on the cross, and made him a trophy of that Saviour's love and grace who was then taking away by his death the sin of the world. It was not by any previous preparation or alarm of mind, or the influence of any outward circumstances, but while celebrating his father's birthday, the conviction of his own unfilial and base conduct entered like an arrow into his heart, and falling upon his knees, he cried out suddenly in distress of mind, like the publican in the parable, "God be merciful to me a sinner."

While in this state of mind, he one Sabbath morning entered the place where I was preaching, and found the sermon remarkably suitable to his state of feeling. He continued to attend occasionally on my ministry, and the attention of some young men in the congregation was attracted by his tall and graceful figure, and his intelligent, earnest countenance, which was rendered more interesting by the hectic flush and marked symptoms of fatal disease. They soon contrived to make his acquaintance, and after a while engaged his help in their works of usefulness and charity. Shortly after this, he was encouraged to offer himself as a candidate for church-fellowship, and I was struck with his candour and his clear knowledge of the gospel, his pungent and deep grief for his past misconduct, and his earnest desire to devote his remaining strength to advance the cause of truth and righteousness. His father was made acquainted with the change, and I received in a letter from him the expressions of his joy and gratitude, but he waited for the test of time to be applied in proof of the genuineness of the transformation before he could fully rejoice in it. When he had received that satisfaction, he said, "I may now unfold to him what has never yet been told him, under the idea that it would be of no avail, viz. that *on the very day of his birth* his mother had solemnly and *with her own hand* dedicated him to the Lord." Words which she had written to the following effect were shown him :—" Thou hast given me this day a son, O Lord : I here present him to thee. Make him and keep him thine." And now, to the joy of the whole household, it was seen that the surrender had been accepted and the covenant ratified in heaven.

His mind was deeply affected while reviewing his departed mother's fervent and persevering efforts in prayer for his conversion, with the contrast they presented to the conduct of a pious female friend of hers in the metropolis, who, after frequent warning and expostulations concerning his course of dissipation, finding that he only became increasingly hardened, said to him in the most solemn manner, that she perceived praying for him was in vain, and that she was about coming to the determination to *pray for him no longer*. Even had she done so, the dedicatory prayer of the dying mother had gone before, and was not to be rejected, though no other lips had been opened on his behalf after hers were closed in death.

He lived but a few short years to ingratiate himself in the esteem and affection of all who knew him. His death was in harmony with his profession and new course of life. So remarkable a change seemed to require a public mention, and a large assembly who gathered to hear the improvement of his death were deeply affected by the foregoing facts. The discourse was printed for private circulation among his friends, and was designed principally to awaken the attention of the young to the things belonging to their peace, lest they should be for ever hid from their eyes.

What mother, after reading the above narrative, can desist from praying for her children? For though she could never see her solicitude crowned with success, yet let her continue to hope that the Lord will fulfil his promises, even though that fulfilment should not be witnessed by her till she meets in heaven those beloved ones for whom she had so earnestly and perseveringly interceded on earth.

JOB.

Perfect Resignation.

"And Job said . . . The Lord gave, and the Lord hath taken away; blessed be the name of the Lord."—JOB i. 21.

THE principle that moved holy Job to his submissive behaviour under accumulated calamities is essential to true piety, and constrains every pious individual to act in the same manner, to a greater or less degree, in similar circumstances. It arises out of a deep and settled conviction that all things are under the control of a Being infinitely wise and merciful, who has brought him into a state of communion and friendship with himself, and also assures him of efficient support in every trouble that may befall him;—of its conversion at length into a real benefit, and of its submissive endurance being crowned with an abundant recompense. It represses therefore the rising of the natural emotions of surprise above due bounds; it repels inquietude and fear at any sudden stroke of misfortune, which would otherwise overpower the dictates of faith and enlightened reason, and disturb the habitual tranquillity of the soul. His language therefore to the Supreme Disposer of events, in all his afflictions and distresses, is that of the Psalmist David, "I know, O Lord, that in very faithfulness thou hast afflicted me, and that thy judgments in all things are right;" thou hast reasons for permitting what has happened to befall me, which, could I now perceive, as I one day shall, would not only reconcile me to it, but compel me to adoring acquiescence, and prompt the fervent exclamation, "Even so, Father, for so it seemed good in thy sight." I take then the cup of sorrow which thou hast put into my hands, and press it to my lips, without for a moment suspending my praises of thee or the hallowing of thy name in my heart.

> "Take all, great God, I will not grieve,
> But still *will wish* that I had still to give.
> I hear thy voice ; thou bidd'st me quit
> My paradise ;—I bow, and do submit.
> I will not murmur at thy sovereign word,
> Nor ask thine angel to put up his sword."

This is not mere passive submissiveness, the result of indolence, or a recklessness of spirit, which troubles not itself about the reasons of events, as if all such trouble about them were useless, but suffers them to take their course, without any consideration of the end they were designed to answer,—the submissiveness of a creature devoid of reason. But this is the mind taking part with God in all his proceedings, justifying him in his severest inflictions, and looking forward for relief to the day that shall restore to us all, and more than all, that we have lost, and consummate our wishes in the fruition of bliss.

How greatly superior is this to the boasted *stoicism* of the ancients. They stifled the feelings and sensibilities of nature, to show an even front in all circumstances, whether of pleasure or of pain, that they might receive the admiration of their contemporaries. They made themselves *less* than human, that they might appear to be *more*. But piety leaves the sufferer in possession of all his natural feelings and sensibilities, yet restrains them from excess, and brings them under the authority of right reason and of God. It leaves us men, while it makes us saints, and trains us up for the companionship of angels. It breathes the sincere and fervent prayer to "the Father of lights," "Thy will be done on earth, as it is done in heaven." Yea, it subjects the human will to the Divine, divesting of extravagance the recorded prayer of Luther—" Lord, let *my* will be done—for *thy* will is mine."

Of several instances of this kind which it has been my privilege to witness, I have recorded one at length with all its attendant circumstances, which I here abbreviate.

An Irish peer and his lady were regular attendants at the chapel where I ministered, at Kensington, and had been so prior to my settlement there, having from early life been conscientiously attached to the services of religion among Protestant Dissenters. They resided in a suite of apartments in the neighbouring palace, in a comparatively retired and private manner. Both of them were sincerely pious and devout, and dignified in person and appearance, though advanced in years, having reared a numerous family. They were affable and courteous, and ready at all times to converse on the doctrines and duties of the Christian religion. Two married daughters occasionally accompanied them to worship, and though remarkably striking in their appearance, were still more remarkable for their devout attention to the things of God. It is of their eldest son, however, that I have now to speak. His early career had not been such as to please his godly parents, but after a residence abroad he returned for a while to Kensington, where he attended my ministry with his family.

I learnt, partly from himself, that while wandering in a foreign land—India, I believe—and in a part of it almost wholly uninhabited, he was seized with an intermittent fever which confined him to a little lonely hut, with only a female of colour, its sole occupant, to attend upon him. Destitute of all medical aid, and but imperfectly understood by his attendant, he felt the desolateness of his situation, and began to apprehend a fatal termination to his malady. In this state, on the alternate day of relief and composure, he ruminated on the instruction he had received in early life, and the wayward course he had pursued. He possessed no copy of the Scriptures, but he recollected large portions of the Psalms which he had read and committed to memory when he was a child, and was so struck with the numerous prophecies of Christ contained in them, and their fulfilment in the Gospel history, as to feel an indubitable persuasion of their Divine inspiration, and a determination, if he should recover, to make that book his study and to receive it as a revelation from heaven. This was but a conviction, indeed, of the understanding, without proceeding any further; for God does not always accomplish the work of conversion at once; but it had prepared the way for his devout attention to the truths which he now heard proclaimed from the pulpit: and, under a conviction of his sinfulness and need of a Saviour, he was led to embrace the Gospel of reconciliation and to yield himself unto God. Deep and sincere was his repentance, and marked and conspicuous the benign transformation of his whole conduct and conversation. He was received into our communion, and became anxious that the knowledge which he had received should be imparted to others, more especially to those whose habitual sentiments and course of life resembled what, unhappily, had once been his own.

He obtained, soon after this, an appointment under government in Ceylon, and embarked for that island with a cargo of Bibles and Testaments, and Books from the Religious Tract Society, which I helped him to procure, resolving to sow there "the seed of the kingdom" broadcast, and to follow it with the assiduous culture of oral instruction, public worship, and the celebration of Divine ordinances; which he did, with considerable success. In this work, it appears, he had the zealous co-operation of his amiable and pious consort. All things thus wore a smiling aspect, and his letters home, detailing the progress of religion in his own soul, and his varied endeavours to enrich the souls of those around him with the same Divine knowledge, delighted the heart of his aged and widowed mother, whose favourite son he was. By the death of his father he had succeeded to the title, and, having acquired ample property, he sent to his mother the joyful tidings of his intended return to England, to reside near her for the remainder of his days, and to be associated with me as an office-bearer in the Church where his name had first been enrolled. I was aware that his rank and station in life would place impediments in the way of the execution of his project, and I therefore dwelt upon it with no sanguine expectations. Still, to have so zealous, consistent, and influential an individual among us as a " fellow-worker to the kingdom of God," would, I felt, be a source of true satisfaction. How often, in the elegant little suite of apartments in the palace, have I sat with his dear mother, counting on the joy with which she would receive him to her arms, and be repaid for all her former anxieties by his honourable and useful career. At last a letter was received stating the day on which he should embark to return home, with all the choice purchases he had made, and the valuable presents and marks of honour with which he had been favoured. I rejoiced with her in the happy anticipations thus awakened, not unchastened, however, with a wholesome sense of dependence upon God for their accomplishment.

About the time of their expected arrival she was all anxiety to learn when the vessel that bore them first appeared in sight. After some unexplained delay—alas for human hopes!—she received official information that the East Indiaman, in which they were sailing, had met with a succession of tempestuous winds, and on a certain coast had foundered and become a total wreck. Himself and his lady, with all their furniture, trinkets, papers, and everything valuable, were destroyed by the waves. With what an aching heart did I proceed to the palace on hearing the dismal tidings. How would she bear them? What should I say to comfort her? How bear up myself under such a trying dispensation? But, on approaching her, I soon discovered how needless were all such fears and surmisings. Never before had I seen such a spectacle of Christian heroism—such an instance of the power of faith in the wisdom, sovereignty, and righteousness of God as was then presented to me. At the door appeared her fine and venerable form, with the fatal letter in her hand; accosting me with these words, as I find them recorded in my diary; " My dear pastor—God sustains me—it is all right—I utter not a murmuring word—'the Lord gave, and the Lord hath taken away,'" and, clasping her hands together, and looking up to heaven, she added with fervent exclamation, "'*blessed be the name of the Lord!*'" I was lost in admiration at the elevation of her spirit. The speech of the heathen matron, who remained unmoved on hearing that her son had been slain in battle, saying, ".I knew that I had begotten a mortal," has in it something unnatural; but the speech of this Christian lady, by showing her sensibilities to be alive, and yet her mastery over them by Divine aid, enlists our sympathies, and calls forth our warmest admiration. That tranquillity with which God had so mercifully endowed her, she never lost, but continued steadfast in the faith and hope of the Gospel, and abounding therein with thanksgiving.

The pious and eloquent Jeremy Taylor, before he was

made a bishop, suffered much from the troubles of the times and the persecuting spirit of the men in power. His living at Uppingham was sequestered, his house plundered, his estate seized, and his family driven out of doors. He found an asylum in the house of a friend, where he composed one of the noblest of his works, his "Holy Living and Dying." About this time it was that he drew the following beautiful and touching picture of the state of his mind.

"I am fallen into the hands of publicans and sequestrators, and they have taken all from me: what now! Let me look about me. They have left me the sun and the moon, fire and water, a loving wife, and many friends to pity me, and some to relieve me, and I can still discourse, and unless I list, they have not taken from me my merry countenance and my cheerful spirit, and a good conscience; they have still left me the providence of God, and all the promises of the Gospel, and my religion, and my hopes of heaven, and my charity to them too; and still I sleep and digest, I eat and drink, I read and meditate. I can walk in my neighbour's pleasant fields and see the variety of natural beauties, and delight in all that in which God delights—that is, in virtue and wisdom, in the whole creation, and in God himself. And he that hath so many causes of joy, and so great, is very much in love with sorrow and peevishness, who loses all these pleasures, and chooses to sit down upon his little handful of thorns."

―――o―――

The Preciousness of Life.

"Skin for skin, yea, all that a man hath will he give for his life."
JOB ii. 4.

IN the thrilling narrative of the wreck of an American steam vessel, in September, 1857, some remarkable facts are stated, which afford striking comments on different portions of Scripture, and disclose the wondrous powers of human endurance in perilous circumstances, as well as the proofs of the preserving care of Divine Providence over human beings amidst the dangers of the deep.

The vessel was on her way from California to New York, with a cargo of five hundred passengers, and the treasure they had obtained in the diggings (about two millions sterling), with which to settle in their native country in wealth and affluence. Soon after leaving Havannah, they encountered a tremendous storm, which continued unceasingly till Friday, the thirteenth day of the month, when, owing to the stoppage of the engines from the want of a proper supply of fuel, the vessel was kept in a trough of the sea, and, a leak taking place, began to fill.

And now, says the narrative, occurred a noble instance of astonishing bravery and generosity. All night long the male passengers assisted the crew in baling out the water, being joined by some of the women, many of whom were on board. Till noon the following day they laboured, hoping against hope to save the vessel till some friendly sail might come to their help. As despair was coming upon them, they descried at a distance the brig *Marine*, which stood off to help those who could reach it. All the women and children, twenty-eight of whom were babes, were got into the boats, and with a portion of the crew, sailed off to the brig, not a male passenger interfering for his own safety till those were all launched. "There was not a tear shed on board the steamer," says a female survivor, "that I am aware of, up to the time we first espied the sail which brought us relief. There seemed to be a perfect calmness, which I could not have believed to be possible for such a number of persons to exhibit under such fearful circumstances. Three or four hundred men, with death staring them in the face, stood solid as a rock, nor made a movement for the boats until they saw us all on our way, at about four o'clock in the afternoon, to the little brig that was waiting to receive us." To the noble intrepidity which was exhibited at that juncture, was owing the safety of many lives. Had there been any scrambling or rushing to the boats, they must have been swamped, and the whole have been lost in the confusion. Presence of mind in danger, if only as a means to keep others cool and courageous, is to be sought after and implored as an inestimable boon.

But now came the struggle for the safety of their own lives, of those who were left in the vessel, as it gave every sign of parting before the boat could return. Here was seen the immense value attached by them to the continuance of their existence above everything else. The adage was indeed verified in the strictest sense, which says, "Skin for skin (or skin after skin), yea, all that a man hath will he give for his life." Their first care was to avail themselves of their "life preservers;" and being abundantly supplied with these, they braced themselves as tightly as possible, keeping nothing about them but what would be subservient to buoyancy, intending to commit themselves at all hazards to the boisterous waves. How differently did they now regard that hoarded treasure which a short while before had engaged all their hopes, and had been as their very life. Many were persons of large means, and there were but few whose immediate wealth did not amount to hundreds of pounds, while numbers reckoned their gold brought from the diggings they had left by thousands of dollars. But as the storm continued to rage, less and less was thought of gold; and when towards the close of Saturday it became evident that they were likely at any moment to be buried beneath the waves, wealthy men divested themselves of their treasure-belts, and scattered the gold upon the cabin floors, telling those who would to take it, lest its weight of a few ounces or pounds should carry them to their death. Full purses, containing in some instances two thousand dollars, were lying on sofas untouched. Carpet bags were opened, and the shining metal was poured out upon the floor with the prodigality of death's despair. One of the passengers, who was subsequently rescued, opened a bag, and dashed about the cabin twenty thousand pounds' worth of gold and permitted any one to take it who chose. But it was passed by untouched as the veriest dust. "They had said unto gold, Thou art my hope, and to fine gold, Thou art my confidence;" but where was it now? They saw it was but a vain hope, and that which would prove an injury to them. Thus is the state of the mind changed by circumstances. How well is it to have this change wrought in our disposition by grace, instead of waiting for it to be effected only by the prospect of immediate death!

They sink in the mighty waters, and to save themselves, cling to the broken spars, barrels, and planks of the floating wreck. Of the few who remained to the last by the *captain*, one survived to tell the extraordinary tale of *his* agonizing feelings and marked intrepidity, as he resolved not to leave his post till the waters should close over his head, "I felt myself," says a Mr. George, "drawn in by the whirlpool of the sinking vessel, which went down at last with the speed of an arrow to her ocean-bed. Night had closed in, and I was carried by her swift descent to a depth which seemed unfathomable, and into a darkness that I had never dreamt of. Compared with it, the blackest night, without moon or star, was as the broad noonday. I was stunned rather than stifled, and my sensations on coming to the surface were almost as painful from the reaction, as those which I endured at the greatest depth. After the lapse of a few minutes, I could distinguish the objects around me; the waves as they rose and fell revealed a crowd of human heads. Those who had lost their 'life preservers' or planks while under water by the force of the whirlpool, were frantically snatching at the broken pieces of the wreck as they were tossed up from beneath. Their cries swelled into one inarticulate wail, when the lustier and less terrified shouted for assistance to the barque *Marine*, which was far beyond hailing distance. At first the waves dashed them one against another, but speedily they began to separate, and the last farewells were taken. It was when I was drifted far from the companionship of any of my fellows in misfortune that I began to realize my situation. The night was dark, and but a star or two was visible, and gave not the faintest gleam of hope that the dawn would be fair and calm. Great was the swell of the sea, and the poor floaters, holding on to their planks with the energy of desperation, were now riding on the brink of a precipice, and now buried in a valley of deep water. I was at this time seized with the fear of sharks, and found respiration, from the masses of water dashing upon me, exceedingly difficult. On the arrival of the Sunday morning, I learnt from the shouts of those in the water that the lights of another brig—the *Ellen*, had come into view. A thrill of hope ran through all our breasts, amounting, it may well be believed, almost to a perfect ecstasy. I never felt so thankful in all my life. I never knew what gratitude was before. I do not know whether I cried or not, but I know I was astonished to hear my own *laughter* ringing in my ears. Why I laughed I could not tell. That verse, 'God moves in a mysterious way,' etc.

kept passing in and out of me—through me, rather,—as if I had been the pipe of an organ. It did not come to me by my own volition, but somehow something made me remember it. As the lights approached, numerous voices sprang up around me, '*Ship, ahoy!*' and I began to shout, too, as well as I was able. For a short while I lost sight of her, but was again drifted to her, and was taken up. When I got on deck, I could not stand, and knew not till then how completely I was exhausted."

In this recital, Mr. George appears before us like another Jonah, coming up from the abyss to tell of the wonderfully preserving care of Providence, and of the bewildering ecstasy produced by the effect of a sudden transition from the gloom of despair to the joy of timely deliverance.

This may put us in mind of the joy of our spiritual deliverance from the fears of a far more dreadful gulf, out of which there is no escape: and of the transports of joy then awakened. "Then were we like unto them that dream." "Then was our *mouth filled with laughter*, and our tongue with singing." "Out of the depths we cried unto the Lord, and our prayer came into his holy temple. He sent from above and delivered us, and put a new song of praise into our mouth, that many might hear it and fear, and trust in the Lord."

One exception, however, there was to the renunciation of worldly hopes in the prospect of speedy dissolution. The *stewardess* of the vessel, a negro woman, seeing the gold thrown carelessly about, had her cupidity excited, and collecting the money thus thrown away, she buckled it round her body for great security. The weight of this money proved the cause of her death, as when she was hoisted into the *Marine*, she was found completely exhausted and breathless, from having so great a quantity of gold about her loins. *She was the only one of the women that was lost*, though several had fallen into the sea at the time of their being lowered towards the boats, but were picked up in time to save their lives.

A little girl in the company showed a different spirit. "About ten o'clock on Saturday," says her own account, "a gentleman came down and took me into the saloon. My father was with us. He handed me his money and told me to keep it. Perhaps I might be saved and he not. After we got in sight of the vessel I handed it back to him. I told him it was *too heavy*. They then called us up to the *lifeboat*. I came in the second boat to the brig. I think the terror will never leave my heart. I felt as though I had almost as lief go down with the ship as to get off. I have not heard from my father since I left him on Saturday. I fear he is lost."

The captain of the brig *Ellen*, which had taken up Mr. George and others on the Sunday, gives a curious account of the manner in which he was directed to the spot. "I was forced by the wind to sail a little out of my course before I came near to the scene, and on altering it, a small bird flew across the ship once or twice, and then darted into my face. I, however, took no notice of this circumstance, and the same thing occurred again, which caused me to regard the circumstance as something extraordinary, and while thinking on it in this way, the mysterious bird for the third time appeared, and went through the same extraordinary manœuvres. Upon this I was induced to re-alter my course into the original one in which I had been steering, and in a short time I heard noises, and on trying to discover what they proceeded from, discovered that I was in the midst of a people who had been shipwrecked. I proceeded instantly to rescue them, and in a short time succeeded in getting several of them on board. Not one of them could speak, being perfectly senseless from exhaustion. After awhile we got another on board, who asked incoherently, 'Where is my wife? Give me something to eat.'" — Upon what small pivots does the Almighty sometimes allow the operations of human nature to be turned!

The sufferings of the numbers that were left floating about in the waves for several days until they were separated from each other, and most of them *lost*, may be gathered from the recitals of the few persons who were almost miraculously sustained and preserved, and by different ways escaped alive. Some were heard calling to others for help, till the waves choked their voices. Complaints of intolerable thirst were heard; wild hallucinations were experienced, and frantic efforts made for relief. Their numbers, however, rapidly decreased, and comparatively very few were left to notice what was taking place. On the vessel going down, twelve had clung to what is called the "hurricane deck,"— a flat board with an oily covering—to which, as it was found to bear them up, others swam, but could not be admitted upon it for want of room, and on account of the weight. One of these, however, clung to it till death reduced their number, and he occupied the vacant place. A pair of oars had been mercifully preserved, and with these they drifted on the board for days and nights, having no food excepting a large dogfish which they caught and ate raw, and no drink but a copious shower of rain which fell on them in their course. In this state they floated for some hundreds of miles out of the track of ships, before they were picked up by one vessel and transferred to another. This conveyed them to New York, but they were a very small portion only of their former number. It appeared that they had drifted some hundreds of miles from the point where the vessel had sunk, and they were little better than skeletons, when they were set on shore. It was hoped that others might have drifted in a different direction, and that the brave and skilful captain who had remained to the last, might not be lost.

Of the number that perished nothing more can be said; but surely those who were thus plucked out of the jaws of death, will feel their obligation to yield the lives all but miraculously preserved to the service of God. An affecting blank will be made in some of their households, but doubtless they will meet with many sympathisers and helpers. We read, indeed, of but few of them calling on the Lord in their distresses; but the life so extraordinarily continued may have a better life added to it, which shall lead to an eternal one. Thy judgments, O Lord, are a great deep! but greater still is thy mercy. " O that men would praise the Lord for his goodness, and for his loving-kindness to the children of men!"

---o---

The Recompense of Uprightness.

"Thou shalt come to thy grave in a full age, like as a shock of corn cometh in in his season."—JOB v. 26.

A LONG life and its peaceful close are here spoken of as the promised recompense of walking uprightly. A long life indeed is chiefly desirable to a good man, as it multiplies his opportunities of usefulness, and the proofs of a paternal Providence watching over him for his welfare. It extends, too, the sphere for the exercise of those virtues and graces which adorn the character and constitute in their full development a meetness for heaven. The death of such an one may well be considered as the *harvest season* both of nature and of grace.

Such was the life and such the death of my own revered and beloved father. His course was that of the righteous, and his end was peace.

As a man, he was of a guileless spirit, amiable in disposition, of a cheerful temper, highly imaginative, incited by an insatiable thirst for knowledge, and enriched with various kinds of information, which he was at all times ready to communicate. As a Christian, his devotion was ardent, and his zeal for the propagation of Divine truth by the ministry of the word, unbounded. As an occasional preacher in connection with the Wesleyan Methodists, he voluntarily travelled on the Sabbath-day for many years to teach the way of salvation to the inhabitants of the surrounding villages at the distance of several miles from his own residence. Among them his name is still hallowed, and, at his decease, letters from several of them bore witness to the power of God that attended his faithful and affectionate ministration, resulting in the conversion of many souls.

All this he accomplished amidst the cares and toils of business and the demands of a numerous family, whom he instructed in the way of righteousness, equally by precept and example. They saw him bearing up under all disappointments with indomitable patience and perseverance in goodness. How did we delight to listen to his counsel, as he taught us while sitting in the house or walking by the way! "The lips of the righteous shall feed many, and the fruit of the righteous is a tree of life." So we found it, for though in the training of us, *no one instance of coercion ever occurred*, yet such was the force of gentleness, goodness, and persuasiveness, that we were kept from the snares of the wicked, and grew up to aspire after all that was truly excellent and holy. He had the satisfaction before his death of seeing most of his children enrolled among the followers of

Christ. Several of them have since followed him to glory, two only remaining on its borders to join them.

Towards the close of his life, having retired from business, he removed to London, where the greater part of his family resided: and greatly did he enjoy the abundant religious privileges which now surrounded him. As these increased, so did his fruitfnlness grow and abound in every good work. Seldom was that promise more strikingly fulfilled than in his case, " Those that be planted in the house of the Lord, shall flourish in the courts of our God. They shall still bring forth fruit in old age; they shall be fat and flourishing; to show that the Lord is upright, and that there is no unrighteousness in him."

For some weeks before his last illness he suffered from depression of spirits and loss of appetite. At this time, having visited his native town for the purpose of addressing some friends on the subject of religion, he returned without having been able to accomplish his errand. His wife and daughters then first perceived in him a melancholy alteration. Dim was that eye which had so often beamed upon them with delight; and languid were those arms which on every former return had been stretched out to them with affectionate ardour! Upon quitting his birthplace he had looked on its spires with the melancholy presage that he should see them no more.

He soon afterwards repaired, for change of air, to the house of his eldest son, at Kensington, contriving to go thither on the evening of a public service, which he attended with considerable emotion and pleasure. But, alas! while present, and most devoutly engaged in the service, several, who knew him, could not help remarking, that "death seemed to be upon him." A disease in the passage from the throat to the stomach prevented his receiving the least sustenance for the space of three days. But while his flesh gave way, his heart did not fail. He referred, in the most touching manner, to the former scenes of his life, delighting to call them up to his remembrance, and wishing his son to preserve some memorial of them. His life was now all retouched, and the variety of events which had composed it crowded upon his view. But there were no dark recollections to haunt him—no sins beyond those of infirmity, as he frequently declared afterwards, in the most solemn moments, to spread their terrific gloom over his mind. With perfect composure he was heard to say, "Well, if I can neither eat nor drink, my career must be short. In this state, he went twice on the Sabbath-day to the house of God, and expressed himself refreshed in mind, though fast decaying in body. Of the morning-service, the subject afforded him so much pleasure, that he declared, if ever he should recover, the text— "If any man thirst, let him come unto me, and drink"— should be the theme of his own meditation, and requested the heads of the discourse to be written down for him in large hand. During the following part of the day, he walked out, leaning on his son's arm, still talking of God, and telling of secret but sacred hours spent in communion with him. On the discourse of the evening, which was founded on the interesting narrative at the close of the fourth chapter of St. John, he made some pertinent remarks. He appeared much to enjoy the religious services of the family. On one occasion he gave out a hymn of his own selecting, from the supplement to Dr. Watts, with great energy, dwelling particularly on the following verse :—

"Fear not that he will e'er forsake,
Or leave his work undone;
He's faithful to his promises,
And faithful to his Son."

He was visited on the Monday by Dr. Baillie, who advised, if the difficulty of swallowing continued, a painful operation, but gave little or no hope of his recovery. With this he was made acquainted, and it disturbed not in the least the holy serenity of his soul. He even inquired into the nature of the operation rather as a subject of science than of painful apprehension; and expressed his readiness to undergo it whenever it should be deemed necessary. But the symptoms of the disorder abating, the operation, of course, did not take place. He amused himself now with some light reading, though still of a religious nature; but he soon recoiled from this, and said, "I must have something more solid—more like the Bible." He was still able to keep up, and walk out occasionally, and even to receive a little nourishment. But the flame of his life now burnt in the socket. Of this, however, he did not appear to be sensible, continuing to talk on other subjects, and to take an interest in what was passing. It had long been the custom of the family to assemble on the Christmas-day, when it was his happiness to rise before them, saying, "Thank God, I have all my family about me once more." As this season was now at hand, his thoughts adverted to the family meeting, and he expressed some wishes relative to the manner in which it should be held. Who that heard him could have supposed that within a few days he would be a corpse! But thus mercifully did it please God to remove him; he had always wished not to die a lingering death, and to be spared painful apprehensions. And had we even known his end to be so nigh, his frame of mind was such that it would not have been necessary to apprise him that he was at this time walking through "the valley of the shadow of death." But there it seemed good to the Almighty a short while to detain him, that all who saw him and heard him might know that his Shepherd was with him, and that his rod and staff they comforted him.

About this time he expressed his firm hope, that God would not leave him. He observed, on being questioned if he thought on any particular passages of Scripture, that he had been chiefly impressed with those which related to the faithfulness of God. He adverted, with great interest, to that promise in Isaiah, which he repeated at full length: "Come now, and let us reason together, saith the Lord: though your sins be as scarlet, they shall be white as snow; though they be red like crimson, they shall be as wool." The following, also, was a text of Scripture which he quoted at this time with great fervency: "The blood of Jesus Christ his Son, cleanseth from *all* sin."

He spoke with great satisfaction of his occasional preaching. On being reminded that his zeal had certainly carried him too far, he replied, "Perhaps so; but I did not serve God by halves. I had only his glory in view. I had often great liberty. I was not altogether left destitute of success. I would not, now, but have done what I have done for the world. I wished, from the beginning of my course, to be *a disciple indeed;* and it has been my constant aim. I often thought of those words—'Well done, good and faithful servant.' Now, a man must not be idle if ever he receives that approbation. Oh, John, I do not repent of a word I have spoken for God, nor of a step I have taken in his service!"

He said he had been courageous in many things; but confessed a recollection, in some instances, of deficiency. He mentioned one person in particular, for whom he had a great affection, and whom he had often wished to warn in the most faithful manner against a neglect of the *gospel.* But her ready assent, he observed, to everything he uttered, deprived his words of their edge, and always defeated his purposes.

On the evening of the Wednesday he found himself considerably worse. The death-like cough was now heard to escape him. "Oh," said he, as he was stepping into bed, "this is the worst night of all!" It was, indeed, a night of great restlessness to him, and difficulty of breathing. He revived a little as the morning approached. Glad to see the light, and to cast his eyes from the chamber to the fields, still green, he exclaimed: "Never did poor benighted traveller long for the morning more than I have done." He was unable, however, to leave his bed. It was the only day he was confined to it. He was told, on awaking, that his wife and children were sent for. "Ah," said he, "how will they be alarmed!" He then joined in prayer, and appeared deeply to feel the importance of the petitions that were offered. On being asked if his mind was calm, he said, "Oh, yes. I can do nothing but cast my soul on the *faithfulness* of God. I wish I had joy—but I look to his mercy, his love —to the merits of Christ. But I want my children to be animated, and to know that I am going to glory."

The following were sentences that fell from him at intervals, in the course of the morning:—

"I have *done* the will of God, and I must now suffer it: but oh, it is harder to suffer than to do."

"I rest on the *truth* and the *faithfulness* of God."

"He has made with me an everlasting covenant; on this I rely."

"What a glorious thing for the soul to escape from the body! I trust I shall see God!"

"I can say to all my children—Follow me, as I followed Christ."

"Call on such a friend [mentioning his name], and tell him I remember his kindness *now*."

"I wish I had attended to this complaint sooner; but there must be something to bring us to an end. I have been too careless of myself. But 'Thy will be done.'"

"I am glad I came hither. Where could I have been so comfortable! O Lord, wash me! Make me fit to see thee! Make me meet for glory!"

"Though I tell you I have not that rapturous joy I wished for, yet I have *confidence* in God. He must save me. Christ came into the world to save those who trust in him."

These words were brought to his recollection—

"No guilty doubt, no anxious gloom,
Shall damp whom Jesu's presence cheers."

He seemed to feel them as appropriate to his case, and remarked, "I have not done the work of God deceitfully; I have finished the work thou gavest me to do. The truth of God—I am fixed upon that rock."

After some further expressions of confidence, he seemed to check himself, and said to the son who was attending on him, "I hope I speak with humility, child?" He was answered, "Oh fear not to trust in God!—You cannot speak with too much confidence of his goodness." "No," he rejoined; "but I attribute nothing to myself, I ascribe all to his grace and mercy."

These words abruptly escaped him, as if musing on his state—"Oh, if I had it all to do now!"

His wife and children assembled about this time; and, upon hearing of it, his countenance was lighted up with joy. He called them all, excepting his younger son, who residing at a greater distance, had not yet arrived, to come round his bed; and, raising himself up, like dying Jacob, to whom he alluded, he first addressed himself to his aged and beloved partner, saying,—"We have lived together many years—God Almighty be your portion—serve him fully—and may all the blessings of redemption, in Christ Jesus, be yours! Amen." He then, in a similar manner, gave his blessing to his eldest daughter, charging her to fear God. Over his son who sustained the office of the ministry, he uttered the most affectionate wishes; praying that, as he already been made useful, he might still become abundantly more so. In the same way he continued speaking to his other children, including his son's wife, whose attention he particularly acknowledged, begging of God to reward her for it. He then requested prayer to be offered up for all. As far as grief would allow of it, his own words, which he had used in blessing his children, were presented to God in the strains of supplication, and evidently received the warm concurrence of his heart. He then fell into a gentle slumber, but upon the arrival of his last-born son he gathered himself up with renewed energy, gave him his blessing, reminded him that nothing but experimental religion would make all things go on well; and, putting two volumes in his hand, upon the subject of private and family prayer, he entreated him to peruse them closely. He received assurances from his children of compliance with all his requests, with which he seemed perfectly satisfied. He now begged to be left a little. His thoughts, which had been called down to earth, seemed to long to regain their elevation. His tranquillity, indeed, was not much disturbed, even by these exercises; but no sooner were they over, than every little agitation they had occasioned him, subsided.

It was now four o'clock on the Thursday afternoon, and he composed himself to sleep as though he had lain himself down upon some common occasion, to be refreshed by a short and easy slumber; or, rather, it was like the sleep which a weary traveller would take when near his home, to recruit himself for the remainder of his journey. His unvarying testimony, through the whole of this day, as well as the two former days, was, that he relied upon the *faithfulness* of God. He had repeated, with great emphasis, those words of Scripture, as applicable to himself, "I will never leave thee, I will never forsake thee:" adding—"never, no, *never.*" He had comforted himself with repeating that appropriate promise, "When thou passest through the waters, I will be with thee, and through the rivers, they shall not overflow thee." "What!" said he, on one occasion, "can He who has done so much for me, and been with me so long, suffer me to perish?" He added, and his eyes beamed with animation as he spoke—

"On this my steadfast soul relies;
Father, thy mercy never dies."

Again, he was heard to say, as if remonstrating with those who could doubt of the mercy of God—"For what did he send his Son into the world?—What is the *design* of the Gospel?—'God so loved the world, that he gave his only begotten Son, that whosoever believeth on him, might not perish, but have everlasting life?'—and 'God sent not his Son into the world, to condemn the world, but that the world, through him, might be saved.' Oh, fear not!" Thus he continued, supporting himself and others; and his supplies did not fail:

"His God sustained him in the final hour;
His final hour brought glory to his God."

The twenty-seventh Psalm (his favourite Psalm) was now read to him, which greatly delighted him. He said, "I can make it all my own." He repeated, as if addressed to himself, "I will make all thy bed in thy sickness." From this time, how did he long to be gone! He inquired of his son, clearly with a desire of being answered in the affirmative, if he thought his end was approaching. A determinate reply could not be given. The surgeon found his disorder so much removed, that he spoke to him in a manner calculated to excite an expectation of recovery. But, though the disease was gone, its effect upon the frame was irretrievable. The storm had spent itself, but the scene of its operations exhibited a melancholy proof of its destructive power. His extremities were becoming cold, and the restlessness of dissolving nature was apparent. To a friend who said to him, "Do you now find happiness in religion?" he replied, "What should I do without it? Be not offended with my plainness;—press after religion in its heights and depths." To another, he addressed a most affectionate warning: "Fear God," said he, "and then it will be well with you. Accustom your children to go to some place of worship on the Sabbath-day." Upon being assured that nothing should prevent them from following their own inclination in that respect, "Oh," said he, "this is not enough; *encourage* them —set them a good example." The person whom he addressed, observing, "*You* are going to a happy place," he hastily interrupted him, saying, "And why should not you? Yours has been a thorny path, but it is not too late." He was too much exhausted to proceed, and again requested to be left. From this time, as the night advanced, he became exceedingly restless. It was now that he apprehended his patience would fail. "Pray," said he, "for *ease.*" This was done with earnestness, several of his family kneeling round him. Surely, that prayer was heard! Even before it closed, his agitations had in a great measure ceased, and they were never renewed. It was said to him, "Hold out, faith and patience a little longer." "Oh," he replied, "but it is hard work!" A little afterwards, he said—"Is not the Lord long? How is my pulse?" "Fainter," it was answered. "Oh, that," said he, "is good news! 'Why are thy chariot-wheels so long in coming?' 'Come, Lord Jesus! Oh, come quickly!'" He said he had not that *rapture* which he had often wished he might have on his death-bed, but yet he could *lean his soul on the faithfulness of God.* It was observed to him, that the frame of the mind might considerably depend on the nature of the disease; that, as a fever, from which he was remarkably free, might contribute to raise the spirits, so, mere decay would naturally sink them; that the end of the upright was said in the Scripture to be *peace*, not *rapture*; that resignation to the will of God, and the calm confidence of the soul in him, were, at least, as satisfactory evidences of divine grace as ecstasy. In all this he acquiesced, but observed, that he wanted rapture only to give effect to his dying testimony, and to animate his children. He acknowledged, however, that the tempter had not been permitted to come near him, and that he had not suffered a moment's uneasiness of mind during the whole of his illness.

Upon his alluding to some remarkably happy seasons which he had enjoyed in the service of God, and some extraordinary exertions which he had made for his cause, it was observed to him, that still all his dependence must be on the righteousness of Christ; when he said, with great eagerness, "Oh, my dear, I mention not these things on my own account, but for his glory—his glory! Oh, yes, it is for Christ's sake alone that I can be saved—

> "I the chief of sinners am,
> But Jesus died for me."

He asked what time it was; and being told, ten o'clock, he said, "What, no more! Oh, how slow!" he still seemed to imagine that he must suffer much more before he could die. That verse was now repeated to him—

> "Who suffer with our Master here,
> We shall before his face appear,
> And by his side sit down:

> To patient faith the prize is sure,
> And all who, to the end, endure
> The cross, shall wear the crown."

Some hesitation was felt in repeating the second line, which he instantly removed by suggesting the forgotten words—"his face." The words of the Saviour were repeated to him, " Into thy hands I commend my spirit." " Oh," said he, " I always intended those should be my dying words ; " and, raising himself up in the bed for the last time, with outstretched hands, and eyes turned towards heaven, he pronounced the above passage in the most distinct and pathetic manner. He was now wearied out with longing to be gone. How truly might those words of Solomon be applied to him, " Hope deferred maketh the heart sick !" His spirit stood, as it were, on the verge of eternity, waiting for the summons to enter. The following lines were exactly expressive of his feelings—

> " Never weather-beaten sail
> More fully bent to shore ;
> Never tired pilgrim's limb
> Affected slumber more,
> Than my weary spirit longs
> To fly to my Redeemer's breast ;
> Oh come quickly, dearest Lord,
> And take me home to rest."

He was frequently reminded of the joys of heaven. The martyr's address to his companion in the flames, was mentioned—" Cheer up, my brother ; one moment of glory will make amends for all." He said in a low voice, " Oh, yes—one moment !"

He now requested that prayer might be made for his speedy departure. Hard request to those who were so unwilling to part with him ! Yet, why should they have wished his continuance here ? All his desires had been gratified—all his work was done. He had said of some little circum-

F

stance that he had mentioned before, "That is the last thing I ever wanted to speak about." The bitterness of death was passed. He had gone through a great part of the valley, and was even at the gates of heaven;—who could wish him to return, or to be kept waiting there? His request, therefore, that his release might be petitioned for, with submission to the Divine will, was complied with. The petition rose, and the answer was at hand. That line of Pope's was quoted to him, and seemed exactly to express his state of feeling—

"Tell me, my soul, can this be death?"

Indeed, few of the usual symptoms of death had occurred. There was none of its cold dew upon his brow—there was no convulsion of the frame. The work, however, of the king of terrors, was going on silently, but not the less rapidly and effectually. One of his children asked, "Do you know me?" He seemed surprised at the question, and said, "To be sure." Shortly after, he began to breathe harder. He beckoned to his ear the son who was feeling his rapidly declining pulse, and said, "I am dying. Oh, hasten, hasten!" The other son he grasped with his hand. His eyes were now turned upward, as if fixed on heaven; and every succeeding breath becoming still more gentle, his spirit quietly withdrew to another world, at sixteen minutes past one, on the Friday morning. At that moment, his dying charge was fulfilled—"When the conflict is over, kneel down, and give thanks to God." So soft, so sweetly impressive was the scene, that it seemed as if angels witnessed the solemnity, and covered the suppliants with their wings.

Thus fell, in the seventy-first year of his age, one whom to know, was to love; and who has left a testimony to his worth in the bosoms of all those who were intimately acquainted with him, that no time or change can ever obliterate.

With what fondness do children recollect the form of a departed parent, endeared to them by so many virtues! His eye still seems to beam affection upon them. The sounds of instruction still seem to issue from his lips, and the bright image of his living worth stands before them in all its loveliness and dignity. "The monitions of wisdom, when they return on us witht his melancholy charm, have a more pathetic cogency than when they were first uttered by the voice of that living friend, who is now silent. It will be an interesting occupation of the pensive hour, to recount the advantages which we have received from beings who have left the world, and to reinforce our virtues from the dust of those who taught them."

———o———

Remarkable Dreams.

"God speaketh once, yea twice, yet man perceiveth it not. In a dream, in a vision of the night, when deep sleep falleth upon men, in slumberings upon the bed."—JOB xxxiii. 14, 15.

DREAMS were one of the modes by which the mind of God was revealed to the seers of ancient times. Other and yet more determinate methods of such miraculous communications were those of visions, personal appearances, and audible voices in the air. These modes, so far as they were miraculous, ceased on the completion of the revelation of the Scriptures; but apart from miracles, God has still many secret ways of conveying instruction to our minds, both in our waking and sleeping hours; yet always *in accordance with the written word.* We are thus put upon our guard against imaginary revelations, or the impulses of our own spirits, and against acting upon them according to the interpretation of our own will or fancy.

The following judicious remarks on the subject are taken from an old author, who is now almost forgotten.

"Luther, observing how many were deluded in his time by dreams and visions which they falsely attributed to God, as the immediate author of them, earnestly prayed for two things:—One, that God would give him a sound understanding of his mind revealed in the Scriptures; the other, that he would not send him dreams or visions: 'Yea,' said he, 'I even contracted with God that he would not.' And doubtless he did this upon a double ground. First, to oppose the wild opinions and practices of those who had nothing to pretend for them but dreams and visions. Secondly, to advance the honour of the written word, in its sufficiency, not only without the help of any human tradition, but without any further Divine revelation.

"And, therefore, though God should please to speak to us now by dreams and visions, yet that were only as the apostle speaks to the Hebrews, about his adding of an oath to his promise, to show that he is willing more abundantly to satisfy our weakness by such a condescension, than that there is any necessity for it, in respect of any deficiency in the fulness of Scripture. And hence it is that if men shall profess they have received anything from God by dreams or visions, concerning either what is to be believed or done, the matter of these dreams must be examined and weighed in the balance of the Scriptures, and is no further to be credited than as it is agreeable thereunto.

"It cannot be denied that men may make profitable use of their dreams at this day. They may see much of themselves when their eyes are shut by sleep. Evil men may see their sins at work in the night, and find out what one is most working and wakeful in them. What is said in story of the ancient Persian kings, that they were seldom seen in the day, but came to view in the night, is true of a man's special sin, or of that sin which reigns and lords it in him. What ugly apparitions of sin hath many a man in his nightly dreams; especially of those filthy sins which are most proper to the night! Thus also good men have sometimes a clearer sight of their graces in the night by dreams than in the duties of the day. What holy frames of heart—what lively actings of grace—what sweet and ravishing communion with God, have many godly men found and felt in dreams! That may at least be somewhat of David's meaning when he said, 'My reins also instruct me in the night season.'

"In fine, though we cannot make any certain conclusions, either as to what we are or what we are to do, from dreams, yet from them those who are wise and watchful may sometimes gather strong conjectures about both or either. To make them the rule or warrant of what we do is extremely dangerous; yet that we may have hints what to do in a dream I nothing doubt, nor can there be any danger in it, while the matter hinted is consonant to the word, both as to that which is lawful to be done, and lawful for us, all circumstances considered, to do. Otherwise, whatever we may think ourselves warned against or warranted to do by dreams is but a mockery or trick put upon us by Satan, or a deceit of our own foolish selfish hearts."

Dreams that are repeated, and make a distinct and indelible impression, and relate to a work of God in progress, but threatened with failure, and foretell or show its certain success, particularly if in a way that is answered by the event, may surely be considered as sent by God to inspirit his servants or confirm his own prophetic word and engagements.

The most remarkable dream of this kind upon record was

that of John Huss, the martyr of Bohemia, which took place in the 15th century, while he was confined in prison at Constance, and condemned by the Papacy to be burnt alive as a heretic. He suffered joyfully at the stake, where Jerome of Prague was soon afterwards burnt also by the order of the same persecuting power. A few days before Huss suffered, he dreamt that he beheld from the bottom of his dungeon the images of Jesus Christ, which he had caused to be painted on the walls of his oratory, obliterated by the pope and the bishops. This dream greatly afflicted him; but the next day he beheld in another dream several painters busily employed in restoring the images in greater number and with increased brilliancy. Having completed their labours, they appeared surrounded by a great concourse of people, exclaiming, " Now let the pope and bishops come, they will never be able to efface them again." The inhabitants of Bethlehem, a place where he had borne his testimony for the truth, were seen to be greatly rejoicing, and he felt himself partaking of their joy.

On communicating these dreams to a faithful friend, he was cautioned against trusting to them, and exhorted to turn his whole attention to the preparation of his defence; to whom he replied in these memorable words :—

"I am not a dreamer; but I hold this for certain, that the image of Christ shall never be effaced. They have wished to destroy it, but it shall be painted again in the hearts of men by painters abler than myself. The nation which loves Jesus Christ will rejoice thereat, and I, *awakening from the dead*, and reviving as it were from the grave, shall thrill with great joy."

A century had nearly passed away, during which the witnesses for Christ and his truth were everywhere silenced; and his image which they had sought by their preaching to form in the hearts of men, seemed about to be obliterated, until the triumph of the Papacy under Leo X. appeared so complete that it was celebrated at Rome by a triumphal feast. A few years before the expiration of that period, however, Luther, the morning star of the Reformation, arose, and was followed by numerous reformers, who renewed in far brighter and more enduring colours the image of Christ in the hearts of multitudes in different places. Thus was the prediction of the Apocalypse fulfilled, that after three days (years) and a half of the total silencing of the witnesses, they should rise up in a new spirit and gain the ascendency (Rev. xi. 11).

In a "Brief" addressed by Pope Adrian, Leo's successor, to the Diet at Nuremberg, he wrote—unconscious of the testimony he was bearing to the fulfilment of that prophecy —" The heretics Huss and Jerome appear *to have come to life again* in the person of Martin Luther."

A tradition has been handed down that Huss named a hundred years as the period after which there should be this revival of the witnessing testimony which had been for a season crushed, and a judgment withal, at the same time, on the Papacy. This was exactly the interval between himself and Luther. It was in 1415 that he was burnt at the stake, and in 1517 that Luther began his protest. A medal exists which represents the martyr at the stake, and has the legend around it—

"Centum revolutis annis Deo respondebitis et mihi;"

which may be thus translated :—

"A hundred years will roll when ye
Shall answer both to God and me."

The evidence is most satisfactory of this medal having been struck *before* the time of Luther and the Reformation.

A facsimile of it appears in the elaborate work of Mr. Elliott, entitled "Horæ Apocalypticæ."

To come to our own times, I may mention a remarkable dream of a more personal and private nature, connected with the spiritual history of an individual of whom I had some knowledge, the late Major-General Burn, who thus records the fact:—

"About a fortnight or more after my brother's death, while I continued in a mournfully disconsolate state of mind because I could not love Christ, I dreamed a very distinct and remarkable dream, which had such a happy effect on my heart that I have ever since looked upon it as the principal means the Almighty was pleased to employ in bringing about my thorough conversion. I thought I was sitting a little before daylight in the morning, with my deceased brother, on the wall of the parish churchyard, where we had lived many years together. We remained silent for some time, and then he asked me if I would not go with him into the church. I readily consented, and immediately rising up walked with him towards the porch, or outer gate, which I thought was very large and spacious; but when we had passed through it, and came to the inner door that led directly into the body of the church, some way or other, but how I could not well conceive, my brother slipped in before me, and when I attempted to follow (which I was all eagerness to do) the door, which slid from the top to the bottom like those in some fortified towns on the continent, was instantly let down more than half-way, so that I now found it requisite to bend myself almost double before I could possibly enter; but as I stooped to try, the door continued falling lower and lower, and consequently the passage became so narrow that I found it altogether impracticable in that posture. Grieved to be left behind, and determined to get in if possible, I fell down on my hands and tried to squeeze my head and shoulders through; but finding myself still too high, I then kneeled down, crept, wrestled, and pushed more eagerly, but all to no purpose. Vexed to the last degree, yet unwilling to be left outside, I came to the resolution of throwing off all my clothes and crawling like a worm; but being very desirous to preserve a fine silk waistcoat which I had brought from France, I kept that on in hopes of being able to carry that with me; then laying myself flat on my face, I toiled, and pushed, and strove, and soiled my embroidered waistcoat, but could not get in after all. At last, driven almost to despair, I stripped myself entirely, and forced my body between the door and the ground till the rough stones and gravel tore all the skin and flesh upon my breast, and (as I thought) covered me with blood. Indifferent however about this, and perceiving I advanced a little, I continued to strive and squeeze with more violence than ever, till at last I got safely through. As soon as I stood upon my feet on the inside, an invisible hand clothed me in a long white robe; and as I turned round to view the place, I saw a goodly company of saints (among whom was my brother) all dressed in the same manner, partaking of the Lord's Supper. I sat down in the midst of them, and the bread and wine being administered to me, I felt such seraphic joy, such celestial ecstasy, as no mortal can express. I heard a voice call me three times by name, saying I was wanted at home. My joy was so great and overcoming that it soon broke asunder the silken bands of sleep, and made me start up in my bed, singing the high praises of God.

"So much was I impressed by this remarkable dream, that from this day I was enabled to begin an entirely new life, which, as I advanced in the saving knowledge of Divine things, proved as different from the life I had led for several years past as it is possible any two opposites can be. Old things were now done away, and all things became new."

Dreams are usually formed out of the last impressions made on the mind before retiring to rest. Especially is this the case if such impressions have been deep and solemn. But if in sleep they should be directed to an issue far beyond that which they had in the wakeful hours, who would exclude from them the presence of a Divine and gracious agency? In connection with this thought, the following incident occurs to my remembrance :—

Many years since, in the city of Bristol, on returning home from a Sabbath evening service, I overtook a young lady of whom I had some knowledge as a regular attendant on my ministry, along with a number of other young persons whom she had in charge, being engaged as an assistant in perfecting their education. On this occasion she was alone, the weather having prevented their accompanying her as usual, and as my way home was in the same direction as her own, I took the opportunity of joining her, and entered at once into conversation on the subject of the discourse she had been hearing—the "new birth." I requested her to ask herself seriously if she had had any experience of the nature I had been describing. She made me no reply. I knew that from her earliest years she had been trained to the services of the Established Church, but was unaccustomed to converse with ministers out of that communion. I could therefore account for the reserve and reluctance she manifested in return to my earnest appeal. Nevertheless, I expatiated on the absolute necessity of this change of heart, as a preparation for eternity, dwelling on the emphatic declaration of the Saviour, "Except a man be born again, he *cannot* enter the kingdom of heaven." "And if not *heaven,*" I said, "what then? There is but one other place—that is *hell.*" At the sound of this word, I felt that she shuddered, withdrew her arm from mine, and would listen to nothing further. It appeared that on reaching her abode she felt excessively annoyed at my having presumed to address her thus on religious matters, since she had been so strict in observing all the ordinances of her church, and so correct and blameless in her deportment in the world— which indeed was the truth, for she was one formed to win the love and admiration of others, and her natural gifts had received all the culture of a polite and finished education. She could not forgive me for my plainness, and retired to rest indignant at the thought of having been told that *she* might at last be found among the "*lost.*" In the night she dreamt that she heard noises as of terrible thunder and dire commotion of the elements, and, in reply to her astounded exclamations, was apprised that it was the day of judgment. She saw the Judge seated on the clouds, and felt that she was being drawn irresistibly towards him. At that moment the words sounded in her ears, *Unless born again, not heaven; and if not heaven, hell.* The agitation of her spirit awoke her. She arose, partly dressed herself, and fell on her knees, praying to Christ that he would have mercy upon her, and give her to know what it was to be "*born again.*"

From this time a change appeared in her whole deportment. At the expiration of some weeks, she came to my house and solicited an interview; I was surprised, but received her most cordially. She wished to speak with me in private, and I think I now see the old garden tree under which she paused, while looking at me steadfastly she said, in a voice trembling with emotion,—"*Dear sir, I shall not go to hell. Jesus has had mercy upon me and changed my heart. I shall go to be with him in heaven. Oh, how I hated you once! How I love you now for your faithful warning!*" She then told me what I have just narrated. A few years afterwards, I was sent for to visit her in the neighbourhood of London, where I found her in the midst of her friends, very near her end. Lovely she looked in death; and, taking my hand, she said, "I wished *you* to see that the work was real. I love you all—you, my precious mother—you, my dearest sister—you, my beloved pastor; but I can give you all up to go to Jesus." And so she died.

I had myself a singular dream during my residence at Kensington, which I noted down at the time, on account of its remarkable impression on my own mind and the instructive lesson it afforded. It related to an individual who had been brought up with me in my father's house in our boyhood, but whom I had not seen for years, and scarcely knew whether he was yet living, much less did I know where he was or what course he was pursuing. But one night, without any previous train of thought to that effect, I found myself, in a dream, walking with him in the darkness of the night, by the side of a hedge, which seemed to keep us in one direction. It appeared as if we had been conversing together about the times since we had known each other well and were often together. The particulars of the conversation escaped me, but the result of it made me very grave. On a sudden, a rumbling noise was heard as of a cavalcade approaching us from a distance, and the atmosphere became illumined with a profusion of sparkling lights. On looking up, the sky wore a lurid aspect, and the clouds seemed about to part in the midst, to be rolled up in heaps. Addressing my companion familiarly by his name, I said,

"It is the day of judgment; what will become of us?" And fully expecting to see the Judge appear, I framed an address in my own mind, in which I appealed to his knowledge of my sincerity in preaching his Gospel and endeavouring to make him known to men as the Saviour of sinners. I was conscious of numerous defects, but felt emboldened by my ability to make this appeal, and an assurance of the benignity and graciousness of him who was about to be my Judge. I now turned to my companion, whom, to my consternation, I saw lying on a bank beneath the hedge, pale and motionless, his tongue swollen and hanging out of his mouth, without the possibility of his drawing it in again; as if he had been attempting to kneel and pray, but in vain. While looking with fear and trembling, I heard a voice above me, saying in the most audible manner, "*His character is adamant: he that is filthy, let him be filthy still; and he that is righteous, let him be righteous still.*" The apprehension of something alarming to follow so agitated me that I awoke, and, on recovering myself, I rose, and, by moonlight, wrote down in my pocket-book in pencil, where it still stands, the very circumstances and words that had passed before me in vision.

The impression it made upon me did not wear away as in ordinary dreams, and after a few days I made it my business to find out the individual, and to visit him at his own abode at some little distance from the metropolis. I learned that though he had formerly given indications of seriousness and religious feeling, his habits and companions were of an unfavourable cast. I took him aside, and narrated to him my dream, premising that I attached no superstitious importance to it, but that he would do well to let it lead him to reflection, and to regard it in the light of a warning. I left with him also a copy of the particulars of the dream which I had written at the time of its occurrence. He listened to me with respect and deference; but I could see no signs of any deep emotion, or of alarm at the prospect of what might one day be his case. He died not many years afterwards, and then I heard that an outward reformamation had taken place after my visit. Although I saw him not at last, nor met with any one able to give me a true account of his views and feelings in the closing scene, I may rest in the hope that the thoughts raised up in me with reference to him, without any concurrence of my own, might be designed for his benefit, and that eternity may prove they were not in vain.

———o———

Divine Teaching.

"Behold, God exalteth by his power: who teacheth like him?"
JOB xxxvi. 22.

WE have been sometimes both surprised and delighted with the clear and consistent views of Divine things entertained by some of the pious and unlearned poor. The light of the Gospel system, meeting in their minds with no opposing systems to obstruct its entrance and obscure its rays, shines into them with its own heavenly beams, and is reflected from them in all its native purity and energy. The truths of Revelation have a quickening influence upon their intellect, so that their very conversation becomes improved and ennobled by familiar acquaintance with them, as read from the Book or discoursed upon from the pulpit. Their unconverted friends and neighbours, though their equals in natural sagacity, are no match for them in conversing upon religious subjects, but are obliged either to confess themselves confuted, or to cover their ignorance and mortification by sneers and reproaches. Even professed divines have been foiled by them in disputes upon points of doctrine and experience, and have felt the truth of the patriarch's axiom, "How forcible are right words." No false shame deters them from declaring what they know to be the truth, as if it were dubious or capable of being refuted; but what they see clearly they state boldly. "We speak," they can say, "that we do know, and testify that we have seen, and ye receive not our witness." The convictions of the blind man, whose eyes Christ opened, and to whom he afterwards revealed himself, could not be shaken by the subtleties of the scribes and Pharisees, for he met them with an appeal to facts and to his own consciousness, that silenced though it did not convince them. Though they put him out of the synagogue, he had previously put them out of the field of controversy.

It is, however, on the bed of death, that the views and feelings of these individuals, both with respect to the world they are leaving and that to which they are going, are expressed with an edifying vividness and force. Hence the learned Grotius confessed to a friend, in whose company he had been visiting the dying chamber of a poor but pious peasant, that he would gladly part with all his learning to have the simplicity and holy ardour of that good man at the last. Then it is that the most solemn warnings and the most earnest entreaties are addressed by them to those whom they are about to leave, and especially to their own dear kindred, in words which seem not only to come from the heart but to bear the heart along with them, and which therefore leave an indelible impression on the memory.

Most ministers have within their knowledge individuals whose history would supply ample illustrations and confirmations of these remarks. They have seen persons in the poorer and humbler ranks of society whose intellects became quickened by the reception of the truth, and whose whole character was transformed under the most disadvantageous circumstances.

A poor woman, residing some years ago at Bushey, in Hertfordshire, was a striking instance of this nature. She had been mentioned to me while on a visit to the place, by the pastor of the congregation in the new chapel, as one of the early fruits of his ministry, and as one who by her holy life and peaceful end had been to him an unspeakable comfort and satisfaction. The particulars he related struck me very forcibly, and at my request he has since added a written communication, the substance of which I am permitted to subjoin :—

"She was born," he says, "at some little distance from the place, of poor but honest and industrious parents, who had brought up a large family, including herself, by their united exertions at the lace-pillow. After their decease, when at the age of thirty, she married an individual of her own station in life, by whom she had several children, all of whom she supported while young, with their invalid father, by her sole occupation as laundress to several respectable families at Bushey, where she had come to reside. She had received little or no education, but was moral and religious to a certain degree, having been under the salutary restraint from her childhood of the fear of God, of death, and of judgment, which several incidents during that period had served to strengthen. Her children were trained to attend the parish church on Sundays, and were taught by her at home, as well as she was able, the fear of the Lord. But her own mind was in a state of inquietude from the uncertainty that she felt about the right way of becoming truly religious and happy.

"In this state of mind she was found at the time of my

entrance on the pastorate; but at my ordination over the people, which took place soon afterwards, curiosity led her, though at some sacrifice of her daily earnings, to be present. The scriptural and lucid description of a 'good minister of Jesus Christ,' which was given by my venerable tutor, who addressed me on that occasion, so arrested her attention and impressed her mind, that she said within herself, 'If the minister there is to be such an one, he is the man whom I will place my soul under.' Accordingly, she resolved from that time forth to attend upon my ministrations, a resolution to which she steadfastly adhered, being present whenever I officiated, not only twice on the Sabbath, but on the Thursday evenings, rising for that purpose, if necessary, an hour before her usual time, which was at five o'clock in the morning, that her allotted work for the day might be duly completed. In winter and summer, fair weather and foul, she never missed an opportunity of attending, though her house was a mile distant from the place of worship. I never entered the pulpit but I saw her, in her red cloak, in her accustomed seat. Nor was she an indifferent hearer of the Word, but devoured it, calling it her meat and drink.

"The result, as I found on becoming acquainted with her, was a proficiency in her acquaintance with Divine things beyond any one I have known. She had no teaching but that of the Scriptures and the public ministry, nor ability nor leisure for reading, but she could pray while at her work, and her mind became receptive of many inspiring thoughts, which, with all her incumbrances and laborious occupation, she could not refrain from committing to writing, with a propriety and correctness, as to the *sentiments*, that was truly surprising. Abundant proofs of this I have before me in the papers she left behind. Thus was she supported under various trials and interruptions, and her mind lifted up by faith and hope into heavenly contemplations and enjoyments, while struggling with the hardships of her situation. 'Ah, sir,' said she to me one day, '*I have taken many a walk in the streets of the New Jerusalem whilst standing here at my work as you see me.*'

"She had, before this time, applied for admission to the Lord's Supper in communion with us, that she might sit, as she phrased it, 'at the table that he sat, and eat and drink as he did, with his disciples'; but from her inability, in consequence of her seclusion, to express herself in the usual way upon the topics of religious experience, she was requested to wait till she was further advanced;—a decision that grieved her much, though she did not suffer it to prevent her unremitting attendance on the means of grace, and her earnest endeavours to increase in the knowledge and fear of the Lord.

"For myself, I was more than satisfied of her truthfulness and sincerity, and of the reality and depth of her piety, and she was therefore soon after gratified with a welcome reception among the communicants. Thenceforward her orderly walking with the Church in the commandments and ordinances of the Lord, and her careful, conscientious, and constant use of the means of grace, both private and public, were such as I suppose no Christian has ever surpassed She has left behind her numerous papers which I have in my possession, and which reveal an inner life of near and most blessed communion with God, which she enjoyed in her obscure dwelling, and which made it like the abode of an angel. To myself she was much attached, owning me as her spiritual father, and opening her whole mind to me in the most frank and artless manner. Never can I forget her many expressions of reverential regard and endearment: they blossom afresh continually in my memory!

" When I left for a while to engage in the service of a foreign mission, she wrote a long letter to me, which I send with this brief recital, the sentiments of which cheered and animated me beyond most other epistles from older and more advanced Christians.

" Her end was peace. She was not surprised by death, though it came upon her rather suddenly. It had often been her expressed wish and desire, that, if it pleased the Lord, she might be spared a long last illness. She was gratified. On Tuesday, July 6th, 1836, she spent the day in her usual health and employment, and in more than her usual cheerfulness; but it was her last day. Having folded the articles she had cleansed, and laid them in exact order, she retired to rest—when death touched her body, and before ten o'clock the following morning released her spirit for the realms of blessedness!

" It is truly surprising to find how, with her inability to write easily, as well as her want of proper materials, and of the necessary leisure, she should, at intervals, have penned so much in the form of a diary, and of letters to some of her acquaintance. Besides her letter to me while I was in Jamaica, and other friends in affliction, she had penned a most affecting epistle, a few days before she died, feeling that her end might be drawing near, to her children, which she desired to be read to them after her decease. She had written also an address to the spectators over her grave, and her own funeral sermon, all of which were read at her burial according to her desire.

" Peace, happy soul! thy days of toil and sorrow are ended. In thy low estate thou didst know and love the Saviour, and he has exalted thee to be the companion of perfected saints and holy angels!

" Two of her daughters have followed her to the skies,

one emulating her piety and zeal; while a son yet living is a preacher of the everlasting Gospel. 'Hearken, my beloved brethren, hath not God chosen the poor of this world rich in faith, and heirs of the kingdom which he hath promised to them that love him?'"

Allusion has been made to some papers of a religious nature, which were found in the handwriting of the deceased after her departure from the world. Several of these now lie before me, and a few extracts from them will shed a stronger light upon her character. The papers seem to have been written at various intervals, and to have been the unaffected expression of thoughts and feelings stirring her spirit, and struggling for vent. No particular object, except in a few instances, is assigned for their production. In transcribing them the orthography has been occasionally corrected and punctuation supplied, but no alteration has been made in the language which she employed for the utterance of her views and sentiments. It was felt that any attempt to improve it would only mar its simplicity, and prevent it from affording, as it now does, a corroboration of what has been stated as to the advancement of intellect and transformation of character by the unaided instruction of the Word itself, and by the influence of the Divine Spirit.

The extracts are as follows :—

To a Friend in affliction, with some account of her own Experience.

"Go on, my dear friend: yet a little while Jesus will wipe away all tears from your eyes. You will soon see your beloved friend again, and he and you will rejoice together. Had I wings I would fly to my Jesus. I do endeavour to be with him in spirit; feeding upon the same bread, drinking of the same fountain; bowing at the mercy-seat, and aiming at the Divine glory. The command is to rejoice always in the Lord. The Lord says, 'Fear none of those things that thou shalt suffer: be thou faithful unto death, and I will give thee a crown of life.' We may be persecuted, but we shall not be forsaken: we may be cast down, but we shall not be destroyed. No; with the eye and the ear and the heart of a friend he attends to our sorrows, counts our sighs and tears, and when our spirits are overwhelmed within us, he knows our path, and adjusts the time and measure of our trials, with everything necessary for our present support and seasonable deliverance. What, then, shall we fear, or of what shall we complain, when all our concerns lie near his heart, all our times are in his hand, and the very hairs of our head are under his care? This is a sufficient proof that he does not willingly grieve us; but when he sees our need of chastisement he will not withhold his hand, because he loves us. The Lord grant that we may all find those blessed ends answered to ourselves by the trials he is pleased to appoint! They remind us that this is not our rest, and call our thoughts upwards where our true treasure is, and where our conversation ought to be. This is a weeping world; sin has filled it with thorns and briers; but the Lord says, 'Call upon me in the day of trouble, and I will deliver!'

"To-morrow is the Sabbath; I am usually glad when it returns, though it seldom finds me in that frame of mind which I could desire. But to count the days and the hours from one meeting of God's people to another is all the pleasure I have in this world. I am glad to go to the house of the Lord. The Sabbath is a blessed day, indeed! —the earnest of heaven. There they keep an everlasting Sabbath! and cease not night or day admiring the riches of redeeming love, and adoring him who washed us from our sins in his own blood upon the tree. For this I sigh and long, and cry to the Lord to rend the veil of unbelief; scatter the clouds of ignorance; break down the walls which sin is daily building up around me, to hinder me from seeing thee. I hope I can say, My soul is athirst for God, and nothing less than the light of his countenance can satisfy me. Blessed be his name for this desire; it is his gift, and he never gives it in vain. He will afford me a taste of the water of life by the way, and ere long I shall drink abundantly at the fountain-head, and have done with complaints for ever. May we be thankful for what we do receive, and earnestly long for more."

A Meditation and Prayer.

"Have mercy upon me, O God! and assist me against myself, for such is my infirmity that there especially do I fall into sin. I am ashamed to think how often I pray with my mouth but not with the spirit! my body indeed is in the closet or the church, but my heart is at a distance; nay, can I hope for any benefit while I pray thus? O Lord! send down thy grace and Holy Spirit into my heart, and lead me into the real truth that is in Christ Jesus: enable me to delight in all thy ways; this is what I do request, O Lord! pray, O Lord! hear me, and give me the desire of my heart. Comfort my mournful soul in time of need! Come! thou strength of the feeble, and raiser of them that fall! Come! thou helper of the poor! Come! thou, my dear Jesus! be thou my Guide, and guide me, for I have no help for myself. I am poor and miserable, blind, and cannot see afar off. Come! Holy Spirit, in much mercy, come; make me fit to receive thee! What is it that detains me from thee whom my soul loveth? It is my sin. Prepare my heart, O

God! to receive thee: forsake not, I beseech thee, thy servant that calleth upon thee; for before I called, thou preventedst my desires, and that I called or sought thee, is from that grace which first of all sought or called me. Thou, my dear Redeemer, hast my whole heart. I know no rival. I delight in the remembrance of no other object. My mind is fixed upon thee. A peaceful calm composes all my thoughts. The load of mortality and misery grows lighter, and the tumults of worldly cares and troubles are hushed in silence. Oh that I had wings like an eagle, that my flight might never falter, never rest till I had mounted up to the glories of thy heavenly habitation, and were filled with the pleasures of thy beauteous presence! O my blessed Redeemer! let my soul ever seek thee! and let me persist in seeking till I have found, and am in full possession of thee, O my dear Redeemer! Oh that there was in me a heart that might always fear thee, a soul that might always love thee! O my God, have pity upon me, and from the throne of thy majesty on high cast down a compassionate look! Enlighten my dark soul with the bright beams of thy Holy Spirit! Give me a good understanding of Jesus, for he is God, of thy substance and of ours. He who is thy Son, is also our Brother, bone of our bone, and flesh of our flesh, and he died that we might live. O my blessed Jesus! give me that adorable love, that true and perfect love in Christ Jesus that casts out all fear! Oh, let me not, I beseech thee, turn back or go out of the way, but proceed continually in the love of thee, till thou at last bring my whole spirit and soul and body into the peaceful mansions where my heart is already fixed. The first-fruits of the Spirit I have already tasted, impart to me thy whole self, and satisfy my soul with the joys of thy Holy Spirit sent down into my heart, O God of mercy! Oh that my sins were blotted out, my pardon sealed! When shall I see my dear Redeemer face to face, and approach that joy of an endless, incorruptible state, conferred upon me by the bounty of God?"

From a Letter to her Pastor, when in Jamaica.

"I have often thought, since your departure, of the undeserved praise you once gave me, when you said you thought I had been growing in grace daily. Ah, could I but see this in myself! But I feel that I am far, very far from being what you imagined me to be; and I think there are thousands of poor, obscure Christians, whose excellence will be never known in this world, who are a thousand times more deserving than I am of the kind and tender regard of their fellow-Christians. Yet I trust I am grateful to my heavenly Father for inclining the heart of his children to look on me with a friendly eye.

"If I have at all grown in grace since you left me, it has consisted entirely in an increasing knowledge of my unspeakably wicked heart. I do hope, however, vile as I am, to obtain an inheritance to that better world where Jesus has prepared mansions for his followers, and will introduce them himself, sprinkled with his precious blood and clothed with his righteousness.

"If love to the children of God is an evidence of being born again, I have reason to think that that is my happy case. I know that I love Christians, and love them most who are most actively engaged in the cause of Christ. At the throne of grace I feel, at times, my soul drawn out in love to them, and in as ardent a desire for their welfare as for my own.

"I think I am quite unworthy to be allowed to do anything for Christ, though I am happy in being allowed to live among them that labour for the kingdom of heaven. But if it may please my Redeemer to make me instrumental in bringing some poor soul to a saving acquaintance with him, my greatest desire—my most ardent wish would be accomplished. But I fear I shall never be used as an instrument in the promotion of the cause of Christ. When I consider the great wickedness of my heart, I hardly dare to approach the throne of grace; but when I recollect that God has promised to hear the cry of the poor and needy, and that he has even given his Son to die for those who are sunk down in sin, I find some encouragement to prostrate myself before the mercy-seat and plead the Divine promises.

"How happy should I be to see you and your dear wife once more in this country. No, I cannot forget you. I have missed you very much both in soul and body, but that is not of much consequence to me. A few more years and you will hear of my death, or I of yours; till then believe me to be your most affectionate child,—for this I think I can say, you have begotten me again in Christ Jesus through the gospel. Sure I cannot forget you. I hope you will have many more spiritual children in that country where you are labouring, and they will be my dear sisters and brethren in Christ Jesus. I will pray for you, that is all I can do. I don't expect I shall ever see you more in this world, but when we meet in heaven,—when all have arrived and find all safe—for ever safe with the glorious Saviour, oh, shall we not be happy, and ever praising him who endured the cross that we might wear the crown!"

From a Letter to her Children, to be read to them after her Decease.

"Now, my dear beloved children, I would wish to give you some good advice as a loving parent and a faithful mother, and this will be the last warning I can give you. Remember, these hands are cold and stiff when you read this, and can write no more! Remember, I cannot come to you, but you may come to me; and I hope, my dear children, I shall meet you all at the throne of Christ, my dear Redeemer, to part no more. But, my dear children, you must follow in my steps, or you can never come where I be. I hope by the time when this is read to you I shall be with my dear Redeemer, for his word was most sweet to me when I was on the earth. He was altogether lovely : he was my beloved, and now he is my friend. O my dear children, you must live a religious life, else you cannot go to Christ. But do not take anything less than this for the religion of Jesus Christ; do not take part of it for the whole. What God has joined together, put not asunder. Take no less for his religion than the faith that worketh by love all inwardly and outwardly holiness. Be not content with any religion which does not imply the destruction of all works of the devil, that is, of all sin. We know weakness of understanding and a thousand infirmities will remain while this corruptible body remains. But sin need not remain. This is that work of the devil, eminently so called, which the Son of God was manifested to destroy in this present life. He is able, he is willing to destroy it now in all that believe in him. Only be not straitened in yourselves. Do not distrust his power or his love; put his promise to the proof. He hath spoken, and is he not ready likewise to perform? Only come but boldly to the throne of grace, trusting in his mercy, and you shall find that he saveth to the uttermost them that come to God through him. And I hope I can say that I have gone to God, through Christ, and I long to go to my Father's house above.

"I have enjoyed sweet Sabbaths here below, but now I

shall have a better Sabbath; I am going to begin an everlasting Sabbath in glory—to begin my everlasting song, 'Unto him that hath loved me, and washed me from my sins in his own blood.'

"Farewell, my dear children. I shall see you no more till I meet you round my Redeemer's throne. When this is read to you, I shall be gone, and then it will be too late to wish I had done such a thing. But I hope I have done my duty by you all, though you would not hear me then; but I hope you will listen to these lines now I am gone to return no more. O my dear children, you have all got Bibles. This is the richest treasure you can possess in this world, and if rightly read, will procure you a treasure in the world to come. But without daily studying this book, and making its doctrines the constant rule of your life, you will live to a woeful purpose. The Holy Bible, my dear children, is the only thing that can give you support under every affliction; it is our comfort in life, our hope in death, and our source of happiness to all eternity. But it is not enough, my dear children, that you are constantly hearing God's word, you must be constantly doing God's work. Be very careful to avoid evil company and idle words. They are the snares which will lead you into temptation. Remember, that every sin you commit, however it may escape your memory, will be noted in the book of Heaven, and produced at the great day of account. Then will you be convinced, my dear children, how safe it was for you to have loved godliness more than greatness. Never forget that a contented mind is a continual feast. Now, as God's love is great towards you, so let your thankfulness be equally great towards him. Never be eager to possess what is out of your reach. It is safer striving to win a heavenly crown by prayer, than earthly riches by fraud. O my dear children, go to Christ for everything you want. He has enough; he said, 'Ask what you will in my name, and I will give it you.' It is because you ask not, that you receive not, and because you ask not for such things that are pleasing to him. O my dear children, ask for all spiritual blessings and temporal blessings, for he knows what you have need of; he will supply all your wants, he knows what things you have need of before you ask. But seek first the kingdom of Heaven, and all other things shall be added unto you. Christ is such a friend to those that love him; he says, Come unto me; ask what you will in my name, I will give it you. Therefore, my dear children, go to Christ with all your cares and all your troubles. He says, 'My grace is sufficient for thee. My strength is made perfect in weakness.' Therefore, if you be weak in faith, then go to him for strength. If you be in trouble, then go to him for comfort; and if you, poor one, cannot get food to eat, then go to Christ, he can satisfy you. If you have but a little crust, eat that with Christ, and that will be the sweetest of all food. If you be overburdened with anything, then go to Christ. I have done many hard days' work in the presence of Christ—but when I took it to him, I could not feel it. Therefore, my dear children, do everything you have to do in the presence of Christ.

"But you may say, 'How can we take all these things to Christ, when he is not on earth?' but he is on earth and in heaven too, both at one time. You must lift up your hearts to him, and always keep him in your minds, and then you will be always with him, and he will be always with you, and then you will feel no more trouble. O my dear children, I trust that we may meet in glory, and then I will tell you wonderful things of what the Lord hath shown me. I cannot tell you now a thousandth part. Our Father, into thine hands I commend my spirit!—to thy eternal care!

"My dear children, hear the last advice from your dear mother. Read your Bibles much, meditate more, and pray most of all. You must strive—pray without ceasing—pray on, persevere! May God bless these last words to the benefit of your souls, my dear children. Begin the day with prayer, and end it with prayer. Your life is but a journey, it will soon be at an end. Weep not for me, but weep for yourselves. I shall be happy."

And she *is* happy—" Behold, God exalteth by his power: who teacheth like him?"

PSALMS.

The Susceptibility of the Young.

"Come, ye children, hearken unto me; I will teach you the fear of the Lord."—Ps. xxxiv. 11.

THE teachers of Divine truth have great inducements to address themselves in that capacity particularly to the young of both sexes, whenever they find opportunity. In youth there is a natural and continual thirst for knowledge, and the young are disposed to listen with deference to any one competent to instruct them upon the most serious subjects. Their minds are in a receptive state, their sensibilities are lively, and their memories tenacious. In them none of the cares and perplexities of the world have by fatal growth intercepted the sowing and springing up of the good seed, nor are evil passions and principles strengthened so by indulgence, as to exert a hostile and effectually opposing influence to truth. With hearts true and tender, with consciences unseared, and with all their perceptions clear and unblunted, at what period of their earthly existence can they be so favourably addressed, and hopefully taught the way of salvation by Jesus Christ, and when can the success of the attempt be of equal moment? In the morning of youth cast broad thy seed. It is the Divinely prepared sowing season. If we are not ready with the precious seed, then assuredly the enemy will step in and sow tares. Some plants will certainly appear in the virgin soil; it rests much with man whether they shall be goodly or evil, productive of fair fruits, or merely weeds and fuel for the burning.

The royal psalmist proposes to teach his young disciples "the fear of the Lord;" at that time a comprehensive phrase for the whole of religion. But under the Gospel our great object must be to engraft upon their tender minds the knowledge of God in Christ, for their salvation. To this point all our efforts must be directed. There must be "line upon line, precept upon precept; here a little and there a little," till they are thoroughly imbued with this knowledge. What though the truth in their minds should have no apparent or immediate effect, we have lodged it there, and its great Author will, in his own time and way, render it effectual for conversion. Down the long vista of accumulated years we may possibly look back and see how the gracious result was the effect of due preparation for it, and then we shall cherish the liveliest emotions of gratitude and thankfulness. Thus are we taught the sovereignty and sole efficiency of Divine grace. The husbandman stores his grounds with the precious grain, but cannot contribute aught to its essential vegetative property. It is the same in the spiritual husbandry. "I have planted," says the apostle, "and Apollos watered; but God gave the increase." To him alone be the praise!

In an establishment for perfecting the education of the young, most of the pupils of which attended my early ministry, there was a young East Indian of engaging manners and personal attractiveness. She had been placed there by her guardians, under a strict prohibition against her attendance at any place of worship not of the Established Church. As is frequently the case, the interdict made her the more desirous of accompanying her companions to our worship, especially after hearing, on their return, their accounts of that in which they had been interested. With this fact I was made acquainted, and on one of my pastoral visits to the house, I found her regarding me with great curiosity, and embracing every opportunity of questioning me on religious topics. On every repetition of these visits her questions were renewed, and instructions were given in reply to her inquiries concerning the important topics of repentance and faith, and the absolute necessity of conversion by the Holy Spirit through the truth. She listened attentively, and appeared to lay up the things that she heard, and to ponder them in her heart. But she was young, and gaily disposed; and even up to the time of her leaving, when her education had been completed, I observed no evidence that any beneficial impression had been made on her mind, or indeed that any of the ideas and principles I had been labouring to implant in her, had germinated and given promise of fruit for eternity. I had prayed for success, but hope was still deferred.

Previous to her removal, I found her at one of my accustomed visits seated at the musical instrument, and playing some favourite airs with great spirit. When she paused for a few moments, I placed before her a sacred air, requesting her to substitute it for another, and to accompany it with her voice, by singing some verses which I would repeat. She instantly and cheerfully complied; and her exquisite touch of the instrument, combined with the melting pathos of her voice, deeply affected me. At length she came to the following stanza—

> "Sweet to rejoice in lively hope
> That when my change shall come,
> Angels shall hover round my bed,
> To waft my spirit home!"

At this moment I was overcome by the emotions springing from a train of sentiments which rose in my mind; and I could not refrain from tears. This she observed, and paused, saying, "Dear sir, what is the matter?" "O Annie," I replied, "you are about to leave us, never, it is probable, to see us again in this world; and you are quitting us in a state of mind which makes me fear that angels will not hover round *your* bed to waft *your* spirit home." "But why not?" she pleasantly rejoined; pleasantly I say, and yet I observed a rising tear, which she brushed away. Having now completed the piece, she joined her companions. From that hour, I saw her no more.

At the expiration of a few years, a young lady from India called at my house. She had been intimately acquainted with this interesting young pupil, and was, I believe, her bosom friend. We conversed about her, and she then related the following particulars. Soon after her return to her native country, and at a comparatively early age, she was advantageously married, and had become thoughtful, serious, and devout. But, through the enervating influence of the climate, she fell into a rapid decline, and was soon laid upon the fatal couch, to fade like a flower blighted on its stem. Prior to her decease, and the departure for this country of the friend who was my visitor, she called the latter to her side, and charged her, when she reached England, to call on me, and to tell me that the words which I had spoken to her at the instrument of music had never gone from her mind. They led her to entertain my fear that what she had been singing would never be hers to appropriate. "But tell him," she said, "that I have been brought to the Saviour of whom I heard much at those early seasons, and have found him to be *my* Saviour. And tell him," she added, "oh, tell him, that angels *are* hovering round *my* bed, to waft *my* spirit home; and that I hope to welcome him in that abode of the blessed, and to communicate to him in heaven what I now commission you to narrate to him on earth."

Doubtless she had other instructors, whose efforts, through the Divine blessing, in conjunction with mine, had contributed to bring her to that happy state of mind. But that the little incident which I have mentioned should have remained to be acknowledged after the lapse of several years, from a spot of earth thousands of miles away, and in the solemn hour of death; that its happy issue should have been transmitted to me across broad intervening seas, and thus prove that the original, and apparently casual impression had survived all external mutations, and had neither been obliterated by new affections, intimate ties, nor wasting malady, was far more than I had ever expected, and deeply engraved upon my mind the truth of the gracious assurance that they who sow in tears shall reap in joy. I had literally sown in tears, nor could absence, distance, nor death itself, silence the glad song of the reaper.

> "All earth may change from pole to pole,
> But Truth lives changeless in the soul."

I now turn to another page in my ministerial history, which speaks to the same purpose, but is marked by a more recent date :—

On once dining at a friend's house in the country, not many miles distant from the metropolis, I met with a gentleman and his wife, who came to join in the social repast. Before, however, we partook of it, I was requested by the partner of the gentleman to accompany her from that spot to one at a little distance. I yielded to her guidance, and was conducted to a rising mound near the front of the house, out of which rose a large and flourishing tree, with seats around its trunk for the accommodation of visitors and travellers. She pointed to a particular one which she wished me to occupy for a few moments with herself. I complied, wondering what might be her intention. She then informed me that several years before on that very seat I had discoursed to her, when the inmate of a boarding-school which I had visited, on the love of Christ for sinners, and his graciousness in being willing, and even desirous, to save from misery and to exalt to happiness and glory all who yielded themselves to him. This casual conversation produced an effect upon her which eventually led her to surrender herself to that Saviour whose disciple she became. She had not felt emboldened to make this fact known to me in any formal way, but could not resist the desire to do so on the very spot which had become endeared to her, and was to me ever afterwards an object of interest. I then reflected that I might have allowed the early opportunity to pass away unimproved. I might naturally have thought it out of place and season to speak so seriously to a mere schoolgirl. But I blessed God that his Spirit had prompted me so to speak at that period that, through all the subsequent fadings and re-appearances of the leaves on that aged tree, a silent process of religious growth had been going on in a human soul, and fruit had been produced from seed once cast upon the wayside and forgotten.

I may fitly introduce in this connection a communication which I have received from a brother minister, with whom I was a fellow-student, and who, like myself, is now approaching the termination of life, and gratefully looking back upon all the way that the Lord his God has led him.

While pursuing a course of study for the ministry, he preached, as he informs me, for some considerable time at a small country town in the county of Bucks. He was entertained during his stay by some pious and devoted friends, who had a large and very interesting family. Early one morning, as he paced about their pleasant grounds, he met one of the little girls of the family, an engaging child of ten or twelve years of age. He joined her, and in a casual way asked her concerning her attention to the sermons on the previous Sabbath-day, and how much of them she could remember? Taken quite by surprise, she was obliged to acknowledge that she could not remember even so much as the texts. Upon this, he spoke to her in simple, earnest, but rather reproachful language, and impressed upon her the importance of always paying attention to the means of religious instruction. His words, though he knew it not, took fast hold on the child's memory and conscience, and she could never shake off the sense of her sin in not valuing more highly her religious advantages. She began from that time to pay serious attention to all she was taught, whether at home or in the house of God, and became a truly pious and useful Christian. She was naturally of a sanguine disposition, and devoted her energies with the utmost zeal to every enterprise she undertook, and so became a pattern of excellence to the other members of the family. Especially in seasons of deep affliction was she both their wise counsellor and affectionate comforter.

"*More than forty years after* my conversation with her in the garden," adds my friend, "she, although then somewhat advanced in life, and having charge of an invalid sister at a watering place within a short distance of my own residence, felt it to be a duty and a privilege to make me acquainted with the fact, that the few words of good advice which I had given her had been the means, under God's blessing, of awakening her mind to the importance of spiritual realities, and of leading her to form that holy resolution of attending to them which has received such a favourable issue." Until the period of that disclosure, my venerable friend and brother in the ministry, who had spent years of active service in his Master's cause, had never enjoyed an opportunity of communication with her, and therefore had been without the gratifying knowledge of the happy effect his casual remarks had produced.

From all these facts great encouragement may be derived to improve every opportunity of suggesting thoughts that shall impress the minds and direct the reflections of the young into a religious channel, thereby leading them to follow the Saviour in the way of righteousness and eternal life. The years that elapsed between these brief interviews and these disclosures, and the joy experienced upon being made acquainted with such gratifying results, corroborate and enforce the direction of the wise man: "Cast thy bread upon the waters, for thou shalt find it after many days." Nevertheless, such results, consequent upon Christian efforts, yet await the revelations of eternity, and will doubtless form the crown of rejoicing which shall grace the brows of all who do their Lord's will, and are faithful unto death.

"Speak ever for thy Lord,
  Where'er thy words may fall;
Cast thou the seed abroad,
  And Heaven shall ripen all.

The harvest may be long,
  The seed may seem to die,
Yet still the reaper's song
  Will gladden by-and-by.

'Tis only thine to sow,
  And sowing, still to pray;
Then rest, and be content to know
  There comes a harvest-day."

In the course of a long and rather unusually protracted public ministry, I have observed several changes in the modes of thought and action characterizing the Church of Christ. This is not to be wondered at, as Christian societies will naturally be influenced by the better tone of general society around them. Unceasing activity, and the development of individual agency, are prominent features of our time. Men now devote remarkable attention and energy to the origination of schemes of philanthropy and benevolence, and private persons carry these into execution with a truly praiseworthy patience and perseverance. Concurrently with this, I have noticed with much gratification the increased attention paid to the private and personal teaching of the gospel, which is, I trust, a marked feature of the Christian Church of our day. I speak now not only of Sabbath-school instruction and its improved character, and of other institutions of a similar kind for those portions of the community who, but for them, would remain unacquainted with the very rudiments of Christianity; but also of the advance made by the hearers of the gospel towards becoming its teachers in their respective circles, so that it may be clearly understood in its essential principles, and soon come to be generally regarded as the ordained instrument for regenerating the nature of man, and affecting the true reformation of the world.

Has there not been among us, for a long time, an undue dependence placed on the public ministry of the word as sufficient for the conversion of all classes of the community? Have not many devolved the duty of seeking to convert men by the truth almost exclusively on ministers, to the neglect of their own co-operation in it, and to the strengthening of that false opinion which makes the priesthood not merely the preachers, but also the principal doers, of the word of God, in relation to personal effort and Christian usefulness? Hence, the large proportion of our population, of different ages and stations, that remains to be indoctrinated with the pure principles of our religion. Nor can we expect to be otherwise, till a still greater movement in this direction be made by the combined efforts of all believers.

We cannot conceive of any other method by which the minds of individuals of all ranks throughout a whole country can be brought into contact with the truth that makes wise unto salvation. Was it not chiefly by this form of instrumentality that Christianity first prevailed, and extended its blessed influence far and wide, so that the world, which had hitherto been under Satanic sway, was transferred to the dominion of Christ? All the early converts to the truth were charged to be teachers of it to those who were ignorant and out of the way, and from the heart they became willing instruments in this labour. The desire to impart the same blessedness to others which they themselves had received, gave wings to their zeal, and transported them to the regions round about as messengers of peace, "bringing good tidings of good" to the respective inhabitants. They did not then tarry to be told and retold their duty; they did not wait to be formally commissioned, or to be arrayed with official authority, and thus attract public notice to their efforts. No; they felt that they could not remain silent, but *must* speak of the things they had known, and found to be the life of their souls : " Then they that were scattered abroad went everywhere preaching the word;" and the primitive prolific blessing was upon them. They "increased and multiplied ;" the little one became a thousand, and the small one a strong nation. But faith declined, and with faith, zeal and charity. The love of many waxed cold, and the world, unhappily, in part relapsed into the sad condition out of which it had emerged.

By what other means than those which succeeded so wonderfully at first can the same blessed results be expected to be renewed? Is it not the prominent feature of most of the prophecies of the millennium, that such is the method to be employed for preparing the way of the Lord? The Lord will give the word, and great shall be the company of those that publish it. Fathers will teach their children, and these teach the next generation. Neighbours and brethren shall instruct one another, till the practice becomes universal: "They shall teach *no more* every man his neighbour and every man his brother, saying, Know the Lord, for they shall all know me, from the least of them to the greatest of them, saith the Lord. And the earth shall be filled with the knowledge of the Lord, as the waters cover the sea."

To this, as emphatically the work of our day, are we called. What is necessary but the universal diffusion of Christian knowledge, and the wide establishment of Christian ordinances, in order to bring mankind into a fit state for the reception of the second effusion of the Holy Spirit, according to Divine promise? Who can adequately realize the immediate result of such an effusion? We may learn from recent awakenings in various places distant from each other, in what an almost incredibly short space of time a religious renovation and moral transformation of our species might be wrought. The "seed of the kingdom" sown in men's minds in all directions may in its growth emulate the rapid vegetation of the East, where, under the influence of genial skies, "the feet of the reapers tread upon the heels of the sower." Simultaneously and universally the same Spirit may then operate, and a "nation be born in a day." In some aspects the fields already appear white unto the harvest. The moral darkness seems to be giving way to the breaking dawn. The first notes of the great hymn of joy seem to fall upon the attentive ear of the hopeful believer. What doubt can there be? "The glory of the Lord shall be revealed, and all flesh shall see it *together*, for the mouth of the Lord hath spoken it." Whether human lips gainsay or confirm, the glorious issue is assured, and may be near at hand!

———o———

Avarice and Bountifulness.

"Surely every man walketh in a vain show: surely they are disquieted in vain: he heapeth up riches, and knoweth not who shall gather them."—Ps. xxxix. 6.

"There is a sore evil which I have seen under the sun, namely, riches kept for the owners thereof to their hurt."—Eccles. v. 13.

"The liberal soul shall be made fat: and he that watereth shall be watered also himself."—Prov. xi. 25.

"But the liberal deviseth liberal things; and by liberal things shall he stand."—Isa. xxxii. 8.

THE Holy Scriptures present us with descriptions of the widely prevalent folly of avarice among the children of men, not merely for the purpose of exposing and reprobating it, but also with the intention of enforcing upon us the duty of the opposite and wiser conduct which they propose to us, and illustrate by ennobling examples. It is for the same purpose that I now narrate some instances which have fallen under my own notice in my ministerial position; and for no other purpose do I wish to detail the sad consequences of believing that happiness consists in the mere possession of wealth, and that it alone can procure for us, in the absence of superior possessions, the real respect of our fellow-creatures, or exempt us from numerous inconveniences and discomforts which we are apt to conceive of as peculiarly attendant upon narrow circumstances and poverty.

The class of persons I allude to are engrossed with the cares of obtaining, and the anxieties of preserving, their portion of the goods of the present life, in which alone, or mainly, their confidence and hopes are centred. Yet the happiness expected from this portion is never enjoyed. The happiness induced by acquiring it, and the solicitudes felt in its preservation, are unfriendly to all true peace and expansion of soul. These habits, indeed, dry up the sources from which peace might flow, within and without. By the narrowness to which they restrict their subjects, and by the obvious self-seeking which they manifest to all watchful spectators, they debar such persons from the gratifications of social life and the improving fellowship of the wise and good. They shut them out from the charms of warm and worthy friendship; they exclude them from the companionship of the liberal and generous; they leave them to those who expect solid repayment for their really reluctant attentions, and whose presence can never be sincerely gratifying to them. They induce such friends to apprehend and calculate the time of their departure from the world, and consign them, when debilitated by the infirmities of age or the attacks of serious maladies, to a dependence upon mercenaries, and upon others whose self-interest and expectations alone prompt them to minister to them in the time of distress or decay.

But it is as death approaches that the evil of such a life becomes undisguisedly manifest. Then he who has lived in this manner discovers that he is deprived of all the reliefs and consolations which he has rightfully forfeited. Instead of enjoying liberty of thought and freedom of mind to devote his whole attention to the duties of piety and the concerns of that other world on the borders of which he is now standing, he is distracted with solicitude about the relinquishment of his property, and the distribution of it to other possessors. If religious or charitable institutions are suggested to him as objects for his attention, the enrichment of which might free his memory from injurious reflections, and thus far give him a pleasing place in the breasts of some survivors, he has thus a new source of care in this very suggestion, and is perplexed either by balancing the claims of one institution against another, or by devising means of securing a faithful execution of his intentions in their favour, or with arranging proper measures for that object. Uncertainty and distraction arising from any such causes are inimical to repose, and any unnecessary disquietude as to the suitable destination or just distribution of property, must inevitably place on a death-bed a pillow of thorns.

In such circumstances, what room is there for thoughts about God and eternity? Surely none; and he who thus made gold his hope, and said to the fine gold, Thou art my confidence, endeavours to find support in a staff which will certainly fail him in the time of his heaviest pressure, and prove but a slender reed in that hour when he needs the firmest support; and when all the trusted and painfully accumulated possessions of a life are about to elude his grasp, and to become as free as though they had never been his.

I now recall some instances of this kind which I myself personally witnessed, and among these most striking are the following.

I once attended at the miserable death-bed of an individual who resided at a little distance from my own neighbourhood. He had amassed considerable property, which he tenaciously retained, and seldom broke in upon by liberality. Though he made a profession of godliness, he lived principally to himself, and was not rich towards God. Age stole upon him apace, and he was then naturally compelled to think of relinquishing all he possessed, and of leaving it amongst his surviving relatives, who displayed great eagerness to lay their hands upon it.

After the service one Sabbath morning, one of his married daughters, who belonged to my congregation, entreated me to accompany her to her father's sick chamber, and in the interval between the services of the day to soothe him and prepare him for his last hour. Little suspecting the other object, which she concealed under this general one, and which she hoped to find me instrumental in accomplishing, I consented. On our arrival, we found the dying man propped up in his bed, wearing a perplexed and anxious countenance, though somewhat relieved by my presence and by the recollection of my character and office. His other married daughter had already arrived, and when I entered the room was occupied in warmly entreating him, ere he departed from this world, to cancel a bond for a considerable amount which he had lent to her husband. Upon hearing this, my guide, his other daughter, as earnestly besought him not to comply with her sister's petition, and thus to deprive her family of what they thought themselves entitled to expect. Hesitating and trembling, he looked first to one daughter and then to the other, and finally to me, and entreated me to persuade his daughters to leave him in quiet, and afterwards to administer to him some religious instruction and comfort. One of them, on the contrary, now appeared to have brought me as an advocate on her behalf, and wished me to use my influence on her side. It was in vain, therefore, that I sought and awaited an opportunity to question and instruct the sufferer. I more than once attempted to ascertain from him the state of his mind, but was interrupted by the renewed entreaties of his daughters addressed to their father, and their altercations with one another. As his strength declined, theirs seemed to increase; their eagerness respecting the bond growing as their father's interest in the topic declined. He desired to turn to more important matters, they to fix him to this. It was not his approaching death that troubled them so much as the approaching decision by death in the affair of the lent money. Scarcely any scene could be more powerfully illustrative of the accursed passion of avarice. Here were four persons present in the chamber of death; the dying man in vain and very feebly, more by looks than words, supplicating repose; two daughters urging their respective claims in the very face of death; and a minister of the gospel deeply distressed at the whole, yet unable to effect an alteration, and prevented from exercising the duties of his office by those who ought to have been the first to wish them performed.

As the time for evening service was now drawing on, I explained the necessity for my departure, and turned towards the door. When I looked back, ere leaving, I saw the wretched man casting at me an imploring look, which exceedingly distressed me, and haunted me as I went to my residence. What followed I cannot recount, for I took no trouble to inquire concerning the parties, having been so pained by that short interview that I was unwilling to recur to the event or revive the circumstances. "Surely," I said within myself, "every man walketh in a vain show; surely he is disquieted in vain; he heapeth up riches, and cannot tell who shall gather them."

Still more deplorable, if possible, were the circumstances in which I found another wealthy person in the closing hours of his life. He resided near to our chapel, and, together with his wife, was a regular attendant at our services. Having received a religious training in Scotland, she was united to us in Church fellowship, but he only continued to correspond to the ancient outer-court worshipper. Though he was not considered to be in very affluent circumstances, yet he had evidently more than enough for a competency, and for the reasonable supply of all his household. No one, indeed, knew the amount of his resources, for he was extremely reserved in all allusion to them, and kept the matter in silence which even his wife did not seem disposed to invade. We never found him otherwise than civil and respectful, yet he was very reluctant to afford any pecuniary help to the societies and charities connected with our sanctuary. Some zealous females determined if possible to overcome his parsimony, addressed him with importunity and with persevering appeals to his sensibilities and his conscience, hoping for some assistance towards the laudable objects which they had set before him. But not even their persuasiveness and repeated solicitations could wring from him the smallest contribution; and this was the more remarkable as his wife added her request to that of the devoted ladies for aid in the important causes for which they pleaded. He still remained unmoved, and they retired disconcerted and depressed. He, nevertheless, continued to be regular in his attendance upon my ministrations, and listened to my public and private exhortations, both in the chapel and at his own residence, with apparent approval and consent to their propriety and truthfulness.

At length his end approached, and I was sent for to offer to him the consolations of religion as he lay upon his dying bed. What was my surprise, after having conversed and prayed with him, to find that he was unwilling to take my hand, muttering that he knew he had not done what was right in reference to the support and furtherance of religion, but intended to amend in that respect. He then requested me to say what I thought would become of him. How could I reply, but by exhorting him to repent, and relinquishing all further thoughts of a worldly nature, to betake himself to the sacrifice and mediation of the Son of God for pardon, safety, and salvation in that world which he was to all appearance soon about to enter? He gazed at me with a look of disappointment. Upon a hint being given me to inquire into his thoughts at that moment, I questioned him very pointedly, and to my astonishment and horror, he reluctantly disclosed to me the fact that, while thus seemingly about to breathe his last, his hands were under the bed-clothes grasping the keys of his cabinet and treasures, lest they should be taken from him! Soon after he departed this life, and there was, alas! reason to fear that, together with his property, he had transmitted somewhat of his fatal passion to those who survived him. It was distressing to me to reflect that a hearer of mine should quit this world with his fingers stiffened in death around the keys of his treasures. How strong, how terrible, was the ruling passion in the death of this man!

This may seem an extreme case; but no one in whom the principle of placing happiness in the mere possession of wealth has taken root, can foretell what prodigious strength it may acquire, if not checked in a way of prevention or cure. It often dates its growth from the first acquisition of property, and is then most carefully to be guarded against. There is one sovereign remedy against its prevalence, and that of every other evil passion, open to all, and which, besides being an antidote to what is evil, is itself the germ of true blessedness. It is the infusion into the mind of a new principle, which is not natural but of grace, and is of a repellent and expellent power to whatever is of a contrary nature. Let the heart be opened to receive the messages of truth and grace from the God of love, beaming in the face of Jesus Christ, and the soul be stimulated to seek above all things his favour as that which is better than life, and to cultivate those dispositions and actions which are stamped with his approbation, and which, besides repelling evil, are in themselves a source of the deepest satisfaction,—then will be accomplished what all arguments, persuasions, entreaties, and the mere exhibition of human folly and infatuation, are seen perpetually to fail of effecting.

It would be unjust in me, after what I have stated, not to allude to some instances of victory over selfishness and covetousness, as well as the blessedness of bountifulness and liberality, of which I have heard, and which have come very nearly under my own observation.

The name of Richard Reynolds, citizen of Bristol, of whom when a resident in that city, I heard much, occurs now most forcibly to my remembrance. His liberal soul devised liberal things, and by liberal things he stands ; his name being gratefully and more lastingly preserved in the memories of living men, than in the outward memorials which have been erected to his honour by the inhabitants of the city which he benefited.

He became connected, through marriage, with the large iron-works at Coalbrook Dale, in Shropshire, which prospered exceedingly, and brought in a large accumulation of property. But as riches increased, so did his disposition to share with his fellow-creatures the bounty he enjoyed. It is not possible to tell the extent of his benevolence, since none but himself and the Being whose eyes are in every place knew the number and nature of his disbursements. His contributions to various charities amounted frequently to five hundred and even one thousand pounds at a time, and appeared under the signature of "A Friend," or some other disguised appellation. In one year it was ascertained that, in this way, and in other more private charities, he had expended upwards of twenty thousand pounds. He had correspondents in various parts of the United Kingdom, who sought out cases of distress in their several neighbourhoods, and recommended them to his assistance. That assistance, however, was never carelessly given or indifferently; but the energies of a mind at all times vigorous and discriminating were exercised to distinguish between the impostor and the real sufferer, being to the former a faithful reprover, and to the latter a cheering friend and benefactor.

In the spring of 1816 he found his health failing him, and though buoyed up with the hope of recovery by his medical attendant, he felt assured that his mortal tabernacle was crumbling under the attacks of insidious disease. He visited different places, indeed, for change of air, or the benefit of their medicinal waters; but this was done, as he himself declared, in compliance with the entreaties of his friends, and to satisfy them, rather than from his own solicitude on the subject; for his mind was at ease, having been brought to an entire dependence on the mercy of God in Christ Jesus. He had not been confined to his bed for a whole day during many years, and although now very ill, he would still rise at intervals during the day to associate with the family, till he could do so no longer. A few days previously to his departure, after something soothing had been administered to him by a female friend, he said, "My faith and hope are, as they have long been, founded on the mercy of God through Jesus Christ, who was the propitiation for my sins, and not for mine only, but for the sins of the whole world." He continued placid under his affliction, and kind to all who visited him. His whole demeanour evinced that all was peace within. He felt no regret at leaving a world in which few had enjoyed more real advantages than himself. The blessedness of giving, and the gratitude, esteem, and friendship of all around him, he had long and largely enjoyed; yet he freely yielded up his spirit to Him who gave it, and had redeemed and sanctified it through the blood of the Redeemer. His hand was in that of his daughter as he breathed his last, and so hallowed was the scene that a devout and solemn silence, which continued for a whole hour, pervaded the good man's dying chamber, the impressiveness of which it is impossible to describe. The thousands who attended his funeral and sympathised with his mourning family in the loss it had sustained; the sobbings of the poor, the widows, and the fatherless, whose hearts he had so often cheered, and whose tears he had caused to be wiped away,—formed an eulogium upon his life and character, nobler and better deserved than any pronounced over hero, poet, or prince.

The city of Bristol has also the honour of possessing as one of its inhabitants Mr. John Whiston, who, in the capacity of servant to a house which fitted out ships with the various commodities of merchandize, rose, by a long course of diligence, uprightness, intelligence, and above all (as he himself devoutly acknowledges), by the favour and blessing of the Almighty, to the position of one of the first merchants of the place, and to be invested with civic honours by his fellow-citizens. He became alderman of the city, twice served the office of mayor, and was several times its representative in parliament. He founded several benevolent institutions, and left the bulk of his fortune, after providing handsomely for his widow and near relatives, to charitable uses, as specified on the monument erected to his memory.

During his mayoralty, in 1603, a *dreadful plague* raged in the city of Bristol. Between July in that year and the February of the following year, 2600 persons fell victims to it, as is recorded in a manuscript in the Chamber of the city. This good Samaritan remained at his post, superintending all plans for abating the disorder, lending personal assistance, and affording pecuniary help in cases of the deepest need and suffering.

In a pious meditation on a review of *his life*, he thus modestly but gratefully alludes to his undiminished vigour and freedom from the disorder during the whole period of its ravages: "As to the two other blessings of *health* and *long life*, I have my portion in them, according to God's good pleasure, and am thankful to him for them; yet I must bid them farewell also, and am ready to give them up when God shall demand them back. My health he has been pleased graciously to continue, in the midst of a *contagious sickness*. I have seen a *thousand fall beside me*, and *well-nigh ten thousand at my right hand*, and yet, by his goodness only, the *arrow did not come nigh me*. And though my sins deserved no less than others, his providence has lengthened my life largely to the time of old age; wherein, though I find some decay of strength, yet he has given me health of body and ability of mind. The sorrows and infirmities incident to such a burden of old age he hath withholden from me, and hath not bowed my back, nor taken away my eyesight, nor smitten me in my understanding, nor weakened my limbs nor my senses, but has preserved my all entire to me to do him service. Blessed, therefore, be his holy name!" Such was his singular preservation.

His "Farewell Meditations," which were published after his death, in a little pamphlet now scarcely to be met with, contain many just and valuable reflections, which, coming from such a man, may well command attention, and may properly close the foregoing narrations.

A Farewell to the World and its Vanities.

"Farewell, in the first place, to *riches*, *wealth*, and *large endowments*, the idols of earthly minds and grovelling affections. It shall not at all trouble me to depart from you, the unnecessary burdens of life, and the clog of all spiritual desires. How grievously have I seen men afflicted in the possession of you; and yet more miserable in the enjoyment, than the greatest beggar in the want, of you. They have not fared nor slept the better, nor enjoyed any portion of content or quiet, nor taken any delight in the glory and respect attending their riches; but the more they have raked up, the more unquiet and distasteful have been their lives. So justly is avarice plagued in itself, that I know not whether be greater, the sin or the punishment. For, as it is far more miserable to be drowned in sight of shore, and starve in the greatest plenty of victuals, than simply to perish either way, so much more wretched is his state that wants what he has, and is a beggar in his greatest abundance, than he that begs from door to door. . . . I had rather want riches than not know how to use them. Yea, I have learned to esteem the abundance of riches to be but a more troublesome kind of life, where they are possessed, for rob a man of his quiet, and take away his time, either in the account of them, or the disposing of them. What care is there to be had of rents! What caution and wariness to be had of bad debtors! What fears of losses and casualties! What distrust and suspicion of our best friends ! What vigilance and diligence that we be not overcharged in our bargains ! What grief if we are overthrown in our suits and vexed with fines and amercements. To be brief, what toil and weariness throughout our whole lives ! Either we be troubled with getting, or cumbered with keeping, and heartbroken with losing, and never at rest with paying and receiving. . . . Farewell, again and again, to these thorns ! I thank my God for the provision he has left me ; that it was competent and not superlative : not so large as to disquiet my peace, nor so sparingly small as to afflict my life with want or fear of creditors. Of what it has pleased Almighty God, of his great mercy and goodness, to allow me over and above my own necessities, I have been no unfaithful steward of *Christ*, nor uncharitable to the wants of my poor brethren. I speak from the confidence of a sincere heart, and being noways conscious to myself of any injustice or of negligence in the employment of my talents, I stand ready to give up my account when it shall please God to call me, desiring to be discharged of my trust and to be at rest with him."

Happy is the man who needs not riches of gold and silver to become rich in faith ; happy also is the man to whom God gives, together with abundance, a heart to enjoy it, a hand to distribute to the necessity of every man with whom he may be brought into connection, and a ruling determination to make the wealth which his heavenly Father bestows, the means of glorifying him on earth, advancing his gospel, and relieving the wants of his servants ; and by all these means laying up for himself riches in that celestial treasury where moth does not corrupt, and thieves cannot break through and steal.

Seasonable Succour.

"God is our refuge and strength, a very present help in trouble."
Ps. xlvi. 1.

THE help of God is afforded to his people in trouble, sometimes in ways unknown to them, and from quarters whence it could not have been anticipated. Not unfrequently it is deferred to the last moment, when every known method of relief has been tried, and failed, and hope is at its extremity. The exigency renders such a Divine interposition the more striking, and constrains the subject of it to recognise an unseen Power operating in his favour, to the strengthening of his faith and the renewing of his confidence in the Almighty. The cases are not few in which this invisible agency is exerted on behalf of believers, in directing the movements of other minds towards them, and causing even strangers to act for their succour, and devise means for deliverance. These sensible and continually recurring proofs of an ever watchful and overruling Providence in the affairs of men in every condition of life and at all periods of time, not only serve to awaken gratitude and demonstrate the value and efficiency of prayer, but cannot fail also to exert a beneficial influence on all who behold them. They testify even to the most careless observer that what the captain is in the vessel, what the magistrate is in his province, and the father in his family, that God is in the world. His paternal government is carried on by the harmonious exercise of all his glorious attributes. He combines a comprehensive knowledge of the circumstances of all beings, with a minute attention to the peculiarities of each. In man, the faculty of generalization is rarely accompanied by that of minuteness and detail; but in God, both subsist in perfection. "He so cares for his creatures," says one of the Fathers, "as if all were only one, and so cares for each as if one were all." He propounds to himself the most beneficent designs, and the most blessed ends; he contrives, disposes, orders, means for their accomplishment. He makes all beings instrumental and subordinate to him, moving all inferior wheels in a regular manner, and all the spheres of second causes in an harmonious way. Such as want eyes he leads, and to others he gives eyes for their guidance.

I have been led to these reflections by adverting to my record of some incidents connected with a brother minister in the neigbourhood of London, with whom I was well acquainted, and whom I highly esteemed for his knowledge, piety, and indefatigable zeal.

In order to meet the necessary claims of a beloved wife and increasing family, he undertook, in addition to the labours of his pastorate, the office of secretary to a religious institution, to the duties of which he sedulously attended in London all the mornings of the week, while the evenings and the Sabbath were devoted to the higher claims of the pulpit. But the incessant labours and sedentary habits of this course, together with the want of recreation, proved too much for his frame, and he became eventually the victim of severe internal malady.

I heard that he was suffering severely, and on visiting him found that disease was gaining upon him rapidly, and that he was already confined to his chamber and his couch. No medical aid seemed to afford him relief, and in the paroxysms his agony was excessive. The mere recital of his symptoms appalled me, and by sympathy had an extraordinary effect on my own health. I even imagined myself threatened with similar pains, and was only relieved from alarming apprehension by the assurance of an eminent physician. I mention this to show that here was no ordinary case of physical anguish, and no ordinary demand on the faith and patience of the sufferer himself and those connected with him.

The additional expenses entailed on my afflicted friend by this calamity, led me to think of making an appeal on his behalf for pecuniary help to a few select friends; and on asking his medical attendant whether I was warranted in stating that his disease was not only alarming but dangerous, he replied in words which I shall never forget: "Dangerous, sir! yes; and so fearful in its nature, that if he knew what was before him, he would thank any one to stab him to the heart!" My appeal was most generously responded to, and a sum raised sufficient not only for his own comfort, but affording a residue for those who might survive him. Meanwhile the faith and patience of my friend never failed him, nor did any expressions ever pass his lips but those of perfect resignation. I found him at times not only resigned and patient, but when his pains abated for a season, thankful and even cheerful. His countenance would then resume its wonted placidity, and his conversation become instructive and cheering. It was good to be with him at such moments in his chamber, to hear the testimony of his conscience that "in simplicity and godly sincerity, not with fleshly wisdom, but by the grace of God, he had had his conversation in the world." His occasional praises enlivened the sick chamber, while his fervent prayers with his wife and family seemed to draw down blessings at the time on all who were present. Verily, "it is better to go to the house of mourning than to go to the house of feasting; for sorrow is better than laughter, and by the sadness of the countenance the heart is made better."

"Woes," says the poet, "love a cluster;" and now a new trouble came upon him, as though it were a last effort to shake his confidence and test the reality of his faith. The lease of his little dwelling was about to expire, and the owner insisted on his leaving at the moment of its expiration. The whole village was explored for another habitation, but nothing suitable could be obtained. What was now to be done? To remove him to any distance was to endanger his life, not to speak of the bodily torture and mental agitation such an attempt must occasion. In this extremity, his soul was kept steadfast by that hope which is "as an anchor of the soul," "and which entereth into that within the veil;" and while he was calmly waiting the issue of events, the proprietor of a neighbouring mansion heard of the circumstances, and was so moved to sympathy that, although personally a stranger, he offered him the free use of that residence which he was about to quit for his winter abode in town. This individual made no profession of religion himself, but said to my friend, "I believe you to be a good man, and my house is at your service and that of your family, until my return." It is needless to add, that not only was the timely offer thankfully embraced, but the wonderful goodness of God, as manifested therein, most devoutly acknowledged. Behold the sufferer now in spacious apartments, attended by his beloved wife and faithful servant, and surrounded by unwonted comforts. There I visited him, and there, the severity of the disease being abated, he lay peacefully and serenely for several months; his benefactor declining to return till he, whom he had thus providentially served, needed an earthly tenement no longer, having exchanged the groans of mortality for the songs of the blessed. He breathed his last without ever having been made aware of the gloomy prognostication of his medical advisers; and the sentence that had thrilled *me* with horror on his account, never reached *his* ear nor troubled his repose. We may learn from this the wisdom of not forestalling griefs and tormenting ourselves with apprehensions that may never be realized. The habit of anticipating evil, not only disturbs the balance of the mind, but weakens its resources alike for present and future service.

I learnt a lesson on this subject in my early ministry which I never forgot. It was from the lips of a pious and gifted woman, the wife of a poet, who, in disposition and genius, seemed to me to resemble the pious Cowper, and who, alas! like him, was the subject of mental aberration. I felt for her deeply, and, on one occasion, when his malady had assumed a most affecting form I was pointing out the difficulties of her situation with a view of offering some advice for her future guidance. "Ah, my dear sir!" said she, "you have not had my experience, or you would have learnt the blessedness of following Christ's gracious command, 'Take no thought for the morrow; for the morrow shall take thought for the things of itself. Sufficient unto the day is the evil thereof.'" *Sufficient*, but not *more* than sufficient. So she found it, and by her faithful trust in this word of her Saviour, she was supported day by day, and enabled nobly to "minister to a mind diseased," till she happily witnessed its restoration.

I have known some good people kept in bondage all through life by the fear—not of death, but of dying pangs, which, nevertheless, were so far from being realized, that on their last bed they were heard to exclaim, "This cannot be dying—it is so easy!" "Lord," said the judicious Hooker, "I owe thee a death, but let it be an easy one:" and

Charles Wesley writes in this strain, as clearly expressive of his own feelings :—

> "Oh, that without a lingering groan
> I might the welcome word receive;
> My body with my charge lay down,
> And cease at once to work and live!"

Better, however, is it to say and feel with the pious Baxter, "*As* thou wilt, *when* thou wilt, and *where* thou wilt—only let me be thine!"

The following well-accredited instance may fitly be subjoined to the foregoing.

An eminently pious minister in the last century, the Rev. J. Corbet, of Chichester, was afflicted with the same malady as that of my departed friend, without however receiving the same relief from medical skill, and the same alleviation from suffering. His disorder was indeed much more severe, and of a much longer duration than that which has been noticed, continuing for many years, with intense agonizing sufferings and alarming apprehensions, yet was he supported, as was my dear friend, and more than supported—comforted and solaced, by the Saviour whose grace was sufficient for him, and whose strength was made perfect in his weakness. He published several learned works, but left in manuscript a little manual which he had penned for his own private use, detailing the inmost workings of his soul under his grievous affliction, and its elevation by the aid he had received from above. It consists of but few pages, and was published in a very small and portable form after his death, with a preface by Mr. Howe, who speaks of it as a most exquisite delineation of the work of grace in the soul, and characterizes it as "a dissection of the inner man, less to be regretted by his friends, now he is out of sight, and much more useful than that of his lately buried body." Few who are the subjects of Christian experience can peruse it, if they have it in their power, without admiring the grace of God in him, and becoming more sensible of their own deficiency. When the late Dr. Lant Carpenter expired on board the vessel in which he was making a voyage for the recovery of his health, this little manual was found in his pocket, as that which he had been in the daily habit of perusing. It is entitled, *The State of my own Soul, according to the strictest search I have been able to make.*

For the benefit of such as have no acquaintance with it, and for the help of others who are under any similar affliction, I transcribe a few of its passages as a specimen of the rest.

The Workings of my Heart in my Affliction.

" The will of God in laying this affliction upon me, I unfeignedly approve as holy, just, and good ; and I am unfeignedly willing to bear the affliction, as it is an evil laid upon me by his will, till the time come in which he thinks fit to remove it. I watch and pray and strive, that I may not give way to a repining thought against his holy hand. On that point 'the spirit is willing but the flesh is weak.' My mind doth really consent to God's dispensation, and to my submission, as being most agreeable to his wise and gracious government and most conducing to my salvation. But my sensitive part, and my mind also, as it is in part unrenewed, weak, and sinful, doth greatly reluctate, so that I am put hard to it, and I must say, I am willing, Lord help my unwillingness ! I have not observed in the several days that a thought of direct or positive discontentment, or vexatious commotion of mind, hath been admitted by me, nevertheless, I see, to my great grief, that I fall exceedingly short of that quietness, contentation, and cheerfulness in my condition, and of that freeness of self-resignation to God's will, that I desire and his goodness calls for.

"I wrestle with God by importunate prayer, that this *thorn* in the flesh might depart from me; that this distemper might be removed, or so mitigated that I might be in some comfortable ease, and get a more cheerful freedom in doing my duty. Yet I would not wrest this relief out of his hands unseasonably, and without his good-will and his blessing. I would wait his time, and desire to have it with his love and favour, and with a saving benefit. And so my earnest desire thereof is limited with submission to his holy will. Yet I find that this submission is no easy matter, but that I must take pains with my own heart, and that it is God who must work my heart to it, and keep under the flesh, which is always ready to rebel. It is hard to be willing to bear my wearisome condition; and oh how weak is my heart, and ready to sink, if it be not upheld by a strength above my own! Oh let his grace be sufficient for me, and let his power be made perfect in my weakness!

"I feel myself bettered in the inner man by this chastening. It hath furthered mortification and self-denial, and done much to the breaking of the heart of pride, and to bring me on towards that more perfect self-examination for which I labour. It hath much deadened the world to me, and my desire to the world. It makes me know in earnest the emptiness of all creatures, and how great my concern is in God. It drives me close to *him*, and makes me to fetch all my comforts from *him*. I see of how little value all outward contentments are; and not only in my present afflicted state, but if I were at ease and in full prosperity. The sense of this benefit to my soul is the great means of bringing my will to that weak degree of submission to God's will to which I have attained.

"I do not love God the less because of his correcting hand upon me. As my necessities drive me, so *his* love draws me, and my love brings me to him. I look to him as my Father; and shall not I honour my Father, and give him reverence when I am chastened of him? The Lord is my portion, saith my soul; therefore will I hope in him. I will wait for the Lord, who hideth his face; I will look after him; he retaineth not his anger for ever, because he delighteth in mercy. Therefore he will turn again and have compassion upon me. If he kill me I will put my trust in him, for he will not cast me off for ever if I cleave to him with faith unfeigned; but even through death itself will he save me. He will bring me forth to the light, and I shall behold his righteousness. When I cry, 'What shall I do in case of such or such troublesome or dangerous consequents?' my heart answers, 'Be not careful, God will provide, I will leave it to him.'

"I am desirous to be delivered from this affliction, if it be the will of the Lord, upon this account, that I might have a more notable proof of my freer choosing of God for my portion, when I am not thus driven to him, as now, because I can go nowhere else for comfort; also of my freer turning from the world even then when I am capable of enjoying it. To have such a proof of these things in myself. I should take for a great advantage, and be greatly thankful. Nevertheless, for the quieting of my mind, I consider that my present afflicted state doth better secure me from temptations which might draw my heart from God to the love of the world, in which respect prosperity is far more dangerous than adversity. Moreover, my present state gives me advantage for a higher proof of the grace that is in me, and of the power of Divine aid upholding me in a life of faith and patience, by which I live upon God alone, when worldly comfort fails me, and by which I am enabled to overcome things grievous to nature, and to get above, not only the pleasures, but the sharp pains of sense; and to live and continue with little natural or bodily rest. Also, it gives me the advantage of exercising a resolved, willing self-resignation to God, in this dispensation, which is harsh to flesh and blood; and resting in hope, when there is no present appearance of help, and as waiting and looking for the Lord, who hides his face, and a cleaving to him by constant love, though he doth sore bruise me.

"If I continue in the exercise of these graces they will give me a good proof that the heavenly nature is in me, and will make way for great assurance towards God, and full consolation in Jesus Christ. And yet further; I trust that I have, long before this distress, chosen God for my portion, and drawn off my heart from the flattering vanities of this world. I know that in this distress I do not come to him constrainedly, or merely as driven, for I delight to draw nigh to him, to pour out my heart before him in prayer and meditation. My meditation of him is sweet to my soul, and I do not love to be diverted from it; and when my distemper is any whit more easy, it works into a rejoicing in him. It is for an enlargement of heart towards him that I chiefly desire bodily ease and rest.

"The Lord will perfect that which concerneth me : thy mercy, O Lord, endureth for ever! Forsake not the work of thine own hands. O Lord, without thee I can do nothing! therefore I must beg, and thou wilt give grace sufficient, without which I cannot subsist; for therein is the life of my spirit.'

Extremes of Trial.

"We went through fire and through water: but thou broughtest us out into a wealthy place."—Ps. lxvi. 12.

Not only one but many kinds of affliction are denoted by these words, and some that are positively contrasted—as much so as the natural elements of fire and water. It sometimes pleases God to bring his people through extreme vicissitudes, that they may be tried with the utmost severity, and the vigour of their faith be thereby manifested—together with his own faithfulness in sustaining, comforting, and delivering them.

Thus they have escaped from some one trouble, in which they have been comforted and supported, to enter into another, arising from a very different quarter, in order, as it would appear, that their faith and patience may be variously exercised and still more strikingly illustrated. In all exigencies they plead these consoling words of promise: "When thou passest through the fire, I will be with thee: and through the rivers, they shall not overflow thee." "He shall deliver thee in six troubles, yea, also in seven." "I will never leave thee nor forsake thee." The instances of this kind upon record are appropriated by them to animate their hopes. They know that although miracles themselves have ceased, yet the power that wrought them remains unweakened, and can and does effect similar results in the course and turns of a regular and ordinary providence.

They are conscious of the Divine presence as a defence against all harm. As the Son of man was present with the "three children" in the fiery furnace, and enabled them to pass through its fierce flames without trepidation and free from injury; as, also, Noah heard the waters of the great flood rushing and roaring around him, yet felt confident in the security of his ark,—so the godly of all ages possess an inward peace and serenity in the midst of many troubles, of which no forebodings and no sufferings can deprive them.

The review of these supports and deliverances, when in the enjoyment of a future state of happiness, will be indeed an addition to that happiness. Circuitous as the route may appear by which we have reached the "holy habitation," it will then be seen, in the full knowledge of our nature and individuality, to have been the only certain way of obtaining an abundant and joyful entrance into the kingdom. The mountain traveller often thinks, when he is at the base of a lofty mountain, that he can ascend to the summit by a direct path which he may perhaps see in soaring outline before him; but when he has proceeded a little way he finds the direct path must be forsaken, and when he has gained the summit he looks down with thankfulness, as he observes that the plain and shorter path he would have chosen was forsaken by his guide in time to prevent him from coming upon abrupt precipices, down which he might have been hurried by his rash confidence. So when from the hill of Sion above we gaze upon the rugged and diversified routes we have been led to take in the long and trying ascent, then in the light thrown down upon all the scene from the throne of glory, we shall admire the skill and wisdom which led us and guarded us at every step and in every emergency.

> "The light that from the glorious throne
> Shines down upon life's varied way,
> Shows that one path, and one alone,
> Led safely to the realms of day."

How thankful shall we then be for the means as well as the end,—for the path as well as the palace: and rapturously shall we join with the mighty host of the saved in singing, "Great and marvellous are thy works, Lord

K

God Almighty ; just and true are thy ways, thou King of saints."

The following narrative, communicated to me by the individual herself who was principally concerned in it, will show the words of the psalmist to have been fulfilled in her experience, both in a literal and spiritual sense. In the land of vision to which she is gone, she may indeed sing with deep emotion, and in the double meaning, " We went through fire and water : but thou broughtest us out into a wealthy place." It was given to me as having formerly been her pastor, upon her return from St. John's, Newfoundland, whither she had repaired to reside with her husband, and had remained until the dreadful conflagration which nearly consumed that place in the year 1846.

"On that fatal night, at nine o'clock p.m., we were aroused by the repeated cry of ' Fire ! fire !' On rushing to the window in an upper room to ascertain the ground of this alarm, we found the whole of the opposite side of the street in flames. The width of the street and the direction of the wind prevented any particular apprehensions of danger to ourselves ; but, alas ! in a few moments the wind changed, and blew the flame directly over our house, which stood opposite the one in which the fire had originated. The street was by this time filled with burning furniture, thrown out of numerous houses which were on fire, and we endeavoured to remove the best part of our own, but were unable for want of assistance. My dear babe was conveyed by the two servants to a place of safety, while my husband and myself remained, still hoping to save the most valuable portion of our property, but were prevented by the rapid progress of the flames throughout the dwelling. Now, our only way of personal escape seemed to be through the nursery window, which looked into the garden ; but on reaching it we found it to be rapidly consuming. We then rushed to the main staircase, which unfortunately was blocked up with furniture hurried to the head of it for removal. Over this obstacle, however, we contrived to climb, and make our way through the hall to a lower window which looked upon the garden; but before which also, in the confusion, much furniture had been accumulated. We now gave up all for lost, and commended ourselves to God, prepared to perish, and locked in each other's arms. At that moment we heard the shouting of our servants, who were asking for their master and mistress, and were urging the bystanders to break open the kitchen window, as they declared their confidence that we had not escaped. Their shouts, however, were soon lost to our hearing in the roaring of the fierce flames and the loud tumult of the people. Yet, exhausted as we were, we endeavoured to raise our voices to their utmost pitch; and were at last happily heard. Instantly the window was dashed in, and we, with our torn garments and bruised and burnt persons, were dragged out safely—the living monuments of a wonderful preservation, and of our Father's merciful deliverance.

"I pass over what immediately followed: but we had lost our all; and my own health, together with that of my baby, had seriously suffered. We resolved therefore, with the assistance of friends, to return to England, and begin life again. Accordingly I embarked with my child, leaving my husband behind to arrange his affairs, to rest for recovery from an accident he had met with, and then to follow us. In the month of January our passage was taken in a fine vessel bound for Cork, and in company with twenty-four other passengers, some of whom had belonged to my most intimate circle of acquaintance, we set sail on the 22nd of that month. We started with a fine breeze, which accompanied us, and made *half-passage* in five days, the wind continuing fair : but on the fifth day it became very boisterous. I felt dissatisfied with several things which I had observed in reference to the captain and crew ; but as there were so many other passengers on board, it hardly seemed within my province to make any remark. That evening I retired with my dear babe to rest at nine p.m., but became so extremely nervous and restless that I could not sleep. Towards midnight I felt certain from the peculiar motion of the vessel that all was not right. I was debating in my own mind whether I should call to any of the passengers, but fearing to disturb the child in my arms, and thus to add to the confusion, should any misfortune occur, I remained quiet and silent a little longer; but presently found the vessel gradually sinking on one side, and a noise, which came down into the state-room, like the gathering of water over my head. The widow lady who occupied part of my cabin cried out, ' Mrs. T., are you awake ? I am sure all is not right!' 'I have been under the same impression,' I replied, 'for some time, but I could not move on account of the child.' 'I will call,' said she, 'to some of the gentlemen.' She arose, and was in the act of throwing on her dressing-gown, when, in an instant, the ship went over on her beam ends ! Wild shrieks were heard, and we were in utter darkness, for both our fire and candles were extinguished. By some means two passengers procured a light, I think from their cigar cases, and by this time all present, with the exception of myself and one other, were thrown into the ladies' cabin. Some were praying on their knees, some profanely cursing the day on which they had come on board, and others calling on all the saints in the calendar, and especially the Virgin Mary, to save them. Few, very few I fear, addressed themselves to Him who alone had the power to save. A second tremendous sea struck us, and deluged the cabin together with every one in it. There was one faint cry, and then the stillness of death prevailed amongst us all, for all were in despair! *My* feelings are to be more easily imagined than described. At the first shock I was too confused even to pray—the thoughts of my poor absent husband, of my mother, and of the many friends who would be overwhelmed with sorrow on our account, for the moment obliterated every other idea. But it was the feeling only of that one moment, for in the next *a whole life seemed crowded into the brief space allotted between the stroke of the first and second seas. As if in a panorama, the whole scenes and objects of the past became present to my view.* This was an awful season; nature shrank and trembled at the thought of the waters closing over us, and none being left to tell the tale.

"But *prayer prevailed!* The light of heaven broke in upon my terror-stricken spirit, and I felt that though the chief of sinners, I was secure, being even then upon the 'Rock of ages.' That place of horror where I lay immersed up to my clinging baby's feet in water, and in the midst of distress, was indeed a 'Bethel!' Never may I forget those happy moments! I now covered the face of my babe with one portion of the sheet I had about me, drew the remaining part over my head, and awaited the awful moment that was to hurry us into the eternal world. A third heavy sea now struck us; but, singular to relate, struck us on the opposite side, and the vessel immediately righted, though trembling to its very centre from the shock and the quivering of its beams! One of the passengers rushed on deck, and in a moment the joyous shout was heard, 'Thank God; we are safe!' Some minutes elapsed before I could believe it, and then the joy was too great, and I became quite hysterical, but shortly recovered, pressed my babe to my heart, and re dedicated it, together with my ownself, to Him who had thus made our lives doubly his care."

The subject of this narrative arrived safely on land, and remained some time with her friends near the metropolis. We did all in our power to soothe and comfort her and her husband, who was a truly pious man. But her constitution had suffered from the repeated shocks, and upon an epidemic prevailing, she was seized with it, when tranquilly, amidst friends and relatives, with every creature help at hand, she left this troubled scene for the haven of eternal rest.

———o———

The Marvels of Grace.

"I am as a wonder unto many; but thou art my strong refuge."
Ps. lxxi. 7.

ON several accounts a converted man may be an object of surprise among his contemporaries. This may arise from the circumstance of his conversion dating at a late period of his life, when his long continuance in a state of impenitence seemed to render it almost certain that he would persist in it to the last. It is indeed a wonder to see any human being's course entirely altered at a late period, and to observe him afterwards moving in a totally different direction, influenced by different principles. Or, to take the instance of another convert, the character he is enabled to sustain, founded upon his great change, is in such marked and continued contrasts to his former habits of life, as to render it difficult to recognise in the Christian of to-day the sinner of yesterday. " Is Saul also among the prophets?" Or, in yet another example, the means Divinely employed to effect conversion may be, apparently, so disproportionate to the magnitude of the result, as to place the result itself under suspicion and doubt. Even godly men, like Ananias of old, may hesitate to admit into their society the persecutor or the profligate of unhappy notoriety, except upon clearly discerning that he has become a new creature in Christ Jesus, and that old, evil habits have passed away. At the same time, his former ungodly associates are malicious enough to promulgate false reports concerning his character and motives. "They think it strange," says the apostle, "that ye run not with them to the same excess of riot, speaking evil of you." Yet to such a convert his God is a sun and shield—a shield from the shafts of cruel slander, and a refuge to him from all the storms of persecution. In all similar cases the language of the psalmist becomes particularly appropriate,—" I am as a wonder unto many; but thou art my strong refuge."

I have been led to this train of reflections by recollecting the case of an individual who was one of the early fruits of my ministry at Kensington, and who himself adopted, and often repeated, the passage I have placed at the head of these remarks.

He was by trade a shoemaker, and resided in one of the narrow courts or alleys of the town. Naturally he was inoffensive and cheerful, and so healthful and good-tempered that his neighbours deeply lamented his association with dissolute and profane companions. At the time I became first acquainted with him he had already degenerated into a notoriously bad man. Two of his children were brought into the Sunday-school that was established in connection with my chapel, the gratuitous teachers in which were indefatigable, scripturally intelligent, and zealously concerned for the intellectual, moral, and spiritual welfare of those committed to their care. One Sabbath afternoon these were publicly examined to test their proficiency, and their parents and friends were invited to be present. By the persuasions of his favourite daughter, the father of these two children was induced to attend. It was the first time he he had ever entered that place of worship, which was his abhorrence, on account of the reformation there wrought in some of his dissolute companions. He was astonished at the knowledge which his own child had obtained, and gratified at the commendations she received. As the company were invited to attend again at the evening service, he resolved to make one among the number. The subject of the discourse happened to be singularly appropriate. It was founded on that passage in the Epistle of Jude, where the apostle speaks of believers as "preserved in Christ Jesus, and called." The aim of the preacher was to expatiate on the many recorded instances of the wonderful preservation of persons while in an unconverted state, who afterwards became eminent for piety and zeal in promoting the conversion of others. The case of the Rev. Mr. Cecil, which at that moment came suddenly to recollection, was introduced in illustration. That excellent clergyman was thrown from his horse on the road just across the rut of a wagon, which in passing crushed his hat and moved it away from his head, without inflicting any injury on himself. The attention of the new-comer was riveted. *He* had in his youth been in a similar situation, unfavoured however by so marvellous an escape, having been much hurt by a cart-wheel which passed over him, and rendered him a cripple for life. When the question which followed the recital was addressed and repeated, to any present who might have experienced similar preservations while in an unconverted state, as to the purpose for which they had been preserved, whether to continue servants of sin, or to become the servants of God; and when they were urged to answer it, as they would at the judgment-seat,—he trembled, for he felt that this question was addressed emphatically to him. The evil of his past life rose with appalling vividness before him. His heart melted within him like wax, and his eyes streamed with tears. That night he passed in an anguish of remorse bordering on despair. Afterwards he came again and again to the house of God. Light broke in upon his mind by degrees, and he sought and found salvation by faith in Christ Jesus. Not only was he now remarked for his constant attendance upon public worship, but for the total change which had taken place in his character and course of life. The drunkard became sober, the profane began to fear an oath, and the Sabbath-breaker to account "the Sabbath a delight, the holy of the Lord, and honourable." He was admitted into Christian fellowship, to the surprise of many; and not only he himself, but his whole family, became worshippers of God at their own abode as well as in the sanctuary. Of course general observation was attracted to him, ridicule was unsparingly heaped upon him by his former boon companions, and every method was resorted to which malice could devise, to drive him from his determined perseverance in his new and better ways. But all this was in vain. The work was of God, and could not be overthrown.

The beneficial influence of this happy change extended where it might have been least expected; for it broke down a wall of prejudice which had arisen in the mind of the young vicar of the place against the nonconformists of his neighbourhood. Of their minister he had formed the grossest misconception; and in his zeal to prevent defections from the parish church, he himself called at the house of the individual of whom I am now writing. He found him engaged at his work in his truly humble abode, and was received respectfully and deferentially. Upon inquiring the reason of the shoemaker's absence from what he affirmed to be his proper place on the Lord's-day, the vicar received from him, while his eyes streamed with tears, such an account of the transformation which had taken place in him, and the manner in which it had been wrought, as greatly affected the prejudiced clergyman.

"O sir!" said the poor man with deep emotion, "what a change! This room was once a little hell; it is now a little heaven!"

Shortly afterwards the vicar called upon me, and entered into familiar conversation with me on the great truths of the gospel, evidently as the result of the impression which the shoemaker's wonderful conversion had produced; thenceforth his kindly feeling towards me never declined, and this was the more to be remarked on account of his high standing in the Episcopal Church, as respected his learning, oratorical power, and zeal for God according to his knowledge. He was comparatively young, but with a magnanimous mind he had early determined to appreciate truth and goodness wherever they were found, and to follow them whithersoever they might lead. Shortly afterwards he fell into a decline, and one evening while we were holding a prayer-meeting, news was brought us of his dangerous illness. I immediately requested those who led our devotions to bear him on their minds before God; I afterwards requested that no mention might be made of this circumstance, as I did not desire to draw attention to ourselves; but a report of it reached his sick chamber, and shortly after, upon the occasion of his removal for the benefit of change of air, I received from him the following note :—

"VICARAGE, KENSINGTON,
April 29*th*, 1824.

"DEAR SIR,—I cannot leave Kensington without expressing to you my grateful feelings for the truly kind and Christian manner in which, during a very critical period of my illness, you were pleased to direct the prayers of your congregation to the throne of grace for my recovery. It has made a deep impression on my mind.

"These prayers were mercifully heard, and by the blessing of God I trust that I am in a state of progressive amendment. Slow, indeed, have been my advances, insomuch that even now I am totally incapable of the ordinary exertions of life; but I trust that a good Providence, whose mercies have indeed been about my path and about my bed, will, in his good time, perform the perfect work of restoration.

"Believe me to be, dear Sir,
"With much respect,
"Your faithful and obedient servant,
"THOS. RENNELL."

The benefit, however, sought for by a change of residence was not obtained, and he departed this life in the midst of his zealous and useful labours, to the regret of his numerous parishioners and a large circle of friends.

The following reply to a circular inviting the inhabitants generally to give expression to their feelings by contributing to a tablet to be erected to his memory, and which was read at a public meeting, will show the estimation in which he was held, and justify the foregoing encomium:—

July 10*th*, 1824.

"GENTLEMEN,—It is with great pleasure that I immediately forward my subscription for the laudable object you have in view, and I am reconciled to the limitation imposed on the subscriptions, only by the consideration that so many more persons will thereby have an opportunity afforded them of showing their respect for an individual of no mean estimation or importance.

"It is rare that so many excellences are found in combination as those by which the late vicar was distinguished. His zeal for the interests of the Church, of which he was so bright an ornament, was happily accompanied with candour and kindness towards those who conscientiously differed from him in some particulars. The virtues of his private character were equal to the energies of his public one; and he was not more admired as an author and a preacher than beloved as a man.

"It is among the mysteries of Providence that he has been so soon removed; but it must be some consolation to the friends whom he has left, and some mitigation of the pangs inflicted on them by the bereavement, that their sorrows are largely shared, and that no monument can be erected to his memory that will adequately express the esteem and affection with which he was regarded by individuals of all classes and parties.

"I hope I shall not be deemed intrusive in offering this testimony, the genuine dictate of my own feelings, and
"I am, gentlemen,
"Your obedient and humble servant,
"JOHN LEIFCHILD.
"To the Committee, etc., etc."

The deceased had, I was told, expressed a hope to some friends who referred to the circumstance of his calling upon and conversing with me, that we should meet in heaven. May this be granted! Will not the above then be recognised as one of those incidental benefits with which the operations of God are fraught, which distinguish them from all the schemes of men? *They* employ a variety of means and expedients to compass one end; He by one accomplishes many, and those the most unexpected. Probably no other circumstance would have overcome the prejudices of my opponent, and converted him into a Christian friend. The tide of prejudice against nonconformists was by this event, in a great measure, stemmed, and persons of high rank and station were frequent attendants at the Sabbath evening services of our sanctuary.

As to the humble individual whose conversion was connected with this occurrence, he continued firm in the new course on which he had entered. He became not only a reformed, but a remarkably different character from what he had been during the former and greater part of his life. "Old things passed away, and all things became new." The profligate persecutor of the Church of God was now a warm adherent of it; he who once stood at the corner of the street leading to the chapel, at the hour of the evening service, assiduously and earnestly attempting to dissuade his associates from entering within its doors, now stood there as earnestly entreating them to come within its sacred walls. His house, formerly the scene of riotous disturbance, was now the humble abode of peace and devotion; instead of the song of the drunkard, the praises of God were heard in it; and his wife and children having been brought into the same state of mind, and thereupon gladly joining in the same religious engagements, they composed a truly happy domestic circle. He formed some societies of a benevolent description, and the neighbourhood was now considerably benefited by his exertions and example—perhaps more than it had been formerly injured by the influence of his bad conduct.

As his inability to move from place to place increased with his years, a chair was made for him, in which he was carefully wheeled about by his relatives and friends. His once bloated countenance now displayed habitual serenity and joyfulness. Whenever he heard that I was about to revisit he town, which I had subsequently left for another scene of labour, he caused his little carriage to be wheeled out to meet me. I saw his eyes glistening with emotion and the tears rolling down his cheeks as I approached him, and then he invariably exclaimed aloud, "I am a wonder to many, sir; but God is my strong refuge." This was the passage of Scripture which, after his first strong impression, he was able confidently to adopt and joyfully to apply to himself. The following stanza was often on his lips, and sung with a jubilant voice :—

> "Amazing grace! how sweet the sound,
> That saved a wretch like me!
> I once was lost, but now am found;
> Was blind, but now I see!"

The above narrative is given in its simple details, without addition of any kind, in order that its desired effect may not be weakened by any attempt to supply ornament or to append further reflections.

―――o―――

Remembered Preservations and Deliverances.

"Bless the Lord, O my soul, and forget not all his benefits; who forgiveth all thine iniquities; who healeth all thy diseases; who redeemeth thy life from destruction; who crowneth thee with lovingkindness and tender mercies."—Ps. ciii. 2-4.

THIS sublime hymn of praise teaches us to record our mercies in our inmost souls, and to summon all our powers to expressions of exulting gratitude. The psalmist himself is an example of pious reflection upon the varied events of his past life, and we see him classifying the multitude of his mercies under different heads; such as, the preservation of life under imminent danger, recovery from severe and threatening maladies, the bestowment of the grace of penitence for sin, and of the gift of pardon and restoration to the Divine favour after temporary relapses, thus "crowning" his following days with peace and gladness.

It is most profitable for us oftentimes to review God's goodness to us in days that are past, and to distinguish special manifestations of it by marked consideration and acknowledgment. If we fail in this exercise the intended benefit will be lost, and any gratitude inspired at the moment of partaking the blessing will prove to be but as the fire of thorns that soon passes away. However signal the forgotten mercies, yet how fruitlessly shall we have been the subject of them if they elicit no song of praise, animate us to no renewed confidence under new perplexities, or prompt us to no becoming manifestations of zeal for the Divine glory, and to no deeds imitative of the Divine benevolence! Forgetfulness such as this virtually defrauds our gracious Preserver and Benefactor of his due return of praise, while it deprives us of the spiritual and moral improvement which the favours themselves are specially designed to produce in us.

The preservation of life in particular jeopardy, and its unexpected prolongation, should appear prominently in our retrospection; for not only is life a great blessing in itself, but the prolongation of it may insure a continual capacity for enjoyment and activity, and thus become the means of glorifying its Divine Author and increasing and maturing our own moral excellence. Yet alas! how many among us fail, while reviewing past life, to regard their mercies in this light, and life itself as the primary mercy and the source of all blessings associated with it! Were they to give utterance to appropriate thoughts under such circumstances, they might cheerfully sing—

> "Thou, O Lord, my life defending,
>   Hast prolonged my mortal days,
> That my love through life extending,
>   E'er may prompt a hymn of praise.
>
> Thanks for gracious preservation,
>   Thanks that thou didst haste to save!
> Gratitude and exultation
>   Shall not cease but in the grave."

How sinful in the sight of the loving Father must be the heedlessness of those who take no account of remarkable escapes during the perils incident to infancy and childhood, or, in after-years, of their safety in trying circumstances by night and by day, on the land, or on the treacherous deep, in ordinary occupation and in peculiar exposures! What! will they not retrace with profound emotions the periods when their heavenly Father's gracious interposition rekindled the fast-waning lamp of life which disease had well-nigh extinguished? Will they not call to mind the dark hours when their uncertain steps wandered on the brink of destruction, and when in one moment, life with all its complexities, engagements, varied attractions, its memories of home and childhood, and its more recent yet equally strong affections, was in peril of sudden termination; and when one turn of that Hand which holds the keys of life and of death would have opened to them the doors of another world? David, at least, treasured all such mercies and all such interpositions in grateful remembrance, when he penned this beautiful ode to Him who had been the Redeemer of his life from destruction, and the Healer of his sore diseases, as well as the Author of his eternal salvation.

Let this inspired bard be a model to those who acknowledge with contrition their lapses of memory, and deplore their failures of grateful expressions to the Divine Source of all the favours by them received, especially for the extension of opportunities to serve him on earth, and to speak his praises with an unfaltering tongue.

I was upon one occasion discoursing from the pulpit on the above words in the 103rd Psalm, and enlarging upon the singular protection afforded in pity to some, who while in an unconverted state, had been in imminent peril, but who had afterwards been happily made partakers of Divine grace—the "crowning mercy;" yet who had nevertheless failed to record and keep in grateful remembrance these merciful interpositions. I then narrated some one or two instances illustrative of the tenor of my discourse, and concluded by endeavouring to impress upon my hearers the heinousness of the sin of forgetfulness under such circumstances, and the injury they suffered in the loss of appropriate emotions, and of strong incentives to holy obedience in the present, and humble confidence for the future.

After this service and the sacramental communion, I tarried at the house of a lady who had been one of my auditors and a communicant at the Lord's table. When she appeared, I was surprised to observe that her countenance wore the traces of deep emotion. Upon my remarking this, she at once said to me, "O sir, what a train of thoughts you have awakened in my heart this morning by your discourse; what mingled feelings of sorrow for forgetfulness, shame for ingratitude, and wonder in reflecting upon the riches of Divine goodness and condescension with relation to myself! The particular cause was connected with the following event in my life. It is now many years since I was sojourning at Margate for the benefit of my health, which had been impaired by a round of fashionable amusements in which I had taken part. While there, I was accustomed to proceed frequently in my own carriage to the adjoining town of Ramsgate, where some cherished friends of mine were also sojourning. I was in the habit of driving, in my open vehicle, a horse, long accustomed to me and my guidance, which, though occasionally high-spirited, was generally docile and quiet. In some places the road at that time ran at no great distance from the tall chalk cliffs which on that coast overhang the sea ; and in such a place as that I was one day met, while driving as usual, by a brewer's dray. Unfortunately, its rumbling noise upon the road, joined with the loud voices of the men who were with it, and the cracking of their whips, so terrified my horse that he suddenly reared, and then backed towards the cliff, the edge of which he reached, despite all my efforts to soothe him and to check him in his retrograde course. At length, to my unutterable horror, I was ejected from my carriage, and literally thrown over the edge of the cliff! This overthrow caused the animal to plunge madly forward at that moment, to draw the empty vehicle from the edge of the cliff, and thus to escape. The men who had witnessed this accident, with others who came up with them, hastened, some to the summit of the cliff, and others, by a downward opening, to the shore, expecting to find me a mangled corpse. But most singularly my fall had been broken by a projecting portion of the chalk, on which I had been lodged. There I lay stunned and without any consciousness, until means were devised to get at the spot and to extricate me from my awful position. Most mercifully I had only received severe but not dangerous bruises, and on recovering from my state of insensibility, I was enabled to return home, a wonder to the spectators, and snatched, as it were, out of the very jaws of sudden death! I am ashamed to confess that this signal deliverance had almost passed from my mind, and that I had of late seldom recurred to it. Your observations, however, this morning, deeply humbled me, and brought the whole scene again vividly before me, with all its attendant circumstances. I was then a thoughtless, world-loving person, and had I but fallen down the cliff, I should have been hurried unpreparedly into the eternal world. What then would have been my everlasting condition? I could not but reflect upon this during the remainder of the service, nor could I refrain from mentally expressing my gratitude to my Redeemer. Now, sir, for the future, I beg of you to omit no opportunity of urging upon me to show my gratitude in all those ways in which I may be able to render any service to my fellow-creatures, or to promote the cause of Christ. I should wish to consecrate my all to his service and glory."

So remarkable a deliverance as the above may not have been the lot of many readers of this volume; and yet it is probable that every one of them has been at one period or another the subject of preservation in extreme peril, or at least of restoration from severe sickness and wasting maladies. Probably, too, this has not been duly acknowledged at the time, or adequately improved afterwards. To all such a frequent review of past mercies, and a distinct enumeration of the principal ones, will be particularly improving; and will stimulate them to thank God for his goodness in sparing them, the "unprofitable servants," and granting them a yet longer space in which to repent of numerous offences, to resolve on more entire obedience, and an unreserved surrender of person and property to the Divine call. If we should neglect such a retrospect, and should miss the fruits of it, nevertheless, providences unimproved will all one day come to remembrance, and then by confronting us, cause shame and confusion of face.

The example of the Rev. Edmund Staunton, an eminent Puritan divine, may be commended for imitation to all who desire to be the followers of them who through faith and patience inherit the promises. He kept a "diary of God's mercies," a part of which only was found after his decease, and was published with his name. In it he recounts several signal preservations and remarkable escapes, appending to each of them an appropriate ascription of praise and thanksgiving to the ever-watchful Providence which presides over human affairs. From this I have extracted and subjoined some incidents which may serve as an incentive and guide to those who are similarly devout, who may be similarly circumstanced, and who may desire to be quickened in their consciousness, and stimulated in their acknowledgments of the goodness and mercy which have followed them all the days of their lives.

He refers to an alarming fever with which at an early period of his life he had been seized, and to the failure of all the remedies devised and administered to stay its progress. His death was expected as inevitable, when under a sudden impulse, for which he could scarcely account, he laid hold upon a pitcher of liquid placed at his bedside for some quite different purpose, and drank it all. To the astonishment of his attendants, it was found that this unexpected draught had arrested the progress of his malady. "I think," says he, in the quaint style of his day, "my good God directed me to the act."

At a subsequent period, and when he was about fourteen years of age, he was exercising himself in a swing in his father's kitchen at Birchmore. The ceiling was lofty, and the floor was paved with rough bricks or stone. In a mad freak he urged his attendant to raise him to the utmost height, that he might touch the ceiling with his hands and feet. When nearly able to do this, the rope of the swing broke, and he was precipitated to the rough pavement below with great force. There he lay stunned and motionless, and apparently lifeless, until a copious effusion of blood from different parts occasioned relief. To this unusually copious effusion, those around who were best able to judge attributed his freedom from permanent injury, and his ultimate recovery.

On other occasions he was delivered from a dreadful death in a remarkable manner. While sleeping in his tutor's chamber at Oxford, a wax-candle, which he had carelessly left alight upon a deal box full of linen, had kindled the box, which, together with all the linen it contained, was burnt, while he lay in unconscious slumber in a closely adjoining bed, and was uninjured. Again, at a later period, in the same city, the partner of his life was busy late at night in the midst of suspended linen. This was accidentally and suddenly ignited by a candle, and would have set the house on fire, and in all probability burnt herself and her husband, who lay asleep in an adjoining chamber, had she not providentially been enabled to tear down the consuming material, and by great exertion to extinguish the spreading flames.

At the time he was deeply sensible of his obligations to praise a kind and vigilant Providence; but much more sensible of this was he, when it afterward came to pass that his life, so signally and frequently spared, was devoted to the sacred ministry, and was honourably employed in the salvation of many souls from everlasting destruction.

With him was contemporary the Rev. James Janeway, one of the five sons of the Rev. William Janeway, minister at Kelshall, in Hertfordshire, all of whom were remarkable for early piety and devotion. On leaving the university, where he had taken his degree, he exercised the office of tutor some time at Windsor, preaching wherever he had an opportunity, without obtaining any benefice. By the act of uniformity he was silenced and separated from the Church. During the plague, he was assiduous in visiting the sick and preaching the gospel, being singularly preserved from infection and from taking any harm. He collected a congregation at Rotherhithe, where he was very useful, and which, after the plague, became very numerous. This so exasperated the high party, that several attempts were made to deprive him of life, all of which, as well as the plague, through the intervention of Providence, had no power to hurt him. Upon one occasion, as he was walking along Rotherhithe Wall, a fellow shot at him, and the bullet went through his hat, but did him no further harm. At another time, the soldiers broke into his meeting-house, and would have pulled him down from the pulpit, but the bench on which they stood gave away, and in the confusion he escaped. The troopers made another attempt to seize him, when he was preaching at a gardener's house, but he threw himself on the ground, and his friends covered him with cabbage-leaves, by which means he escaped. He died in the prime of life, in the thirty-eighth year of his age. In his last illness he had some clouds of melancholy, but it pleased God to dissipate them, and not long before his death, he said, "I can now as easily die as shut my eyes;" adding, "Here am I longing to be silent in the dust, and to enjoy Christ in glory."

He was the author of several excellent works, among

which is to be noticed, "A Token for Children," which has been greatly owned and blessed of God in the conversion of the young.

These incidents, together with others of a like nature, are deserving of notice, not, perhaps, so much on account of their marvellousness or rarity, as on account of the practice of the good men concerned in them, who, when thus preserved, perpetuated the instances of Divine care by erecting a verbal memorial of praise. Many good men have, in the absence of such a habit, omitted to record as striking and even more striking interventions in their behalf, and have suffered such, though they may have impressed them deeply at the time, to lapse from their memory, and to be effaced by the ever-recurring tides of the business of life. Sometimes, indeed, when quickened to a careful retrospect of what they have lived through, such deliverances start up into view, and rebuke their slumbering thoughtlessness and negligent gratitude.

And surely the holy men of Scripture reprove us by their superior conduct in noticing the hand of God in whatever befel them, and in recalling such proofs of his intervention as invest their writings with undying interest to future believers.

For many years it was my practice, in order to avoid the unprofitableness of desultory conversation, to request the friends in any Christian company which might meet together socially, at the house of one of my people, to call to mind and to narrate any such providential interposition in their own lives as might lead to useful reflections and contribute to united thankfulness. No one was strongly pressed to speak, and thus it often happened for a while that no person had anything to bring forward. Yet in the end it almost invariably occurred that one recital, when completed, led to another; and in due time a store of singular narratives was called forth, and stimulated memories reproduced the materials of the past for present wonder and gratitude. Occasion was thus furnished for caution and for exhortation, as well as for renewed confidence in the Great Deliverer, to whom all united in singing an appropriate hymn of praise, and thus terminated, not merely a happy, but a lastingly useful meeting. Some, now grown old in the service of their Lord, have referred to these unions with distinct recollection and pleasant associations.

On one of these profitable meetings, an individual who was a member of our Church Society, and whose zeal and usefulness were noteworthy, though accompanied by humility and backwardness to make himself prominent, narrated the following incident, which at my request he committed to writing:—

"During the Christmas season, 1830, in the north of Scotland, the discharge of fireworks was a favourite amusement of the younger part of the community. At this time, while a boy at school, I had saved up my pence and purchased a pound of gunpowder. The servant-girls that same evening being in another part of the house, and the kitchen being perfectly clear, I retired thither, accompanied by my two sisters and my brother, all younger than myself, and constituting the whole family, with our parents, the latter being then in an adjoining room, but ignorant of the manner in which we were employing ourselves.

"In order to empty the gunpowder out of the paper in which it was wrapped up, it was poured into a large bullock's horn with a wooden bottom, and a common cork for a stopper. A great fire burnt brightly and freely in the grate, a jet of gaslight protruded from the wall above, the door was at the farther end from the fire, and behind the door stood a large tub of clear water for domestic purposes, while round a table which stood in the centre of the room we four children were engaged as described. The bullock's horn being filled, and packed as tightly as possible, was corked and placed on the table; about an egg-cupful remained which could not be got in. This my brother wished for, and I refused him, upon which we quarrelled, and he seized it by force, but I, being the stronger, forcibly wrenched it from him. Stung at the disappointment, he went deliberately to the table, took up the powder-horn, walked directly to the fire-place, and in an instant thrust it into the centre of the burning coals. Fear so paralysed my frame as to prevent me from being able to arrest his movements. The mischief done, he immediately ran out of doors. My sisters, ignorant of the precise danger, still lingered between the table and the fire; I, suffering at the time from lameness, through a recent burn on my foot, could only cry out to them to save themselves by getting out of the room, while limping myself as fast as I was able towards the door. I ran behind the chink of it, and was now watching the expected consummation. My eldest sister, having accompanied me, ran into the passage beyond, while my youngest sister in her dread ran into a corner of the kitchen, and the very corner nearest to the grate.

"An agony of suspense ensued, and a dizziness from excessive fear came over me, in the midst of which my eldest sister, behind me in the passage, walked past me into the kitchen again, and went straight up to the grate without uttering a syllable. In the coolest manner she took up the tongs, thrust them into the fire, grasped the powder-horn, now crackling from the heat, and its wooden bottom one red charred mass, and taking it the whole length of the kitchen, loosened her hold, and calmly allowed it to sink into the tub of water, where it hissed for a short while, and all danger was over. But for this *extraordinary promptitude* of mind, we should all probably have been dreadfully injured, if not destroyed.

"My parents in the next room knew nothing of what had happened till some time afterwards. Nor did we ourselves then fully understand the greatness of our deliverance. Our dear sister to whom we owed so much, became herself the mother of an interesting family, but died, regretted by the whole community, at the age of thirty-five years. She fell asleep in Jesus. My youngest sister is well and comfortably settled in Scotland, but never, since she arrived at an understanding age, was the protecting care of our God in this matter forgotten or unacknowledged."

———o———

Light in Darkness.

"The entrance of thy word giveth light; it giveth understanding unto the simple."—Ps. cxix. 130.

THE living power of the Bible, and its wonderful adaptation to the human heart, is a truth almost universally acknowledged. Yet how many who admit the fact, have but the faintest experience of its reality! Those indeed who have been familiar from childhood with the contents of the Sacred Volume, can scarcely estimate the mighty effect of its simple but sublime disclosures on the minds of persons previously utterly ignorant and unawakened. The astonishing facts, the moving scenes, and remarkable personages of the Old and New Testament, strike them with all the vividness of a first impression; seizing the imagination and affecting the heart so powerfully as sometimes to engross the whole powers of the soul. How many dark and neglected minds, fast locked in the chains of ignorance and sin, have been thus secretly opened by this Divine key, and insensibly peopled by objects of fresh and undying interest. The mysterious capacities of the human spirit for communion with the unseen world being awakened from their death-like slumber, new desires, affections, hopes, and joys spring up within the soul. It is then that the consummate wisdom of the Book of God is seen in its perfect suitableness to meet these wants, and to nourish them with appropriate supplies. Those of whom we speak have little power to enter into the abstractions of truth, or the mysteries of Christian doctrine, and may be incapable of appreciating the force of reason and argument in its favour; but they can understand the histories of men and women of like passions with themselves, and enter into an experience that is similar to their own. Above all, they can see Jesus, the Friend of sinners and the Saviour of the lost, as the very Friend and Saviour *they need*, and to him, when Divinely taught, they yield the unquestioning love and trust of little children. " Blessed be ye poor; for yours is the kingdom of God !"

Instances might be multiplied of those who, though like the subject of the following narrative, they may have no place in the visible Church of Christ, will yet assuredly, at the day of his appearing, be found among the Lord's chosen ones, to swell the chorus of his praise: " And they shall be mine, saith the Lord of hosts, in that day when I make up my jewels."

Many years ago I visited an aged woman in the city of

Bristol, at the request of her son, who was in decent circumstances. He told me that his mother had been a constant attendant on my ministry, but was now very aged and infirm, and at the point of death. It was the afternoon of the day when I reached her house, which was at some distance from my own. Following my guide, I ascended to the topmost room, and found it meanly furnished, and so far from cleanly as to render it unpleasant *for me* to remain. I saw lying on a bed before me, an aged female, with her grey hair matted about her head, her eyes dim with age and disease, and her whole appearance most painful and repulsive. "Mother," said her son, "I have brought a gentleman to see you."—"Who is it?" she mumbled, "I don't know anybody, and can hardly see at all." "I thought," said I, turning to the son, "that she would not know me." At the sound of my voice, she started, and aroused herself, saying, "Oh yes, but I do. Ah! you are the gem'man that I ha' walked so many a weary mile to listen to, and after my walk on my old legs, I had always to stand in the aisles, as you call 'em, for want of room; but I didn't mind. Oh, often's the time when I waited to pull you by the sleeve as you came down from the pulpit and passed me, that I might tell you how I loved you for talking so much about my old friends and acquaintances!" "Your old friends and acquaintances?" I inquired, "whom do you mean? You and your friends are quite strangers to me." "Why, I mean," said she, "Abraham, Isaac, and Jacob, and them like. Dear me, didn't you often tell me how that good old man walked with God, when he went out not knowing where he was going to? And how poor old Jacob lost his son—dear Joseph? They bound him fast in the prison, and the iron entered into his soul; and," continued she, as if talking to herself, "I've got a Joseph.

He's far away from me, and I shall see him no more, but I shall leave him this book" (a large folio Bible, which had been purchased in separate parts, and which was lying before her), "I bought it for him a long while ago. I have got no other book, only 'The Holy War,' them be all I ever had; but him (directing her attention to the Bible), I'll give him; he'll find it wetted in many places with his old mother's tears. Ah! don't you remember," she continued, "that poor dear creature who went into the house after him, and stood at his feet, and wash'd 'em with her tears, and wiped 'em with her hair? I got no hair to wipe 'em, but *I* could wash 'em with tears too, and they'd not be tears of grief—no, but of love, like hers was, for he said to her—oh! did not his dear lips say to her—Your many sins be all forgiven you; and has not he forgiven mine, quite as many as hers? and don't I love him?" Then the big tears rolled down her furrowed cheeks, and her strong emotions almost choked her utterance, while her hands were clasped together and lifted up, as if she would have embraced something which she alone could see. So graphic were her descriptions, and so animated was her manner, that I stood beside her listening, as it were entranced, and unmindful of all around me that had seemed unsightly and unpleasant.

The son had quitted the chamber and left us alone; but she, as if heedless of the presence of any one, and occupied with her own musings, went on, and once or twice spoke as if she saw before her the very individuals about whom she was conversing. "Yes," she exclaimed, "the ill-natured Pharisee—(ah! them be always ill-natured to poor folks and sinners like me)—huffed her, and said, if the Master knew her, he wouldn't ha' let her come so near him,—wouldn't he? Ah! *he* didn't know him, bless his dear lips and his tender, loving heart. No, says he, she has much forgiven her; and didn't he look into her heart, and tell her to go in peace? Why, they put him between two thieves! they thought to disgrace him; but he took one on 'em to heaven with him! didn't he make a jewel of him? Ah, and he can make me one of his jewels! But la, sir," said she, just then recognising my presence, "how I ha' been talking, and *you* here, who I've so wanted to hear talk again. Oh, do tell me more about my friends and acquaintances (meaning the Old Testament saints), for I think about them all day and night, and I go about with them and hear all their tales, and see how they wept and how they prayed; and I see the angels, too, coming and talking to them, and then I talk to them, and they to me. And I thinks it'll not be long before I do talk to them *really*." So she went on till, having to attend an evening service, I reluctantly left the room, promising to see her the next day. My mind was so full of the images and personages she had conjured up before me, that they formed the whole matter of my address that evening; and at the close I told the friends who composed my audience what I had seen and heard. Some pious females requested the address of the aged saint, and repaired early the next morning to her humble abode.

"Ladies," said the person whom they saw, "she scarcely spoke after the gentleman left her, but folded her hands upon her breast, and died in the night."

She was not, for God took her. In her lowly path she had walked with God, conversed with the angels, and held intercourse with the spirits of just men made perfect, for whose holy society she was, as far as man can judge, prepared far above many of her superiors in gifts and privileges.

May we not be incited by such instances as the foregoing to seek out more diligently and habitually these hidden ones whom the Lord hath chosen, and bring them to the light to show forth his praise? He that is seeking after goodly pearls, regards not the unfavourable situation in which they may be found. He recognises their true value apart from all appearances; while he who possesses not the requisite knowledge for discerning the hid treasure, passes it by with indifference. In proportion as our own souls are earnestly concerned in this matter, shall we find ourselves rewarded by ever fresh illustrations of the Divine wisdom and goodness amongst the simple annals of the poor.

While lately visiting some friends in Leicestershire, I was taken by them to view the remains of Bradgate Hall, the birthplace of Lady Jane Grey. After surveying the ruins, and listening to the traditions of the spot, we adjourned for refreshment to the little inn of the neighbouring village. While we were conversing together on religious subjects, it was hinted to me that a very aged man, the father-in-law of the person who kept the inn, was sitting by the fire in an adjoining room, and that he appeared desirous of speaking with me. Approaching him without any formality, the friends following me to listen, I entered into conversation with him, desirous of eliciting from himself the state of his mind, and the views he entertained of this life and of another. He was tall, respectably clad, and though enfeebled by age, of an agreeable appearance. His communications were so artless and free, and so evidently the genuine expressions of an untutored mind, enlightened with the rays of gospel truth, that, assisted by the recollection of my companions, I put upon record the following dialogue, in which, as generally in such instances, I preserve, as far as I can, the words and imperfections of the respondent :—

"You look very old, my friend, and have passed your 'threescore years and ten'?"

"I am ninety-two years old," said he, "this last month; and, excepting that I have been very deaf, I am not very infirm."

"Well, you have had enough of this life, I should think; are you not tired of it?"

"No; I am waiting till God Almighty sees fit to take me out of it."

"Not trusting, I hope, to your own works?"

"No; I put them off long ago."

"Where is your hope?"

"In the Lord."

"Are you in Christ?"

"Yes. I hope: I know't. I ha' the sweetest union with God on my bed. It's like meat to my corporal frame. I cannot read, nor hear; but the Spirit of God, I thinks, has taught me. I know whom I have believed. I have a peace that passes all things. I know that when my heart faileth, and my flesh too, God will be the strength of my heart, and my portion for ever. I am sure on't;—and sure the Spirit will keep me steadfast."

"How came you, my friend, by this knowledge?"

"I was very hard, sir, to be moved; but the clergyman came to me, as I could not hear him at church. And he was so kind: I was a great rebel against him; I thought he would ha' given me up; but he didn't, and at length he overcame me, and I could tell him all my mind. I had told him before that I could not feel what he said, but afterwards I opened my whole heart to him. He's gone, but another good man is come in his place. But, may I ask, sir, who I am talking to?"

On being told that I was a minister of Jesus Christ, he rose, took me by both hands, and with a glistening eye, said—

"Oh, I am so thankful that a good minister should come to talk to me! My heart is full. I could go down on my knees to thank you."

Wishing to remember him, I asked his name, and was surprised to hear it announced as "*John Wesley*," which his daughter informed me was the family name, her parents and grand-parents, who lived in Shropshire, having been so called, and she believed they had been originally Methodists.

"Ye see your calling, brethren," says the apostle, whose words meet with a striking exemplification in the foregoing recitals, "how that not many wise men after the flesh, not many mighty, not many noble, are called: but God hath chosen the foolish things of the world to confound the wise; and God hath chosen the weak things of the world to confound the things which are mighty; and base things of the world, and things which are despised, hath God chosen, yea, and things which are not, to bring to nought things that are: that no flesh should glory in his presence. But of him are ye in Christ Jesus, who of God is made unto us wisdom, and righteousness, and sanctification, and redemption: that, according as it is written, He that glorieth, let him glory in the Lord."

PROVERBS.

The Backslider Restored.

"The backslider in heart shall be filled with his own ways."
PROV. xiv. 14.

A BACKSLIDER is indeed filled with the fruits of his own misdeeds. He has nothing else as a spiritual possession, for he is destitute of all true peace and solid satisfaction. Even if he be apparently at ease while a backslider, yet upon his being aroused from his sinful lethargy, his state of mind will be most distressing and fearful to witness. The various expedients to which he had recourse, in order that by pre-occupation of mind he might ward off the shafts of conscience, and avoid the tendency to condemnatory self-comparisons in contrasting his previous and present states of soul, all begin to fail him; and their lulling efficacy, like that of natural opiates, soon spends itself, and then leaves the wretched sufferer to deeper desolation of spirit. Conscience now *will* be heard, and severely reproaches him with the deep-dyed ingratitude which has marked his conduct, a conduct more injurious to the cause of religion than even the sins of his unregenerate life. He cannot shut out the thought that he has given too much occasion to the enemy to blaspheme, that he has supplied the scorner with another opportunity for the exhibition of his powers of sarcasm, that he has emboldened the hesitating sinners, and filled the quiver of the infidel with poisoned shafts ; and that all these will reiterate and enforce the calumnious assertion that those who have loudly boasted of the happiness of a religious life, and have professed that spiritual enjoyments arising from piety and holiness far surpass all the vaunted pleasures of earth and sense, have proved the falsity of their profession by their subsequent declension. He bewails also the cause for dark triumph which he has given to spirits of evil, and the emotions of sadness (if such can be entertained by happy spirits) which he has awakened in good angels, who had once made the heavenly courts to resound with songs of joy when he had been enrolled amongst the penitents of earth.

There remains a still deeper wound in his breast, a still more prominent stigma of ingratitude, and it is this :—What offence has he not given to him, who did not hesitate to die for sinners, and whom he, the backslider, had once openly professed to love and adore as his Saviour ! Perhaps he imagines that he beholds a tender yet upbraiding look directed to him, like that which once met the eye of Peter, when the discovery of his baseness was made, and when his guilt flashed suddenly upon him ; and then the backslider of to-day, like the one of old, goes out and weeps bitterly. He now conceives of the obstacles which he himself has accumulated in the path of his return as insurmountable. He doubts the possibility of restoration. Knowing that a relapse is in nature more dangerous than the original malady, he fears that it may be impossible to renew him again' unto repentance. The doom of apostates looms darkly before him in that awful saying of Holy Writ, which announces it in terrible form : nor are evil spirits, of whose agency he can have no doubt, slow in their hidden but never-remitted efforts to fasten around the captive the last links of the chain of despair. With a wound which he fears is incurable, and under terrors which continually affright his soul, he cries out, as though in the agony of broken bones, or as if he were a tortured culprit upon the engine of cruelty, for the gracious help and relief of Heaven, and for restoration to spiritual health and vigour.

If he be restored, and if Heaven hear his strong cries and supplications, then let him declare himself as an example; let him unveil the darkly curtained picture of his own soul; and this for the sake of those who are still pursuing the right course, that he may thereby address to them a seasonable and salutary warning against the deceitfulness of sin, and may prevent them from being in any degree lax by conceiving that, even if they should backslide, the cup of salvation may again be put into their hands. It may be: but those hands must first have held a cup of trembling, and their lips will first have tasted a draught of wormwood and gall, the embittered remembrance of which will cling to the entire future of their lives. Escape does not diminish peril, nor does it warrant rashness. To become emboldened by another's deliverance, is to read the intended lesson backwards. Spiritual deliverance is designed to awaken gratitude and to inspire caution.

"Sin no more, lest a worse thing come unto thee."

I find amongst my records a narrative which well falls in with this train of reflections.

In the neighbourhood of a large town in the North of England, I met with a respectable individual, at whose house I was partaking of some slight refreshment, and who, after some serious conversation, narrated to me the following circumstances, mostly in the plain terms preserved:—

"Sir, I have been a *backslider*. In connection with the Primitive Methodists, I had powerful religious feelings, and made a flaming profession. But after some years of consistent conduct, I fell away, by little and little, and contracted habits of dissipation. I resided in a village not far from Nottingham, and rented a small farm, which I kept in good order, but was too passionately addicted to the culture of flowers, being ambitious of obtaining a prize at the annual show, in which I succeeded. Yet I was ill at ease. I had lost true peace, and while I kept from the way of seeking its return, I lived a random sort of life, with occasional gloomy fears and forebodings. One day a young man from a neighbouring village met me, not very far from my house. He was on his way to be married the next day to his affianced bride. He had purchased a watch, some trinkets, and little household utensils, which he showed me, and told me they were for commencing housekeeping. As we had been acquainted long, and he was fatigued with walking, we adjourned to a small public-house, where he soon became inebriated, while I, perhaps more used to the beverage, remained sober. He showed his trinkets, and an itinerant musician coming into the place, he was excited by the music and began to dance. His trinkets fell out of his pocket, which some low-minded fellows who were present sought to pick up. I, however, secured them and put them in my own pocket. On leaving the place, I accompanied him to a certain spot, where I gave him the articles I had secured, and we parted. He was never seen afterwards. Inquiry was made the next day, and as his path lay by the river Trent, it was supposed he had fallen into it and was drowned. The river was dragged for a considerable distance for his body, but in vain. As I was last seen with him, and also known to have possessed myself of the few valuables he had about him, suspicion fell upon me, that I had robbed him, and afterwards made away with him. To clear myself, I caused the river to be dragged again most carefully, and stated explicity all I knew of the matter. In vain. I now perceived myself gradually shunned as a suspected murderer. All kept aloof from me, and at length my nearest and dearest friends did not like to be seen with me. You may try, sir, but you cannot conceive the isolation I endured. For seventeen months this lasted. Life was a burden; and but for the recollection that I had back slidden, and justly deserved the anger of the Almighty, and for the supposition that He might be thus meaning to bring me back to myself, I should have repeated the attempt, which I had more than once made, to destroy myself. I appealed to a magistrate to try me, but as there was no charge against me, he could take cognisance of no confession or declaration. At last a man who was fishing in a boat farther up the river than had been dragged, met with a piece of flesh on a bone floating on the surface. He carried it to a surgeon, who pronounced it to be part of the thigh-bone of a man. The river was dragged just where this human relic had been found, and the remains of the body of the missing man were brought up from the rushes beneath, in which they had become entangled, together with his watch, trinkets, and other articles. I was then acquitted from all guilt in public opinion, and a feast was made among my friends to testify their joy at the accidental vindication of my innocence. But the neighbourhood became intolerable to me, and I have removed to this spot, have repented of my backslidings, and turned to the Lord; and I now enjoy a quiet satisfaction in his service which I never expected to enjoy in this world."

I may add that, on inquiry, I found this story confirmed in all its essential particulars.

In the course of my ministry in the metropolis, I had one Sabbath evening been most solemnly warning the large congregation of my hearers against tampering with temptation, and against imperceptibly declining from the good ways of God. I pointed out, in the most effective terms I could command, the insidious nature of spiritual declension, and the bitter pangs of remorse attending it in after-life. I addressed those who had fallen into such a state, and affectionately besought them to return unto the God whom they had forsaken, assuring them not only of his ability, but also of his willingness to receive them again into his favour. After my return home late in the evening, a letter was put into my hands which is here subjoined. On the following morning I sent one of the elders of the Church to converse with the writer, and to afford him any advice or assistance he might need. He found, however, that the writer had just departed, with a view of immediately returning to America; and heard that, to all appearance, he was a young gentleman, and had behaved in the most correct and proper manner, but that he studiously avoided giving any clue to the discovery of his connections, or even, as was surmised, of his real name.

"REVEREND AND DEAR SIR,

"It is not for the broken-hearted and disconsolate stranger to practise either dissimulation or flattery. I have been aroused and edified by your faithful ministry, because the Spirit of the Lord of hosts was with you. Your graphic description of the humble but successful pleader with God this morning, and especially your thrilling allusions to the poor backslider, stirred within me such recollections of the past, that I fain would have cried aloud, '*O Jesus, after all, I am thine! save me!*

"Yes, your voice still echoes in my startled ear, and an

indescribable influence is in my heart, which I fear, alas!—
I fear may leave me on the morrow. O man of God, I
know my weakness, the treachery of my heart, the restlessness of my wayward will, the unhallowed passions of my
nature! Verily I am the *veriest chief* of sinners! I dare
not trust myself in aught, dare not even form one resolution,
yet the vows of the Lord are upon me, the holiest of vows.
But how have I violated them!

"I have heard you preach thrice, and on each occasion
barbed arrows seemed to transfix my soul. This acknowledgment I make for three reasons: first, that I may humble
my naturally *proud heart;* secondly, that I may secure an
interest in your prayers (which will assuredly be heard);
and thirdly, that you may receive an additional assurance
that your labour is not in vain in the Lord. Sir, I feel that
my spirit is drawn out after you, which is my only apology
for thus intruding upon your valuable time. It may be that
a few days may terminate my stay in this country. I came
to find employment; but am not likely to succeed, simply
because I am a stranger, and devoid of patronage. Perhaps
I looked too high,—the fault of my education, and family
pride. But when oceans roll between your holy ministry
and my pilgrim path, in saintly compassion remember me!
I have always dealt honourably with men, but what of that?
Have I not unbuckled my armour, and deserted the
standard of Christ? Base desertion! in such a time as this,
when the great spiritual and moral conflict is waxing
mightier than ever, and when infidelity so alarmingly prevails!
But I am the man that have seen affliction by the rod of his
wrath, and righteous are all his ways!

"Adieu, reverend sir; may the spirit of Elijah's God
impel you to yet more extensive conquests in the name of
the Lord Jesus, is the humble but heartfelt prayer of

"THE DISCONSOLATE."

The foregoing facts impressively illustrate the facility with which professors of religion may fall into a backsliding state, and the misery thereby brought upon their own souls. It is a sad and solemn reflection that many such never return to the fold of Christ, but wander to the end of life in the deceitful paths of sin, "waxing worse and worse." Notwithstanding these painful cases, we have scriptural grounds to believe that no case of backsliding which admits of penitence or prayer can be hopeless; for Jesus himself has said, "All manner of sin and blasphemy shall be forgiven unto men." No instance of backsliding can be more aggravated than that of the apostle Peter, and yet no recovery was more signal. While that stands upon record, no traitor to his Lord and Master is justified in saying, "The door of hope is closed against my return." The Scriptures contain several instances in which the lamentable and disgraceful lapses of God's people are shown to be followed by their recovery and restoration. Frequently such characters, after they have been corrected and chastened of the Lord, have risen to stations of great eminence in his Church. David in the Old Testament, and Peter in the New, while both illustrating the shame and sorrow of a backsliding state, stand forth as monuments of that sovereign grace which can forgive the penitent wanderer, and once more infuse into his heart the "peace that passeth all understanding."

It appears to me to be very desirable to distinguish Backsliding from Apostasy. I do not purpose in so doing to enter upon a theological disquisition, but simply to present a few brief suggestions in relation to this important topic.

It is manifest that these terms are not convertible, and that Scripture draws a strong line of demarcation between them, which may be distinctly traced by studying the context where the terms are employed, and by collating our own experience and observation with the Scriptures. I conceive that the chief distinctions and contrasts are these :—

The Backslider never altogether loses his respect and regard for religion. The knowledge of it has been too closely wrought into the texture of his mind to be readily removed, and his judgment in its favour has been too decided to be easily or entirely perverted. He sighs as he calls to recollection his former happy days, his seasons of holy communion, contrasting them with his present desolation of spirit. At such a time he requires only, it may be, the under-shepherd of the fold he has left but still fondly remembers, to follow him, and by the constraining power of love and brotherly persuasion (to which he feels that he could readily yield himself), to bring him back to it, and occasion a joy even greater than that which accompanied his conversion. There is in his worst state always ground for appeal, always room for hope, always a possible echo to a beseeching voice. There is always a probability of the triumph of grace over sin. None can be warranted to say of such a man that he has gone too far to return. Religion is rather left off than cast off, and rather overshadowed than extinguished.

Contrast with these marks of character those of the Apostate. The two men may be alike for a time, but are never alike for life. Both go out from the Church, both forsake the people of God to wander amongst strangers; but the one goes out only for a sad season, the other to return no more. The apostate never knows a returning step; he places a fatal barrier in the way of his restoration by decidedly renouncing and perhaps openly reviling the principles he had once professed to embrace. He attempts to justify his defection by the proclamation of defects in these principles, or in their professors. He believes, or declares that he believes, his former profession and sentiments to have been all illusory. He brands as deceivers or deceived all who persist in their religion, and, as the corruption of the best things turns to the worst, so his former love degenerates into present hatred—a hatred far more bitter than that of those who never knew, though they always opposed the truth. Who amongst the persecutors of the Church of God was so relentless as the once professedly Christian Emperor Julian, surnamed emphatically "The Apostate"? Of such an one Saul, king of Israel, was a fit prototype.

Among the disciples of our Lord himself, were the two standing examples of backsliding and apostasy, Peter and Judas. The distinctions between their characters have often been touched upon, and therefore I shall not here renew any such attempt; nor indeed can any careful reader of the incidents of their lives fail to see the broad differences between these two men, whose biographies seem to have been sketched in order that their examples might afford, in all ages, on the one hand, due encouragement to penitent backsliders, and, on the other, a dreadful warning to apostates.

Successful Reproofs.

"He that rebuketh a man, afterwards shall find more favour than he that flattereth with the tongue."—PROV. xxviii. 23.

"BEFORE we reprove," says the learned John Hales, in his "Golden Remains," "let us know the condition of our brother; whether he be not like the young vine, soft and tender, and so to be cured, rather by the hand pulling the branches away, than by the knife. And if he be grown so bad that he shall need the knife, we must not rashly adventure on it, but know that there is a skill in using the knife; like a skilful physician of whom we read, who, having to heal an imposthume, and finding the person to be afraid of lancing, *privately wrapped up his knife in a sponge*, with which, while he gently smoothed the place, he lanced it. So, when we encounter an offending brother, we must not openly carry the dagger in our hand, but with words of sweetness administer our reproof, and so effect the cure."

I once had occasion to travel, in the days of stage coaches, from Plymouth to the metropolis ; and as the journey would extend through the night, I took my place inside. Being informed, that beyond Exeter, where the coach would arrive early in the morning, we should have a view of some beautiful scenery, I requested the guard to arouse me at Exeter, and to give me, for the next stage or two, an outside place. He did so ; but feeling exceedingly drowsy, and the morning air being chilly, I altered my mind, and kept my seat, intending to continue my slumbers. But before I did so I observed a young man, a sailor, who had returned from a voyage the day before, taking the place outside which I had bespoken, and behaving loosely and wildly. He was in part inebriated; and was vulgar, boisterous, and exceedingly profane. He insisted on stopping at every convenient place to drink and to treat the coachman. I was soon, however, lost in sleep, but after proceeding some miles I was roused by an unusual motion of the coach, as if it were going round. In a moment it was partly on one side, and then it speedily overturned.

Extricating myself and my fellow inside passenger as quickly as possible, I beheld a scene which appalled me. At a considerable distance behind I perceived the cause of the overthrow in a dislodged wheel lying on the road. The coachman lay on the ground, pale and affrighted, leaning on his right arm. Some of the passengers who had been thrown off were but little hurt. The young sailor was prostrate, swearing at, and loudly bemoaning his fate. I approached him, and found that his leg was broken, the bone partly protruding through his rent boot. I cautioned him about his profane language, and threatened to leave him if he did not desist; and as it appeared that I was the only male passenger who was totally unhurt and able to take care of him, he became silent. With the assistance of the other passengers and the directions of the coachman, I raised the coach, and he replaced the wheel, having at hand the materials necessary for fastening it on the axletree. We placed the young sailor inside, on my former seat, while I sat by the coachman to assist in driving the vehicle slowly to Honiton, the next stage of our journey.

On our arrival, the wounded sailor was conveyed to a bed, and a surgeon was immediately sent for to set the fractured limb. He called me aside, informing me it was a compound fracture, and would detain the sufferer some weeks before he could be removed with safety. On going to the disabled patient I found him much easier, the place being swollen and the pain abated. "I am ready," he said, "to go on." On my informing him of the communication of the surgeon, he bitterly lamented it, saying he had only just returned from a long voyage, and was proceeding to his parents and relations, who knew that he was approaching home, though not that he had landed. I procured for him a Bible, and putting it into his hand, prayed with him, and for him, and counselled him to read it, and to abandon his profane and dissolute habits, offering at the same time to go to his friends and apprise them of his situation. "Not for the world," said he; "I will not see them till I recover." He was now humble and grateful, and I left him to pursue my journey, reflecting by the way on the merciful providence by which I had been induced, apparently without any strong motive, to retain my inside position.

Some months afterwards, when returning from a short journey to my residence near the metropolis, and hailing one of the long stages passing, I took my seat on the box beside the coachman. I soon discovered that it was the very same coach in which I had met with the disaster above related. Upon this I narrated the circumstance to the coachman, who informed me that he had heard of it, and that the young sailor had removed, but that the coachman had been quite disabled, and prevented from resuming his employment. Just as I was about to alight at my residence, a young woman, an outside passenger, having overheard my narrative, addressed me, saying, "Are you, sir, the gentleman that gave the young sailor a Bible and reproved him for swearing?" "I am," said I. "Then, sir," she rejoined, "I am a servant in the family of that young man. I have heard him relate the whole affair, and mention your kindness with much emotion. I am happy to tell you, sir," continued she, "that he has never sworn an oath since, and is an entirely altered young man." I was about to make further inquiries, but the coachman became impatient and drove on, and I had to regret that in my haste I had forgotten to ask the name and residence of the youth, and could only hope, from what I had heard of the effect of my speaking to him, that the exhortation, the gift of a Bible, and prayer, had not been in vain. There was, indeed, some reason to believe that my prayer as well as my reproof had been successful.

The following narrative has been derived and abridged from a religious publication of a passing nature. It is to the same effect as my own just given :—
"A minister had taken his place in the train for a distant place on the coast of the sea. As it was about to start, a young gentleman, in a hurried state, entered the carriage where he was seated. On the porter accosting him somewhat rudely with the question, 'Where are you going?' he peevishly replied, 'To hell!—away with you!' and immediately the train started. The minister was startled by the expression, and carefully observed the person of him who had uttered it. He was well dressed, and had much of *nonchalance*, but was somewhat pale and sickly. As the minister was seated at a distance from him, he waited till the other passengers had removed, when he watched his opportunity and contrived to sit near the young passenger. Entering into conversation, he made himself very agreeable to him, and they continued discoursing till the evening drew on. At length he said to him, with somewhat of a serious air and tone, 'When do you expect to arrive at your journey's end?'

"'I can hardly tell,' replied the youth, 'as I am going to a place (which he mentioned) beyond sea, for the benefit of my health, which I am told is the only chance of my recovery.'

"'Oh, I did not mean that,' rejoined the minister; but the place to which you told the porter you were going, on entering the carriage.'

"His companion paused; the recollection forced itself upon him, and he observed with an air of thoughtfulness—

"'Perhaps it may be so.'

"'Perhaps it may,' replied the minister, and proceeded to point out from the Scriptures the end of a course of sin. 'But,' he added, 'there is a way of escape!' and being encouraged to proceed, he unfolded the gospel to him.

"On reaching the place of his destination, he was thanked by the young man for the interest he had taken in him, who expressed a feeling of regret that he was to part with him. But the minister, having procured a Bible, went with him on board the vessel, and putting it into his hand, conjured him to read it with prayer, which, with great emotion, he promised to do, the tear glistening in his eye. They took leave of each other, never, most likely, to meet again, except in a world where the interview and its results may perhaps be referred to with exceeding joy."

To reprove a man openly for swearing, and while he is heated with passion, just after the act, generally exasperates him, though he may have nothing to say, and indeed can say nothing, in justification of it. But this may be done so courteously as sufficiently to wound the conscience, while it does not inflame the passions. It is reported of the late Robert Robinson, of Cambridge, that on taking his seat in the mail-coach at night, for a long journey, he found his only companion to be an agreeable gentleman in other respects, but addicted to the practice of interspersing his sentences with profane language. Perceiving that this would make the journey unpleasant, he, after some general discourse, observed that as they were likely to be some time together, he hoped his companion would grant him one favour.

"Certainly," was the reply, "if it be in my power."

"Oh, nothing," rejoined Mr. Robinson, "is more easy;

it is only to be so obliging *as after this to let me swear the first oath !"*

" I understand you, sir," said the gentleman ; " and thank you."

His discontinuance of the habit during the whole of that journey may have enabled him to break himself of it afterwards. This was Christian courteousness for a Christian purpose. It could not have been resented even if it had proved unsuccessful.

Of Dr. Annesley it is recorded that taking coffee one evening at an hotel, he heard one of two gentlemen in the next compartment swearing violently in conversation with the other, upon which he rang for the waiter, and ordered a glass of water. When brought to him he said—

"Take it to the gentleman in the next box."

The gentleman was surprised, and said he had ordered no such thing.

" I thought," said the venerable doctor, gravely, " to cool your tongue, after the fiery language you had been uttering."

This brought a challenge from the other, but the doctor appealed to his cloth as a reason for declining to accept it. Some considerable time afterwards, as he was sitting on a chair in the park, a gentleman passing was struck with the sight of him ; and, after a pause, inquired if he remembered reproving an individual for profane language, by sending to him a glass of cold water.

On being answered in the affirmative, " I am," said he, " that individual, and am happy to have an opportunity of acknowledging an act which I resented at the time, but which cured me of a fatal habit; and I now offer you an apology, with a grateful acknowledgment of your fidelity."

In the "Life of Gerhard Tersteegen," a work too little

known in this country, we meet with several incidental proofs of his fidelity, adroitness, and success in administering reproof.

"Being once on a journey to Holland, and finding in the passage-boat a number of merchants and people of respectable appearance, he leaned his head backwards, and closed his eyes as if he were asleep. After all kinds of tales had been told, and a game of cards had been proposed, he opened his eyes, and said that he had an excellent pack of cards in his bag. Upon being requested to produce them, he drew forth a New Testament, on seeing which they said that was a book to make people mad. He replied, 'Is it not you that are mad?' and rehearsed all their foolish and unprofitable conversation, and sought from their own words to convince them how foolishly they acted in squandering away their valuable time with such useless things. Some approved of what he said, and the rest were restrained from carrying their intention into effect.

"The year before, being in Holland, a person of high rank invited him to be his guest. This individual imagined himself to have attained to a state of peculiar inward peace, and therefore took occasion during dinner to criticise Tersteegen for being too active, and for not sufficiently knowing the ground on which he wrought. Tersteegen attended meekly and silently to all that was said; but when dinner was over he offered up a fervent prayer, in which he commended his host to the Lord in terms of such affection and compassion, that this great and warm-tempered man was so much struck and affected by it that his feelings overpowered him, and he fell upon the neck of his guest and begged his forgiveness.

"The overflowing of his heart with love and compassion for his erring friends invested his necessary reproof of them with such an air of tenderness as made it seem only a kind of gentle remonstrance. Thus it was shorn of everything that could irritate, and won its way with efficacy into the heart of the offender. 'I had,' writes one, 'for several years enjoyed many blessings in Tersteegen's society, from his edifying walk and conversation; but after some time had elapsed I became disobedient to the grace of God, so that my corruptions and the devices of the adversary occasioned me a grievous fall. Having by this afflicted the good man so much, and being ashamed of myself, and fearful of receiving a rebuke from him, I ceased visiting him. After he had observed this for some time, he sent for me. I went to him in the full expectation of being sharply reproved by him, which I was fully conscious I had merited; instead of which he met me with the affection of a father, and tenderly embraced me, by which my heart was deeply affected, and my love and confidence in God and his dear and faithful servant were awakened afresh. He gave me at the same time the necessary instruction respecting my conduct, and exhorted me to obedience to the grace of God. After this he kept a more watchful eye upon me to the day of his death.'"

Many years ago I was journeying through the west of England to fulfil a public engagement, and in order to enjoy the scenery and breathe the fresh air, I and my companions were seated outside the mail-coach. The day was sunny, the roadside views were attractive, and we were approaching the city where the fine square towers of the cathedral rose over the surrounding buildings, and added architectural to natural beauties. We were all in good spirits, and willing to enjoy the scene.

A respectable young woman sat on one side of me, and near to me on the other side, a vivacious and talkative gentleman, who seemed to think that he proved his high breeding by frequently using oaths. Presently he addressed the young woman alluded to, in a free and not very refined style, mingling an oath or two with his speech. She looked uneasy and abashed, and did not reply. Upon her silence, he rudely remarked to her, "Why don't you answer me? What are you afraid of? I suppose you have said your prayers this morning?" As she continued silent, I spoke to her, and said, "You see the gentleman has *said his prayers!*" "Yes, sir," she added, "and shocking ones they are." The profane swearer now appeared confused, and after a time thought fit to apologise, and to confess that he was ashamed of himself. I and my companions now raised a favourite tune, and each one taking a part in the strain, the effect upon our fellow-passengers appeared to be very favourable. Our late swearing neighbour was very attentive, and seemed interested in us, and anxious to learn who and what we were. We continued our singing, and as I gave out verse after verse of the hymn before the strain of harmony, it was very pleasing to observe how all around us, from the coachman to the fellow-passengers, listened with evident gratification. It was certainly a remarkable change of scene, and we had been enabled to turn the current of speech from profanity to the high praises of God. At setting out we should little have anticipated singing psalms or hymns or spiritual songs on such an occasion, and in such company; but having begun so successfully, we did not fail to continue, and we received courteous adieus from all who were with us when we arrived under the shadow of the cathedral towers, and alighted at the hotel.

The incidents above narrated are not merely interesting in themselves, but they may be serviceable in encouraging the friends of true religion and of good morals, to avail themselves of every favourable opportunity to speak wisely and decisively, though considerately, to such as offend by the use of profane language or by unseemly conduct, in public vehicles and elsewhere. The word of God, indeed, expressly says, "Thou shalt in any wise rebuke thy neighbour, and not suffer sin upon him." Without question, reproof is a painful duty, and many pious persons fear to make use of it, lest they should be betrayed into anger or hasty expressions, or provoke an unpleasant recrimination. Nevertheless, in most cases, some method may be devised, and some opportunity found, of courteously, yet plainly intimating disapproval, and I have brought forward the above instances in order that they may suggest methods and measures of Christian reproval.

It may not, indeed, in the present day, be our misfortune to listen to outspoken profanity so often as in preceding times; but yet we are bound to rebuke and discourage language of any kind which is disrespectful to religion, subversive of morality, or openly insulting to what all good men hold dear and sacred. We ought not to be silent when our consciences prompt us to speak, and we ought so to speak that our consciences shall not compel us to repent of what we have uttered.

ECCLESIASTES.

The Vanity of Human Pursuits.

"'Therefore I hated life; because the work that is wrought under the sun is grievous unto me : for all is vanity and vexation of spirit."— ECCLES. ii. 17.

NO theme is more trite than the unsatisfactory character of earthly good. From the time of Solomon to the present day it has been commented upon even to satiety, assented to by all, and yet, strange to say, practically disbelieved by most. While no man will deny this conclusion of the Preacher, to which he was led by a long and large experience, yet every man secretly wishes to make proof of the assertion for himself. He is convinced at heart of its truth before he begins life, yet he must needs come towards the end of life before he openly consents to that which he could not deny in the beginning.

It might appear strange that our present dissatisfaction with what we possess at any given time, does not demonstrate to us that this will be the rule of a carnal life. The dissatisfaction of one day is the type of all days; yet we join with the multitude of men in the eager pursuit of something unattained, but which is conceived of as attainable, and as conducive, when attained, to perfect happiness. Not one of the multitude of pursuers ever announces that he has seized the prize; or, at least, not one long persists in such a declaration; yet generation after generation of mankind wear out their lives in the false but alluring chase; and the sentiment of their hearts is this :—" We are wearied in the greatness of our way, yet say we not there is no hope : because we have found the life of our hand, therefore we are not grieved;" that is, because we have found some present help, stay, or support, therefore we are not grieved so as to abandon the expectation and to relinquish the pursuit. It was the brief expression of a whole public life condensed into a few words, when a dying senator, of brilliant rhetorical triumphs, exclaimed, "What shadows we are, and what shadows we all pursue!"

In confirmation of these remarks, the following account may be adduced, as taken from my own private notes when a traveller on the continent :—

The hotel at Brussels where I took up my abode, was frequented by a well-dressed Frenchman, of apparently little more than thirty years of age. His countenance was intelligent but grave, and his manner listless and indifferent. He usually sat alone in one compartment of the room where we assembled, and glanced cursorily at the papers, but seldom entered into conversation. I learnt that he had been staying there several months, had abundance of money, was regular in his habits, but had no particular object in view, and seemed, as it was expressed, like a man who knew not what to do with himself. My curiosity was awakened; I endeavoured to render myself agreeable to him, and as we always met at meals, and frequently, also, at other times, I got into familiar conversation with him. His coldness and indifference gradually wore off, and at length we sat together for hours, conversing in an unembarrassed manner.

In answer to my inquiries, on several occasions, he gave me the following account of himself :—

" I was left, at a very early period of my life, heir to a very considerable estate, the annual revenues of which soon came to be at my disposal. I had an eager desire to see different countries, to make myself acquainted with their several aspects, and the customs, manners, peculiarities, and language of their respective inhabitants, with the most interesting particulars of their history. I therefore set out on my travels, and spared no expense for the accomplishment of my object. With this view I have visited Europe and the East, have been in both the Indies, and through Switzerland, France, and England. · I have also visited other places, too numerous to particularise, and I have met with but few disasters, and with but little interruption to my health, while, as yet, my resources are unimpaired."

He said all this with coolness and with no apparent desire to excite my astonishment. He surprised me by the extent of his information and the accuracy of his knowledge. I found by his ready answers to questions which I put to him relative to those parts which I had traversed, that he was perfectly correct in his statements. He had read much, and, indeed, as he said, all the books that came in his way, till he found succeeding authors only repeating the former in a different mode and form of expression.

"And now," said he, "I am at a loss what to do. I know not where to go or what to see that I am not already acquainted with. There is nothing new to sharpen my curiosity or to stimulate me to exertion. I am sated. Life to me has exhausted its charms; the world has no new face for me, nor can it open any new prospect to my view."

I strongly impressed upon him the necessity of seeking and serving the God of the Scriptures, and of proposing to himself some ennobling and worthy object of pursuit in life. This, I assured him, from my own experience, was the unfailing antidote to *ennui*, and the cheering solace of our present existence. I left him with the hope that my arguments and appeals were not in vain, and we parted in a friendly manner, though he still exhibited on his countenance a feeling of languor and disinclination to exertion.

Surely here was a practical comment on Solomon's conclusion, "Vanity of vanities, all is vanity and vexation of spirit."

To the same effect is the subjoined confession and lamentation of the celebrated Frenchman, Lamartine, eminent as an historian, politician, and poet, of whom it is observed in a critical English work, "All in all, M. de Lamartine will be remembered as one of the most remarkable and high-minded Frenchmen of his generation." The following passage is translated from one of his books, but little known in this country :—

"Of all the multiplied men who lived in me, to a certain degree—the man of sentiment, the man of poetry, the man of oratory—nothing remains in me but the literary man. The literary man himself is far from being happy. Years do not yet bear me down. I bear more heavily the weight of my heart than the weight of my years. These years, like Macbeth's phantoms, pass their hands over my shoulder, and point out to me, not crowns, but a sepulchre : would to God I was now asleep in it! I have nothing in me wherewith to smile to the future or to the past. I am growing old, without children, in my desolate house, surrounded by the tombs of all those I loved. All that remains to me of life is concentrated in a few hearts and in a modest inheritance. And even these hearts suffer because of me, and I am not sure that I shall not be dispossessed of that inheritance to-morrow, and go and die upon some stranger's road, as Dante says. The hearth on which my father placed his feet, and where I now place mine, is a borrowed hearth, which may be torn up at any hour; it may be sold and resold at any caprice of the auctioneer; and so may my mother's bed; so may the dog which licks my hand in pity when he sees my brow in agony as I look at him. The children of the Samians insulted Homer, because, said they, Homer obstructed the highways of the island by singing poetry before the houses. I am not Homer; but my critics are more severe than the Samians. Upon these pages where they reproach me for heaping piles of vanity, it is not ink you read; no, believe me, it is not; but the sweat of my brow. It is not my name I seek to magnify, but the pledge of those who have no estate and no existence save that name. My name!—ah, I know as well as you do what that name is worth, and what will be its fate! I would, with all my heart (God is my witness), that name had never been uttered. I would give all that may yet remain to me of life, if it were entirely buried, with him who bears it, in the silence of the tomb—noiselessly borne to the graveyard there, forgotten here. Life to me now is as nothing worth. What have I now, I pray, to regret in life? Have not I seen all my thoughts perish before me? Do I design again to sing in life, with an extinguished voice, strophes which would end in sobs? Have I taste for returning into those political struggles which, were they even opened again, would no longer recognise my posthumous accents? Have I any firm hope in those forms of government which the people abandon with as much fickleness as they adopted them? Am I so insane as to believe that I shall cast, or that I shall sculpture—I alone—in bronze or marble, a colossal statue of the human race, when God has given wherewith to do so but sand and clay to the greatest of sculptors? Of what use is life when one can contemplate nothing but the ruins of those things which are recorded in his mind! Happy the men who die at their work, struck down by the revolutions in which they were engaged. Death is their punishment—ay, but it is their refuge!"

The declaration of Solomon, however, at the head of these observations, calls for some explanation that may serve to fix its meaning, and point out the salutary use that should be made of it. The meaning is not that the good things of earth are incapable of affording any degree of satisfaction or pleasure, for this is contrary to reason and experience. They are not *vain* to this end, but vain if they occasion neglect of God, who claims man's heart. Let but the mind be in possession of the Divine favour, in communion with the blessed God, and animated by the well-founded hope of a glorious immortality, through a risen and exalted Redeemer, and then the good things of earth are received with thankfulness, and are productive of enjoyment in accordance with their nature and the design of their Author, "who giveth us richly all things to enjoy." They are not vain as accessories, but as substitutes for spiritual food. After the wants of nature are satisfied with suitable provision, delicacies are tasted with pleasure, but are sadly disappointing if substituting for the former.

The common mistake, therefore, consists in the wrong uses to which they are applied, and the false position they are made to occupy. Their inadequacy to satisfy the cravings of a soul not previously at peace with God, and not reconciled to him through the Son of his love, must ever inflict upon the most ardent and successful of the votaries of pleasure the punishment of vexation and disappointment.

Regarded merely as an end, life is even sadder and more fruitless than moralists have discoursed and poets have sung. As an end, it is empty as a dream, and wearisome as a thrice-told tale. But as a means to an end, it is great in its aims, glorious in its conquests, which are ever renewed as long as it endures, and hopeful in its issues, though now often beclouded, and for the present full of cares. As a traveller's pathway, it is pleasant when recognised as a pathway to perfect rest. The hope that beams down upon it from above and the expectation of an enduring good to come alleviate its toils, and render it what the best men have ever found it to be—a traveller's track to a radiant home—a narrow but certain approach to an eternal city.

Such, in other words, are the lessons to be derived from this book of Ecclesiastes. If Solomon wrote it in his last days, as several critics suppose, and penned it while reviewing his character and condition after he had departed from the living God, and had yielded himself to the seductions of idolatry; then it is a vivid and sententious expression of the impossibility of substituting the creature for the Creator. Having given up the one true God, he employed his vast resources and his rare capacities to extract the essence of enjoyment from created objects. Wealth in abundance poured in upon him. The gold of Ophir shone in his crown and gilded his royal palace. Silver hid itself in its paler modesty, as if of no account. The cedars of Lebanon waxed mighty, and waved in sombre shadow upon their lofty mountain, to frame his dwellings and to span his roofs. Ships crossed the ocean to bring to him foreign treasures, and to convey to him the tribute of far distant princes. His eyes lighted on nothing but the scenery of natural and artificial beauty; his feet trod the pathways of richly adorned gardens. His ears were saluted with the sweetest sounds that art could educe from lyre and reed. His palace was refreshed with rarest dainties and choicest drinks. And far more than these to a mind like his, all the stores of knowledge were unfolded to his search. Nature revealed to him her secrets, and the lordly cedar and humble hyssop were alike subjects of his careful study. Kings and queens of distant kingdoms were attracted to the feet of his throne by the fame of his glory and his wisdom. Seated on his ivory throne, clad in gorgeous robes, covered with a gilded canopy, surrounded by ranks of servants who watched his casual gaze and interpreted his lightest look, he received the embassies of remote empires, accepted the homage of royal personages, and amidst profound silence dispensed words of wisdom which gold could not out-value, and which were recorded amongst the wisest sayings that the world had heard.

This was earth's happiest man, and this the experiment he was permitted to make, that all generations might know and confess the vanity and insufficiency of all earthly pleasures, and the necessity for Divine teaching to make men truly wise. "Let us hear the conclusion of the whole matter :— Fear God and keep his commandments, for this is the whole duty of man."

———o———

Sowing and Finding.

"Cast thy bread upon the waters : for thou shalt find it after many days."—ECCLES. xi. 1.

IT has often been remarked that there is in these words an allusion to the annual overflowing of the Nile at a certain season, by which the neighbouring fields were watered and fertilized in an otherwise very dry climate. It would appear, however, to be more consonant with the locality and knowledge of the sacred writer to presume that he here refers to that remarkable system of irrigation which was devised in eastern countries, and of which some remains are still visible in the plain of Jericho. A recent traveller, Dr. Olin, encamped in that plain, and mentions the broken aqueduct over the Jerusalem road, just before commencing the ascent of the valley. Other ruinous aqueducts are to be noticed in a journey of an hour or more farther north. "Taken together," says the traveller, "they must have formed, when in successful operation, a splendid system of irrigation, unequalled, perhaps, by anything now in existence; and they point to a degree of national and individual affluence and civilization almost inconceivable to the traveller of the present day, who finds himself in the midst of a vast arid desert covered with thorns or encrusted with salt." Josephus declared, with reference to his time, that it would not be easy to find any climate on the habitable earth that could well be compared with it, as what was there sown came up in rich clusters. He ascribed the fertility of the soil partly to the warmth of the climate, but more to irrigation. Now, the sowers would go forth into the fields while yet wet with the irrigating streams, and cast their seeds or bread corn literally upon the waters. When these were fully dried up or imbibed by the soil, the seed would spring up, and would be found after many days.

The application of this metaphorical allusion would seem to be, that the sower of spiritual seed should not refrain from his labours because the soil may not seem to be yet fully ready to receive the seed, but that he should cast it broadly and believingly upon the waters; on the subsidence of which, however flooded the field may now seem to be, it will be conveyed to the ground, and after many days it will be seen to be springing up, and in the end will produce its proportion of fruit. Christians should at all fit times, and in all suitable places, sow the seed of the word, nor impatiently expect to witness its immediate sprouting. Years may elapse, and they may have forgotten the sowing time; yet when, perhaps, they are little disposed to expect it, they shall *find* it, and give to God the glory.

It has been narrated of the late Thomas Wilson, Esq., Treasurer of Highbury College, that he received an impulse to greatly enlarged liberality from a discourse by the Rev. Andrew Fuller on this text, especially from the following observation. "Observe," said the preacher, "it is not said, cast thy *crumbs*, but thy *bread*, thy *substance*, *the whole loaf*." Few men of modern times have more completely embodied the spirit of this passage, and more fully realized its truth. He was not afraid to cast his bread upon the waters, and we all know how abundantly it was restored to him, and how the fruits of his liberality survive him for the encouragement of his successors.

A short time since I was visiting a locality of considerable historical interest in Leicestershire. My name having been communicated by one of my companions to the pious and aged female who kept the house we had come to inspect, and which had been the birth-place of one of our early reformers and martyrs, she accosted me in a most earnest and affectionate manner, as one whom she had long wished to see, since she had in her possession a letter in which I had been spoken of in terms most gratifying to her maternal feelings. It was, she said, from a son of hers, who, when he wrote it, was at Worthing for the benefit of the sea-air, but who had since died, leaving behind him satisfactory evidence that he had, through the grace and mercy of Jesus, entered into "everlasting rest."

I rather doubted the correctness of her narrative, not recollecting at the moment that I had preached at that place.

With a view of refreshing my memory she reminded me that it was at the period when the cholera prevailed in this country. She persisted in her statements, and after searching through a large packet of letters, which she had carefully preserved, she at last found the one referred to.

It was addressed to her by her son, in most affectionate terms, acknowledging the kindness and tenderness of both of his beloved parents, informing them that his health was improved; and proceeding to say that he and his wife had heard a sermon which had deeply affected them, and that they hoped they were truly profited by it. "The text," said the writer, "was from Hebrews iv. 3, 'We which have believed do enter into rest;' and the preacher showed, in a striking and beautiful manner, what the rest itself was, what was believed concerning it, and how it was entered into in this life, preparatory to a full enjoyment of it hereafter." The preacher's name, which he mentioned, was my own.

By these details I was enabled at length distinctly to recall the fact of having preached from that text, at the place named; and I also called to mind that the people to whom I was preaching, with few exceptions, appeared to be so utterly unimpressible and unsympathising, that I considered the effort to be fruitless and my services lost. I had indeed preached respecting the fearful visitation then and there so fatal, and in the afterpart of the day had repeated my labours, and, as I thought, to an equally cold and unimpressed audience. Scarcely any public exhortation of mine had appeared to me at the time so utterly ineffectual, and I had been so deeply penetrated with the idea, that I was glad to escape from its remembrance. How could I then have supposed that, after a period of nine years, I should, in quite another district, be cheered with the intelligence that my labour had not been in vain in the Lord, that two hearts had been touched, and two at least of my auditors benefited by what I was enabled to unfold and apply respecting the spiritual rest?

Were it desirable, I could introduce numerous similar instances having reference to my own past ministry—instances in which, "after many days," indeed, I have been privileged to hear of the blessed results following my exhortations. The original circumstances might have passed from my recollection, and so far had been virtually lost; yet, after an effort of memory, I have been permitted to *find* what I should never otherwise have sought, and to discover that the seeds cast upon the uncertain waters had nevertheless taken root and prospered abundantly.

---o---

The Soul's Mirror.

"For God shall bring every work into judgment, with every secret thing, whether it be good or whether it be evil."—ECCLES. xii. 14.

"And they which heard it, being convicted by their own conscience, went out one by one, beginning at the eldest, even unto the last."—JOHN viii. 9.

THAT every man's conduct and character shall be fully manifested at the great judgment of the world, is the clear assertion of Holy Scripture both in the Old and New Testaments. In the former we are assured that, "Our secret sins he will set in the light of his countenance;" that is, as all the previously invisible atoms that float around us are suddenly made visible by the bright shining of a sunbeam, so all our previously unknown sins shall be made manifest by the clear and all-revealing light of God's countenance. In the New Testament, we are told by our Lord himself, "That every idle word that men shall speak, they shall give account thereof in the day of judgment;" where the term *idle* may be rendered *false* and *calumnious*, the reference being to falsehood combined with calumny, as in the instance of the Pharisees. But the warning extends to *deeds* as well as words,—" For we must all appear before the judgment-seat of Christ, that every one may receive the things done in his body, according to that he hath done, whether it be good or bad,"—a passage which seems to be the counterpart in the New Testament of that one in the Old Testament, which I have prefixed to these observations.

The multitude of thoughts which have passed through any one human mind, and of deeds which have been performed by any one individual, especially in the course of a long life, would appear to be too vast for specific remembrance and revival; and to elude any ordinary powers of comprehension at one and the same time. As these thoughts and deeds have been protracted through a long series of years, so we are apt to attach the idea of a lengthened period as essential to that circumstantial review of them which we are enjoined to anticipate. It would be well, however, in connection with this topic, to bear in mind the wonderful power of memory and conscience to throw their concentrated rays on all the transactions of the past, and to illumine them with a brightness above that of the sun. Instances are not wanting in which the vividness of retrospection, under certain conditions of mind or body, has been such as to re-enact the whole history of a life, and to cause it to re-appear as if on a stage before the eye of the mind. In sleep, too, the details of a dream sometimes appear to occupy a long period; but, on awaking, we discover perhaps that a few seconds have sufficed to build up the entire fabric. Such facts surely furnish us with intimations as to the latent powers of the mind, and its independence of the lapse of time in its mysterious operations.

In the narrative of a shipwreck inserted in this book, the sufferer records such a revelation of her whole life to have been made to her in an instant, as she thought she was going down into the deep; and another instance of the same kind has been very recently furnished to the author by a writer, whose known piety and veracity attach importance to her communication.

"After attending the morning service on the first Sabbath in the year 1848, I ascended a flight of stone steps, fifteen in number, leading into the schoolroom, and I had reached the thirteenth, when my foot caught, and I fell backwards, my head coming in contact with the edge of one of the steps. I have no recollection as to what followed, but I suppose I turned over again, and so fell on the stones below. In the moment that elapsed between the time of catching my foot and the blow I received on my head, *all* the events of my life rushed into my mind. Everything that had occurred from my earliest childhood—my school-days, and all that had transpired since—(a period of eleven years), with all their various incidents, passed before me in rapid succession. I thought of all my friends, those who were still living and those who had departed, how many of them I should meet in that world which in another moment I expected I *must* enter; and I thought, too, of the service to which I had just been attending; that I should never again be seen in that pew; and how truly it is said, 'We know not what a day or an *hour* may bring forth.' And I thought not only of the past, but of the future. Should I on awaking to consciousness find myself in heaven or hell? Was I prepared for thus suddenly being summoned into eternity?

"I expected that as soon as my head came in contact with the sharp edge of the stone steps I should be killed, for I had no means of saving myself; and then reflected how entirely I was in the hands of God. I shall never forget that feeling. He had the power either to spare my life, or take it away in a moment; and my recollection closed with the prayer of the publican of old, and of Stephen, 'God be merciful to me a sinner;' 'Lord Jesus, receive my spirit.'

"It seems incredible that all these thoughts should have passed through my mind in these few seconds, but *it was so*. My remembrance is so distinct of that wonderful preservation of life, that I can truly say I have exaggerated nothing."

I remember to have read of an eminent foreign painter who was engrossed by his art, and devoted to the delineation of natural scenery, striking groupings of common and domestic life, and the strife of battle-fields. His canvas represented such scenes with wonderful fidelity. Ill-health, resulting from too close attention to his easel, compelled him to retire to the country. There he declined rapidly, and lay in almost solitude and poverty in a retired sick chamber. While there, and in a state of delirium, he was overheard describing, in artistic style, the several scenes and groupings which he had successfully studied and painted. He died while gathering around him and imagining before him, in his sick chamber, the varied originals which he had contemplated. Thus he recalled and described the peaceful cottage and the wandering stream, the populous market-place, and the domestic interior, the battle array and the sanguinary field,—passing rapidly and confusedly from quiet homes and placid pastoral scenes to busy life, to the death-charge of excited troops, and the victory or defeat of the heroes of a country's history.

In this instance, again, we see that the strong impressions of former years were revived in all the vividness of present reality. His pictures have been delineated in the dying artist's mind. His mere mental impressions were more lasting than his own pictures. What others saw only on the outward canvas he beheld in the recesses of his own mind; and thus his death-chamber became to him literally "a chamber of imagery," a gallery of glowing representations of his creative skill. He had observed, designed, and forgotten; but memory had all this while painted for herself, and what she had once delineated, indelibly remained.

Another instance illustrative of the same tenacity of mental impressions, I may cite, as mentioned by Coleridge in his "Biographia Literaria," a case which occurred in a Catholic town in Germany, a year or two before his arrival at Göttingen, and which had not then ceased to be a frequent subject of conversation. It is in substance as follows :—

A young woman, who could neither read nor write, was seized with a nervous fever, during the prevalence of which she continued incessantly talking Latin, Greek, and Hebrew, in very pompous tones and with most distinct enunciation. The case had attracted the attention of a young physician, and by his statements many eminent physiologists were led to visit the town and cross-examine the subject of this visitation. Sheets full of her ravings were taken down from her own mouth, and were found to consist of sentences, coherent and intelligible each for itself, but having little or no connection with each other. Of the Hebrew, a small portion only could be traced to the Bible; the remainder seemed to be in the rabbinical dialect. All trick or conspiracy was out of the question; so the young physician determined to trace the past life of the young woman step by step. This he did with great care and at no small cost of time and patience. He found that she had been, when nine years old, charitably received by an old Protestant pastor, and had remained some years with him, even till the old man's death. A niece of the pastor's remembered him and the girl. On further inquiry into this pastor's habits, it appeared that it had been his custom for years to walk up and down a passage of his house, into which the kitchen door opened, and to read to himself with a loud voice out of his favourite books. A considerable number of these were in the niece's possession, and among them were found a collection of rabbinical writings, together with several of the Greek and Latin Fathers. From these the learned minister was in the habit of declaiming, and the inquisitive physician succeeded in identifying so many passages with those taken down at the young woman's bedside, that no doubt could remain concerning the true origin of the impression made upon her nervous system.

Here we have a proof that relics of sensation may exist in the mind for an indefinite time in a latent state, and in the very same order in which they were originally impressed. What more, then, at any period of its existence, would be necessary, than to stimulate the mind by some exciting action in order to reproduce the long latent sensations in their original force? Other instances of the same nature, which have been recorded by observant physiologists, might be narrated. They all tend to prove the indelibility of thought, with the permanence of original impressions made under exciting circumstances; so that we may be as accountable for impressions and sensations permitted and cherished as for our actions, and may be rendered as capable of clearly recalling and reviving the one as the other.

There may, at first, appear to be less difficulty in recalling deeds than thoughts and words. The thoughts of a past life, extending, as they do, over many years, seem to us as innumerable as the sands upon the sea-shore, and as easily and entirely obliterated by the ever-recurring tides of events as are our foot-prints upon the bordering sands of the ocean. We can without difficulty entertain the possibility of remembering actions, but to remember thoughts surpasses our apprehension and appears impossible.

To apprehend such a retrospect the more clearly, consider for a moment the vitality and enduring character of thought itself. If it be regarded as far more evanescent than deeds, and that the deed may survive even when the thought perishes, then it should be remembered that the thought prompted the deed and lives in it, and lasts as long as its remotest consequences, being in fact part and principal of them, inasmuch as the deed partakes of the character and tendency of the original thought from which it sprang. Not that a thought always ripens into action, but that such is its natural result, and, therefore, account must be taken of the origin of such a result. Thoughts are the motive powers, the fruitful sources, the fresh fountains of actions. And hence it is that we are exhorted, "Keep thy *heart* with all diligence, for out of it are the issues of life."

To the same effect are the following words of Coleridge, appended to the narrative before cited :—

"It is possible that all thoughts are in themselves imperishable; and that if the intelligent faculty should be rendered more comprehensive, it would require only a different and duly proportioned organization—the body *celestial* instead of the body *terrestrial*—to bring before every human soul the collective experience of its whole past existence. And this—this, perchance, is the dread Book of Judgment, in whose mysterious hieroglyphics every idle word is recorded. Yea, in the very nature of a living soul, it may be more possible that heaven and earth should pass away, than that a single act, a single thought, should be loosened or lost from that living chain of causes, to all whose links, conscious or unconscious, the free will, our only absolute self, is co-extensive and co-present."

With such views as these of the imperishableness of thoughts as well as of deeds, we might well look forward with trembling to the great day of account, were it not that He who will then be our Judge is now our compassionate Redeemer, easily touched with the feeling of our infirmities; able, not only to pardon the sins of our lives, but to "cleanse the thoughts of our hearts by the inspiration of his Holy Spirit."

ISAIAH.

Premonitions.

"And thine ears shall hear a word behind thee, saying, This is the way; walk ye in it, when ye turn to the right hand and when ye turn to the left."—ISA. xxx. 21.

IN certain states of mind or body, sometimes even in sleep, the imagination may be so excited as to persuade the individual that he hears or has heard a voice distinctly speaking to him, and for the moment he cannot doubt but that some audible sound has been uttered. Yet on being sufficiently aroused, the illusion has generally been dispelled, and the passing emotions produced by it have subsided, and soon been forgotten. Yet who can question that God may, even in these later times, speak to men by an inward call or a powerful impulse upon their spirits, unknown to any one else, and directing them what to do or say in an emergency. The several extraordinary ways in which he revealed his mind to men of old have indeed ceased, having been superseded by an authoritative and standing revelation to which we do well to take heed. But the "Spirit of the Lord is not straitened," so that he may not still avail himself at times of some secret methods of influencing the mind, and of making spiritual communications to human beings which neither add to nor in any way affect the written Word.

It is indeed a difficult and delicate task to estimate our mental impressions aright. We have only to peruse the records of ecclesiastical history, to learn how grossly mistaken some men have been who fancied themselves to be acting under a Divinely communicated impulse, but yet were betrayed into open shame, and sometimes into dreadful impiety, and even blasphemy. We may, however, in a great degree guard ourselves against erroneous estimates of our impulses, by subjecting all our impressions and intended actions to the rule of the written Word. The human soul is as open to influences as the hanging leaf is to every passing wind. It is like a clear mirror which is overclouded by the breath of every one who stands near it. Nevertheless, it would be contrary to all experience to say that, because the soul is so easily affected, therefore, all impressions are alike uncertain, and unworthy of being accepted as right impulses to action. We must learn rather to distinguish than to deny—to distinguish the casual emotions of the mind and caprices of the imagination from such direct, forcible, and apparently providential influences as may be appropriately traced up to a holy and heavenly source, since they tend to holy issues, and to the glory of God rather than of self.

If the issues justify the impression, we can doubt no more, and the particulars of such instances will qualify us to form an opinion of others that may come before us. I have met with several instances of sudden and remarkable impulses of mind not to be accounted for satisfactorily by human reasoning, and which either by the hopes they have raised, or the purposes they have suggested, have led to the most benign results. Among these I may be permitted to mention one that occurred to myself in early life, and exercised a real and lasting influence on my subsequent course.

When about seventeen years of age, I left home for the metropolis, where from too close application to my pursuits, and the want of country air, I lost my health, and soon fell into a state of extreme debility, with all the threatening symptoms of consumption or decline. Medical aid seemed unavailing, and but slender hopes were entertained for my life. In this condition, I was brought back to breathe my native air, and experience the unparalleled tenderness of a mother's love. I well remember how shocked they all were at my altered appearance, and how the hushed exclamations of my beloved parents increased my own apprehensions of danger.

Strictly speaking, I had at that time no religious character, although I was no stranger to prayer and the Scriptures, and had been, when in health, a regular attendant on the outward means and ordinances of Christianity. Now, however, my thoughts were chiefly occupied with my bodily condition, and the best means of restoring my lost strength. One morning as I was sitting as usual in my sick chamber, ruminating on the bare possibility of my recovery, my dear mother entered the room, and I heard the sighs that escaped her, as she looked anxiously in my face. The Bible was lying before me, and as I glanced on its open page, my eye was arrested by a passage that came to my heart at that instant with a power not to be described. With a strength of voice that startled my dear parent, I cried out, "O mother, I shall recover! See here it is written;" and I pointed to the memorable words which were then sealed upon my heart in the 17th verse of the 118th Psalm—"*I shall not die but live and declare the works of the Lord!*"

For a moment she caught the feeling that inspired me, but soon shook her head in doubt and sadness. To her surprise, however, and my own, for the first time since several months, I felt my appetite returning; and that very day gained strength enough to bear being carried out into the garden, where I distinctly remember the reviving scent of the fresh turned mould which I was encouraged to inhale. I slept the following night as I had not done for weeks, and step by step grew again into vigour and manhood to pursue my appointed course.

I need not say that at that time I had not the remotest idea of ever becoming a teacher of Divine truth. It was enough for me, then, that the power of God's word rested on my spirit and increasingly influenced my life. Severa years had to pass away with their various experiences of sorrow and of joy, before the premonition of my youth was completely fulfilled by my dedication to the work of the Christian ministry. From that time forth it was the honour and privilege, as well as the delight, of my prolonged life, publicly to "*declare the works of the Lord.*" To this day that passage always looks to me as if an angel pointed to it with his radiant finger, and surrounded it with a halo of glory !

I do not mention this as an extraordinary case, but as one, the *issues* of which may safely determine its character. The same remark will apply to the following incident related to me by the individual who was concerned in it—a brother minister, in the neighbourhood of London. He was a man of great intelligence, courage, and piety, and prompt to acts of benevolence and mercy.

A young relative of his, having been ordered to Margate for her health, and finding no one else able to accompany her, he undertook that duty himself, and stayed with her for some time at that place. On one occasion, having retired to rest as usual, some time after midnight, or rather very early in the morning, he was startled out of his slumbers by the sound of a voice pronouncing, as if close to his ear, in a loud tone, "Ramsgate, Ramsgate!" He endeavoured to discover the quarter from which it came, and to account for it, but in vain. Again it was repeated, in a tone that seemed to him to summon him to that town. He rose, and still the call was renewed. It was useless to think of recovering sleep after this event, which impressed his mind deeply; and he, therefore, in a leisurely manner dressed himself, and prepared to comply with the mysterious summons. As soon as convenient he departed for Ramsgate, and arrived there without any definite aim. He repaired to the beach, and sauntered along, musing upon the extraordinary cause which had moved him, and half blaming himself for having yielded to an impulse which, as he then in the full daylight conceived, might have misled him. Yet he still remembered the solemnity and loudness of the voice that came to him through the darkness.

He was now unexpectedly accosted by a friend of long standing, whose invitation to join his family at dinner he complied with, and repaired with him to a house situated upon an adjoining eminence, and fronting the sea. In the afternoon he parted with his host and strolled out to amuse his leisure upon the beach, which was nearly in front of his friend's house. There he contemplated the receding tide, and came upon a retired spot where several youths were preparing to bathe. Amongst those who went into the sea, he observed one venturing farther than the others to the distant waves, which he seemed to buffet with evident pleasure and courage. While watching him, however, he saw the youth suddenly succumb to a stronger wave than the preceding ones, nor did he reappear, as my friend anxiously looked for and expected him. He was horrified at the sight; and keeping his eye steadily fixed upon the precise point where the youth had gone down, he hastened to his companions, and inquiring for the most expert swimmer amongst them, directed him most earnestly and encouragingly to the spot, and besought him to attempt the rescue of his friend. His request was complied with, and the noble lad plunged into the sea and swam as directed, till he arrived at the exact place which was indicated. He then boldly dived, and with great difficulty brought up the body, and conveyed it to the shore, where it lay, unhappily, to all appearance destitute of life.

The minister now secured as speedily as possible a private room to which he conveyed the senseless body. He then devoted himself with all his strength and judgment to the labour of restoring suspended animation. He had formerly listened to a recital of the means suitable to be adopted for this purpose, and he employed them all according to his ability. He used continual friction, he breathed into the youth's mouth, and left nothing untried which he thought would conduce to the anxiously desired result. For a long time, however, no success appeared to crown his labours, and some of the few bystanders, who had at first proffered assistance, discouraged further efforts by pronouncing them to be hopeless. My friend himself now began to fear this opinion was too well founded. Yet his spirit was strong within him, and the impulse he felt to renewed exertions was uncontrollable. Again and again did he assiduously operate, and at length he perceived faint tokens of life begin to manifest themselves. Still he was in sad suspense, for his own strength was failing him, but he persisted once more; and now not without more evident signs that life was slowly returning. Slowly, very slowly—almost doubtfully—but yet, at last, certainly.

A warm bath was now instantly procured, and accelerated

the returning animation. Nor was it long before the speech of the youth came back to him, and, after a slight convulsion, he fell into a profound slumber. My friend watched beside him with unspeakable interest while he slept. When at last he awoke, he seemed like one beside himself, impatiently asking where he was, who was near him, and how he came there? It seemed as if a veil of oblivion had fallen upon him from the moment of his disappearance in the sea to that of his returning consciousness. He was gently and gradually informed of what had taken place; when, in spite of all entreaties, he was so overcome with emotions of gratitude to him who had thus determinately persisted in recovering him, that he sprang from the bed and threw himself at his feet, exclaiming, "Oh, my more than father!" In that one moment my friend was recompensed for all, and returned to Margate to recount his adventure.

At the ensuing annual meeting of the Royal Humane Society, this philanthropic man, whose benevolent assiduity had become known, was invited to be present. He described to me, as I myself cannot describe, the tide of emotions which flooded his soul when, at a certain stage of the proceedings, the doors of the large room in which they were assembled were suddenly opened, a procession began to enter, and slowly passed along the lines of the company. Each constituent of this procession was a human being who had been rescued from a watery grave and restored to life, at least instrumentally, by the exertions of a fellow creature.

As the procession moved along my friend scanned it carefully, and at length his heart beat violently, when he saw the youth he had restored approaching him, animated, and anxiously peering into every countenance he passed. When at last the eye of the young man caught that of his restorer, his emotions were too powerful to be restrained.

He broke from the rank, fell at his feet, and embraced his deliverer from death with a fervour that kindled the sympathies and visibly affected the hearts of all the spectators. Soon the chief officers of the institution summoned my friend to the chair, and publicly presented to him an annual medal of the Society, adding to it their united and hearty acknowledgments of his successful services.

Often during his after life did my friend thank God that he had yielded to the impulse that had mysteriously summoned him to that special act of benevolence.

The meeting of this recovered young man and his humane deliverer in the hall of a public assembly, and their joyful recognition, naturally suggests to us a meeting of a higher and holier character between a faithful minister of the Gospel and the souls instrumentally recovered by him from the death of sin to a life of righteousness, in the presence of God and of the holy angels. What a meeting will that be, and what honour will redound to the human instrument, even while he ascribes all the glory to God, as the author of every good work and the inspirer of every holy thought! It should much encourage ministers to reflect that one who is thus employed by Divine grace as the medium of conveying the truth of God to fallen beings, and as the instrument of restoring them to their Father's favour, as new creatures in Christ Jesus, will be more gladly greeted by the souls he is enabled to benefit than the great and honoured ones in the record of earth's benefactors. "Though ye have ten thousand instructors in Christ," says the apostle to his converts, "yet have ye not many *fathers*, for in Christ Jesus I have begotten you through the Gospel."

There is, then, a relationship, like that of a father to his children, established between them, which, being purely spiritual and existing only in *the mind*, is invulnerable to that stroke of death which will dissolve all earthly relationships, and will be made manifest for ever in the heavenly state. How soon do children recognise a parent after long separation, though in the midst of a multitude, and cause him to recognise them! With what transports of joy do they renew their former associations, and advert to the scenes and circumstances in which they have mingled! With similar emotions of a perfectly sublime and exalted nature, may the redeemed in heaven hail those who were the chief means, though not the source, of their bliss, and each of whom will be filled with ecstasy on receiving the expressions of their endearment. They will be his crown of joy and rejoicing in the day of the Lord Jesus, and he theirs.

A persuasion of this joyful recognition prevails in the breasts of most Christians. The idea, though communicated to them in no formal manner, is welcomed and cherished, and felt often most strongly at the moment of their separation for awhile by the stroke of the last enemy. The following touching narrative, communicated to me by an esteemed Wesleyan minister, will explain and enforce the meaning of what has been stated :—

"A Wesleyan missionary was called to visit a native in Ashantee, then on his dying bed, who had been his first convert, and was thus addressed by him :—' I hear you preached last night about heaven. I could not be there; but I am going to heaven itself; and when I get there, I will go to my Saviour and throw myself at his feet, and thank him for his mercy in sending a missionary to this land to tell me of the truth. Then I will come back to the gate and sit down until you come, and then I will take you to my Saviour's throne, and say you are the man who first told me of the cross of Christ.'"

The same idea was conveyed to me by an incident which took place not long since in one of the public vehicles of conveyance in the metropolis. Two very respectable females expressed the liveliest satisfaction on meeting with me, as the minister of Christ who had brought them to believe on him to the salvation of their souls. They evidently thought that I must recollect the circumstance of receiving the account of their conversion when I admitted them into church fellowship, although that had taken place many years before. They mentioned their previous names when single, and many other particulars, which all failed, however, to answer the end of recalling them to my recollection. I then overheard one of them (there being but few passengers beside ourselves) consoling the other for the disappointment by saying, "*Ah, well! he will be obliged to acknowledge us for his spiritual children in heaven.*"

Pleasing thought! to be thus hailed in the world of perfect knowledge, in the presence of glorified saints and angels, and of the approving Saviour, whose own joyous words we may then, in our humble measure, adopt—"Behold I and the children whom God has given me!"

———o———

Marvellous Issues.

"This also cometh forth from the Lord of hosts, who is wonderful in counsel and excellent in working."—Isa. xxviii. 29.

THE instance I am about to record affords an admirable illustration of the providence and grace of God, in preventing much evil and producing extensive good, by what would appear to us small and insignificant means. The narrative was communicated to me by a friend now living, who, when

ISAIAH.

he was in Paris some years ago, had an opportunity of hearing all the facts confirmed by undoubted authority :—

A young man of fine talents and prepossessing appearance had obtained a situation as secretary to a general of the Swiss guards, in which capacity his associates were persons who encouraged sceptical principles and fostered habits of dissipation. His bright prospects in life were soon clouded by the breaking up of the company, and for a maintenance he was compelled to descend to a lower station in life. He entered into the service of a jeweller as a traveller. In this situation large sums of money passed through his hands and were entrusted to his care. On one occasion, through some emergency, arising either from dissipation or the fatal practice of gaming, he was tempted to abstract a part of his employer's property and to convert it to his own use. The tempter now had him fast in his toils, and he from this time became the prey of uneasiness and dread.

His guilt sat heavily on him, and his disturbed imagination painted to him the horrors of discovery, apprehension, and condign punishment. Sleep departed from him, and his whole bodily system underwent a change threatening a settled melancholy and despondency. In this state of mind he formed the determination to end his troubles by a plunge at night into the river Seine, that too common resort in France of the duped and ruined votaries of vice and extravagance. Having planned everything necessary to the accomplishment of his fatal purpose, behold him on his way to the river's banks.

The night was dark; a thousand horrid thoughts brooded within him. He was certain of the discovery and recognition of his body in the morning at the *Morgue*. He felt the suspicion to which this would give rise, the consequent examination of his accounts, the inevitable exposure of his villany, the disgrace attaching to his memory, and the degradation of his friends. His invisible foes were doubtless exulting at the thought of the speedy termination of his wicked career about to be made, and the arrears of vengeance for all his crimes which they should be commissioned to inflict. But a better influence was secretly making its way to his heart. The recollection of a discourse he had heard some time before from an Evangelical Protestant minister in Paris, flashed across his mind. It had the effect of diverting his thoughts into a train of reflections directly opposed to the step he was meditating. He paused: he retired into a neighbouring *café*. He sought to relieve his mind by that best of all reliefs to a wounded and broken spirit—the disclosure of his case to another person, and the solicitation of his advice and sympathy. This resolution dissolved the spell which bound him. He recollected the name of the minister, penned a note to him, and despatched a messenger with it. The servant of God was soon at hand, retired with the penitent youth, and heard the whole of his unhappy tale, concluding with the desperate intention which had been thus singularly arrested in its execution. After considering the matter awhile, the minister advised an immediate surrender of himself to justice. This advice was complied with, and the customary formalities having been completed, his punishment, in consideration of his voluntary confession and agonizing remorse, was mitigated to three years' imprisonment.

It does not appear that, at this time, any religious change had taken place in his mind beyond a vague impression of his guilt and folly, and a conviction of the existence of a gracious Being who had secretly restrained him from self-destruction. But in the deep retirement of his cell, and during the heavy hours that passed over him, he was led to serious thoughts and reflections on the subject of religion, aided, no doubt, by the counsel and suggestions of the excellent minister who never forsook him.

At the expiration of about a fourth part of the period of his imprisonment, an incident occurred that fell in precisely with his state of mind, and turned his powers and thoughts in a direction which had never been anticipated. A benevolent Englishman at that time in Paris, struck with the ungodliness of the place, and anxious to do what lay in his power for its removal, suggested to a friend the propriety of translating one of our most popular little works against Deism and Infidelity into the French language, for gratuitous distribution, intending himself to defray the cost of a small impression. But the great desideratum was a translator who understood both languages sufficiently well to render it spirited and elegant enough to please a Parisian ear. Our young prisoner was immediately thought of, as possessing in an eminent degree the requisite qualifications, while, it was thought, the work itself, if it should engage his serious interest, would agreeably beguile the remaining period of his imprisonment. The prisoner caught eagerly at the proposal, entered into it with the greatest ardour, and at the same time with great seriousness. His careful reading of the book repeatedly, for the purpose of making himself well acquainted with it before he began to translate it, was attended with the happiest effects. The doubts of the authenticity of the books of Scripture which had lingered in his mind, fled like vapour before the rays of the rising sun. His task now became his joy.

When the translation was finished, it was shown to competent judges, and elicited the warmest approbation. A society in this country designed to assist in the distribution of religious books, being applied to by the friend before-mentioned, generously consented to patronize a large edition of the work, and to aid in its circulation. The young translator craved and obtained permission to prefix an expression of his own convictions, with an appeal to individuals of his own class on behalf of the claims of inspiration. Who shall trace the good effects of this work? Who can tell to what good ends the existence preserved by the re-collected fragments of a single religious discourse may yet be applied? How " wonderful is God in counsel! how mighty in working!" "There are many devices in a man's heart, nevertheless the counsel of the Lord that shall stand!" "He will do all his pleasure."

A similar case occurred in the course of my own ministry. A pious young man, deeply concerned for the conversion of his brother, while listening to a discourse addressed by me to the young, was strongly possessed with the idea that if he could obtain permission to publish it, his brother, who was a compositor in a printing-office, might be led to read it first for the press, and afterwards for publication, and thereby the subject might arrest his attention, and impress him with its truth and importance. He had not indeed heard of any such instance of success, and there was little reason to expect it, as it is a well-known fact that what is read for such a purpose passes away from the mind as soon as it escapes the eye. But the venture was not great, and he resolved, after praying for the Divine direction and blessing, to take the risk. The success was even beyond his expectation, and he lived to see that brother united to the Church of which he himself was a member, and also employed in missionary labours, in which he has now been successfully engaged for many years.

Who shall teach God knowledge, or prescribe to him the manner and time in which his providence shall concur with his grace in affecting that momentous change in an individual's character and destiny which awakens the highest interest in two worlds ?

> "The soul of man, Jehovah's breath,
> That keeps two worlds at strife,
> Hell from beneath attempts its death,
> Heaven stoops to give it life."

Surely there is no link in the chain of incidents which terminates in so blessed a result but must be considered as worthy of the particular attention of the Divine and benignant Intelligence. The greatness of the event itself, when considered in connection with the train of circumstances leading to it, and the momentous consequences arising out of it, forbids the supposition of a merely human arrangement, or a fortuitous concurrence of circumstances. From his own deep consciousness the subject of such a change is constrained to recognise the immediate action of Him who is wonderful in counsel and mighty in working. However weak and carnal men may attribute these issues to second causes, and to the ordinary working out of things, they to whom the Spirit of God has given a faculty of spiritual discernment see in them the very finger of God, and are not ashamed to own their convictions of his gracious interposition.

----o----

The Soul's Triumph over the Body.

" He giveth power to the faint ; and to them that have no might he increaseth strength. Even the youths shall faint and be weary, and the young men shall utterly fall. But they that wait upon the Lord shall renew their strength ; they shall mount up with wings as eagles ; they shall run, and not be weary; and they shall walk, and not faint."—Isa. xl. 29–31.

A CONTRAST is here instituted between natural and spiritual strength, and the superiority of the latter to the former is pointed out. Natural strength, having reached its maturity, after awhile begins to decline, and continues to do so till it dwindles into feebleness itself, and finally fades away in death; but spiritual strength is exempted from any such law of decay. It is susceptible of perpetual increase, even to the last, and is often most sensibly felt when physical power is nearest extinction; as the eagle is said to moult afresh in old age, and to renew its youthful might. Thus, the Divine life in man has its maturity still in prospect when death approaches, and that maturity once attained in the immortal state will suffer no decay.

I have often been struck with this contrast in the case of infirm and aged believers, but never so much so as in the case of a brother minister, the Rev. Joseph Slatterie, of Chatham, with whom I was intimately acquainted.

For nearly fifty years he was at that place the pastor of the church and congregation which he had in a manner raised, and which he left at his death in a state of great religious vigour and prosperity. As a native of the sister island, he was possessed of a ready wit, a lively imagination, and great fluency of speech; and was, therefore, an acceptable and popular preacher, not only at his own place, but, at intervals, in the metropolis and other parts of the country. He possessed a retentive memory, and was remarkably well acquainted with the Scriptures and with portions of sacred poetry, especially the hymnology of Drs. Watts and Doddridge. In the early part of his career, he was accustomed to preach several times in the same week, and never felt exhausted. This, however, told upon his constitution, and he declared, in my hearing, that he would earnestly dissuade young ministers from pursuing the same course. "I would as soon," he quaintly said, "have lain under a cart-wheel then as not have been so frequently engaged; but I now see that it was zeal without knowledge, or at least without discretion." His preaching was, of course, extemporaneous, but not without previous care, reading, and preparation. His own mind was his book while teaching publicly, and he employed no other. So unfitted was he by this practice for reading a discourse in public, that when he once attempted it at a missionary meeting, he soon paused, and putting his manuscript aside, took another text—one, of course, with which he was familiar, the faithful saying referred to by the apostle Paul—and preached from it for an hour in the most impressive manner, carrying the souls of his hearers— already burning with missionary zeal—along with him to the close. A series of afflictions, however, at length brought down his strength, and incapacitated him for continuing his former exertions. Seven long years of distressing illness in his wife, the untowardness of some of his family, and the difficulty of meeting the mental demands of a large and intelligent congregation, affected his nervous system to a degree most painful to witness. His natural strength abated; the fire of his vivacity burned dimly; and, finally, he was reduced to a state of utter imbecility. He was now rendered entirely dependent upon the care of his two daughters, whose devoted attentions to him during his melancholy prostration, lengthened as it proved to be, never flagged nor suffered any abatement.

The contrast which has been noticed of spiritual with natural vigour, was strikingly exemplified in him, in a way which, to those who have not witnessed similar facts would appear incredible. His memory, which no longer retained the images of once familiar persons and things, still supplied him in the readiest manner with passages of Scripture and verses of hymns, which he repeated most accurately, and sometimes with all his wonted zest and fervour. When the mention of the scenes and objects of this world with which he had been conversant excited no attention, the utterance of some well-known verse or fact of a religious nature would instantly awaken a lively recognition, and cause him to break forth in an animated strain for some minutes. A veil of oblivion seemed to be drawn over what was temporal and material in his past experience, and a view *only* of what was spiritual and eternal presented to his mind. His occasional significant sayings ; his repetition of hymns and Scripture in long paragraphs ; and the earnest breathings of his soul to be with Christ, a record of which his daughters have carefully preserved, would fill a volume, and afford, in every page, matter for devout admiration and praise.

Hearing of his prostrate condition, I purposely paid a visit to his house. I found but the wreck and remnant only of what I had formerly known him to be. He was sitting in the middle of the room, apparently listless and thoughtless, hardly looking up at my arrival, and even then showing no sign of recognition, nor any revival from his state of indifference. He seemed wholly taken up with trifles, and was muttering a request for sweetmeats, as though he were in reality again a child. I was confounded and appalled at what I saw, and exclaimed, " What, my old friend, do you not know me ?" He gave no response, but simply repeated his former request. One of his daughters then said to me, " Ask him something about the Scriptures or the Saviour, and you will soon see a vast difference." Upon this, I said to him, as if complainingly, " Well, I see you do not know *me;* do you know *Jesus* whom I serve in the gospel ?" He started and looked as if just aroused from sleep ; when, lifting up his eyes, he exclaimed :—

"Jesus, my God, I know his name ;
His name is all my trust ;

> Nor will he put my soul to shame,
> Nor let my hope be lost."

He then relapsed into his former imbecile state; but, wishing still further to be satisfied of the contrast, I repeated the beginning of one of his favourite chapters—the 40th of Isaiah—when he instantly took up the strain, and went on repeating far more readily and correctly than I could have done, till he reached the close of the chapter. After this I could elicit nothing more from him than a few incoherent sentences, with some additional hymns. In this state of corporeal imbecility, and contrasted spiritual vigour, I found he had remained for many months; and he continued in the same for many more, waited upon by his daughters, who watched dutifully and affectionately over him until he breathed his last.

These faithful attendants had been induced, at the request of myself and other friends, to take down many of the expressions which fell from their father's lips at those periods when his singular hallucination had less power over him, and when the temporary re-animation of his mental faculties and spiritual perceptions permitted him to return to and speak of religious subjects. I have before me the paper on which these observations were founded, and from which a few extracts may be made, illustrating still further the force of long habits of piety, and the invaluable benefit of having the memory stored with passages of Scripture and portions of other works of a religious nature. Many friends and ministers during these long months of affliction came to visit this good but sadly altered brother. With most of these he held some snatches of pious conversation; though hardly recognising their persons when they entered his room, or becoming conscious of their absence when they had departed. It will be seen from some of the questions put to him, how deep was the prostration of body and mind into which he had fallen in the apprehensions of those who proposed them; for they were questions far more suited to young beginners in the spiritual life, with a view of ascertaining the objects of their faith and hope, than to one, who for many years had been the instructor and counsellor of hundreds on all these points from the ample stores of an enlightened intellect and his own treasures of Christian experience. Yet such was his present sense of deficiency and unworthiness, that instead of resenting such questions as an insult to a man of his years and standing, he answered them with the simplicity and deference of a child under examination.

In the following unadorned yet touching style do his daughters head the manuscript notes of their father's last experience.

"A few sentences taken from the lips of our beloved father, after he had ceased to feel any interest in the concerns of time, and when his memory was so far weakened as to forget continually the occurrences of the past hour, and even at times hardly to realize his own identity, or the relation he bore to his own children.

"When his mind became a blank to earthly things, his hold on spiritual ones never abandoned him; and in his darkest seasons of despondency, he would exclaim in the most affecting manner, 'Have pity upon me, my friends, for the hand of God hath touched me. But thou art a faithful God; cast me not off in my old age, forsake me not when my strength faileth me.' His supplications for continued forgiveness were often accompanied with a profusion of tears. 'Oh that my head were waters,' he would say, 'and mine eyes a fountain of tears, that I might weep day and night for my sins.' Sometimes he would continue in prayer so earnestly, that nature became quite exhausted, while nearly the whole was couched in Scripture language.

"On being asked if he knew the day of the month, and his replying in the negative, he was informed that it was nearly the last day of the year, upon which he broke out: 'Oh may we be prepared for *our last day!* and for our great change! Enable us, O Lord, to yield our all to thine entire disposal. Oh that I could give over sighing, and be looking for that blessed hope, and the glorious appearing of the great God and our Saviour Jesus Christ. Lord, confirm my hope, and shelter me under the shadow of thy wings.'

"He was much affected during the early part of his infirmity, by the news of the almost sudden death of two dear young friends, brother and sister; and, as if insensible of his weakness and debility, he spoke as though he were still in the exercise of his ministry, and expressed his determination to attempt an improvement of this dispensation to the people of his charge. 'Oh that it may be sanctified,' he ejaculated repeatedly, 'sanctified to the people. Let me go down to the chapel, and try to do good to the souls of the people!' Nor could he be dissuaded from his purpose. For hours he could scarcely be restrained from tottering to the door to go out to the place of worship. One day he managed to open the door unperceived, and had gone a few steps. Most unwillingly he was brought back, saying he had got his text ready, and quoted Isaiah xvi. 12, referring, perhaps, in his mind to his own desire and inability to accomplish it; thus evincing his familiar acquaintance with Scripture in being able to fix in a moment on such a singular, yet appropriate, passage—' It shall come to pass, when it is seen that Moab is weary on the high place, that he shall come to his sanctuary to pray; but he shall not prevail.'

"One evening, after many days and nights of weakness and exhaustion, he retired to rest greatly debilitated, and all but totally insensible to what was passing around. At this moment, one of his sons entered the chamber, and, without knowing which, he aroused himself, and asked for his Christian name. On being informed, he spoke to him with great animation, as though he had been inspired, and continued so speaking for a whole hour. 'O my son, I am glad to see you once more; what an unspeakable mercy will it be if we meet at last in heaven! Seek the salvation of your soul above all things! May you fall into the hands of a precious Saviour.' These, with many similar expressions he uttered, the tears flowing down his cheeks the whole time. When his son was gone, it was found that in a few moments the remembrance of his visit and of what he had said to him had vanished from his mind.

"The ordinary movements and conversations of the family engaged none of his attention. He seemed completely abstracted from them, as in a reverie. But if any spiritual topic were touched upon, in a lively way he would start, as if with a sudden burst of feeling in relation to it; after which he would relapse into his ordinary state of stupor.

"A friend who had called was reading us a letter which she had received from one who had become a Unitarian, giving an account of his sentiments. For awhile the sufferer appeared totally indifferent to what was being read. but when she came to some bold and positive assertions respecting the inferiority of Christ to the Almighty, he became violently agitated, and, with indignation in his tone, exclaimed '*Stuff! poison! Oh, let it not come into your minds!*' and then repeated, with great emphasis, the hymn of Dr. Doddridge on the words, 'Unto you that believe,

ISAIAH.

Christ is precious,' dwelling with great emotion and earnestness on the lines—

> 'Yes, thou art precious to my soul,
> My transport and my trust;'

and having consoled himself with these thoughts, he became again totally indifferent to what was passing.

"His predominant feeling all through life had been one of gratitude and thanksgiving. This did not forsake him in his present extremity. An instance of it appeared in a striking manner when imploring a blessing on the provisions of the table. We had finished the repast, and some fruit was put upon the table as a little dessert. Of this he took no notice, but ere we had begun to partake of it, he stopped us, saying, We have not returned thanks; and putting his hands into an attitude of supplication, he gave thanks in so expressive a manner that we took out our pencils and noted what he said. In a few minutes, oblivious of what he had been doing, he broke forth again with the same interruption and action, but not in the same words; for these, although relating to the same subject, were varied most appropriately on every repetition of the act, which occurred no less than eight times at the same sitting. One or two of these devout aspirations are mentioned as specimens of the rest : 'Father of mercies, we bless thee for thy bounty to us : crown all our hopes with immortal happiness, for Christ's sake. Amen!' 'Heavenly Benefactor, thou hast been with us for good up to the present moment! may we know by happy experience that thou, and thou alone, art the God of salvation, through Christ. Amen.' 'We bless thee, heavenly Father, that thou hast supplied our wants; may grace Divine be inscribed on our hearts, and love Divine be our portion :, for Christ's sake. Amen.' Thus, however mechanical the words and the action might seem, the variation of the expressions, with equal significance and point, proved that the same spirit was stirred within him by the recurrence of the former outward acts. Habitual piety, that does not degenerate into formality, is an invaluable blessing.

"During the dreary months that followed, he was visited by several friends and by other ministers from different parts of the country. They were surprised at the debility of his outward condition, and equally at the undiminished vitality of his inward principles and sentiments; occasionally flashing forth as they did, and wanting only permanence to be the same as formerly. He conversed by fits and starts, but almost always in Scripture language, and in that of sacred poetry. One whole day, though he spoke much, he was observed to have uttered nothing but in such phraseology. The pertinency of his quotations manifested not only his intimate acquaintance with the sacred records, but also their remarkable adaptation to the ever-varying scenes and minutest circumstances of human life. He heard the sound of music, and exclaimed,

'How sweet the name of Jesus sounds
In à believer's ear,' etc.

and followed it with another appropriate hymn—

'Jesus, I love thy charming name,
'Tis music to mine ear;
Fain would I sound it out so loud,
That heaven and earth may hear.'

emphasizing '*so loud*' with the whole force of his utterance; thus showing what was ever uppermost in his thoughts, and to what he was as apt to turn as a bird to fly at the first startling sound. Once he attempted to sing, but failed; on which it was said, 'You will sing ere long;' he promptly replied, 'You will then be thinking of a believer singing in heaven.' On the idea being suggested of the possibility of his giving up this hope, he said with great energy—' Oh no, no, no ; I cannot, I would not, I dare not : I trust a faithful God.' He dwelt on Philip Henry's three unchangeables, 'An unchangeable God, an unchangeable Covenant, and an unchangeable Heaven.' But these broken and disjointed conversations at long intervals became at length less and less frequent, and ceased to enliven the dulness. The wine of life had lost all its flavour, and nothing remained of it but the dregs."

It was during this period of his long illness, or towards the close of it, that he and another neighbouring minister, who had been paralysed, met together. It must have been a singular meeting, when two laborious and faithful ministers of God's word were thus brought together in their enfeebled and shattered state. Yet no debility could prevent them from resuming, in the best way they were able, those religious exercises in which they had frequently in their best years been mutually engaged. Our friend repeated some whole chapters and favourite hymns from memory ; his companion discharged that part of the service which the other was unable to perform—a connected prayer. They shook hands previous to what proved their final separation for this life—our friend saying, in the most solemn, affecting, and collected manner, "*Brother, we part at the footstool ; we shall meet at the throne!*" a prophecy that has long been fulfilled to the joy and rejoicing of their hearts.

Thus passed away the three closing years of his earthly existence, whose dreariness so sadly contrasted with the vivacity of all his earlier years. His wit was then sparkling, his cup of joy, save some bitter drops of domestic sorrow, was full. But how clouded the setting of that sun whose rising and meridian had been so splendid !

Q

What a comment on those words of the inspired preacher, "If a man live many years, and rejoice in them all, yet let him remember the days of darkness; for they shall be many."

The time, however, drew nigh for his sorrows to have an end. His last tears, and they were many during his illness, were now to be shed, and to be succeeded by the never-ceasing joy of his emancipated soul. He had more than once thought he was dying, and had taken leave of his affectionate attendants; but partial revivals proved their misapprehension. Yet it served to slope the descent into the valley, and to familiarise them with its deepening shades. Some verses were repeated while he was expiring, the inclination of his head serving to prove that he understood them, and entered into their import. One verse particularly struck him,

> "Jesus can make a dying bed
> Feel soft as downy pillows are,
> While on his breast I lean my head,
> And breathe my life out sweetly there."

"*My head!*" he ejaculated; and fell asleep in Jesus, in the seventy-first year of his age.

It is a matter of relief and comfort to reflect, that during the whole time of his illness, he was under the constant care of his affectionate daughters. He met, in their treatment of him, with that tenderness, skill, and indomitable patience which are the characteristics of the sex. The ties of affection bound them to him, and the recollections of the many years of fatherly affection and support he had afforded them, made them more than willing to discharge in some measure the obligation under which he had laid them. Such service God in his kind providence reserves for us, when no other could suffice for our necessities. Nor is such a service without its reward to those who so voluntarily and cheerfully render it; in the present joy of giving relief, the approbation of their own minds; and, as in the case before us, the esteem and friendship of all those who were the friends of their parent, and have continued theirs for his sake. What consolation in the thought of meeting in a happier clime with those whose complaints we hushed, whose tears we wiped away, and whose suffering hours we enlivened, while they tarried here below! When we fail, doubtless they will receive us with unusual joy "into everlasting habitations."

EZEKIEL.

Special Answers to Prayer.

"Thus saith the Lord, I will yet for this be inquired of by the house of Israel, to do it for them."—EZEK. xxxvi. 37.

AN objection to the exercise of prayer has often been derived from the immutability of God and the comprehensiveness of those decrees which the Scriptures represent as embracing all things; but it should be remembered that the same Scriptures enjoin upon man the obligation to pray, and consequently, the prayers of men are included among the means which were foreseen and destined to be conducive to the fulfilment of the Divine purposes. As in all other cases men employ means for the accomplishment of ends, so in this case also, prayer is the appointed agency which God commands men to employ, and which reason itself approves as the most direct method of obtaining Divine blessings. Whatever the decrees of God may be as to future events, it is quite certain that they are hidden from us, and can never become the rule of our duty. We are responsible for the faithful use of all the means we possess, and are never commanded to regulate our conduct by abstract conceptions of the attributes and purposes of God.

Prayer not only harmonizes with the appointed method of receiving spiritual and temporal benefits, but is eminently calculated to prepare the heart of the suppliant for the right reception of them. The mind is thus put into a posture of desire and expectation, and hope and faith are quickened into lively exercise; the pure affections of the soul are called forth in holy aspirations towards the true, the perfect, and the eternal; hope lays firm hold upon these, and in imagination realizes the fulness of joy which their possession will afford, while faith grasps the Divine promise as a security for the blessed consummation.

The Scripture makes it manifest in many places that there is an established correspondence and vital connection between the *special* favour God designs to bestow, and the desires after it awakened in the heart of man by the Holy Spirit: "Likewise the Spirit also helpeth our infirmities; for we know not what we should pray for as we ought; but the Spirit itself maketh intercession for us with groanings which cannot be uttered. And he that searcheth the hearts, knoweth what is the mind of the Spirit, because he maketh intercession for the saints, according to the will of God."

One part of this gracious assurance should always be connected with the other parts. We shall never be prompted by the Spirit of God to pray for what that Spirit knows to be detrimental to us, and not, "according to the will of God." Yet every humble suppliant is conscious of inward promptings and assistance which have both given shape to his thoughts and aided his infirmities of expression.

Thus, too, do we account for certain impulses in prayer, and a certain fervour in pleading, which liken the pleader to the patriarch who had power with God by his importunity, and prevailed. Assurances of success in prayer are constantly attached to importunate perseverance. This was remarkably the case with the apostles and their coadjutors in founding the Christian Church. Their "prayer of faith" proceeded from Divine impulses which inspired them with confidence that the answer would be such as the Spirit had impelled them to ask. Some of the promises made in the

New Testament, if interpreted literally, must be limited to these cases. Such are the following: "The prayer of faith shall save the sick;" "Whatsoever ye shall ask, believing, ye shall receive;" "And this is the confidence we have in him, that, if we ask anything according to his will, he heareth us; and if we know that he hear us, whatsoever we ask, we know that we have the petitions that we desired of him."

Nor can it be denied that in later, and even in modern times, good men have often experienced a liberty in prayer and a spirit of importunity by which they have been led confidently to anticipate a favourable response to their supplications, and it has been according to their heart's desire. Yet we have no Scriptural warrant to expect an immediate answer to prayer, or to dictate the time and manner in which the benefits implored shall be conferred. Neither have we any positive promise of the bestowment of *special temporal* blessings. It is sufficient for God's honour and our welfare that, if the petition be sincerely and scripturally preferred, it shall not return void, nor be eventually fruitless. I now chiefly refer to temporal blessings, but, as it respects spiritual gifts, we have specific encouragement to the effect that, if we seek we shall find, if we ask we shall receive, and if we knock it shall be opened unto us. This line of observation will be illustrated and enforced by the following facts:—

The Rev. Mr. Kilpin of Exeter, an eminently zealous and useful minister of Christ, relates that a young woman, on his asking her if she had read the tracts he gave her, answered with embarrassment, "Yes;" though conscious that she had not done so. He then gave her others, entreating her to pray over them. She took them, and when she got home, threw them behind her chamber door, saying, "Pray over them, indeed! No, I shall not begin to pray over books!" But as they lay there her eye often rested on them, and she thought she heard them say, "Pray over us! Pray over us." Probably her conscience reproached her at such times for the falsehood she had uttered in telling Mr. Kilpin that she had read them, and her imagination made the tracts vocal in repeating again and again the minister's injunction to pray over them. At length she thought she would read them, merely that she might know what she was asked to pray over. The first contained an anecdote which interested her; the next was on eternity, and affected her; the third was on prayer, and brought her to her knees. How remarkable and appropriate were the tracts to her case, as well as the order in which she was guided to their perusal! Was there not a special providence in the subjects presented to her, and Divine influence exercised to lead her to pray! She soon became a member of Mr. Kilpin's church, and an active distributor of tracts. She afterwards continued to be an honourable member of the church, married, and became a mother; and two of her children, as Mr. Kilpin believes, were brought into the fold of the Saviour by her pious care and instruction.

It is not merely dispersion of tracts that should satisfy us, but we should seek by some appropriate words accompanying their distribution to secure attention to them, and devotion in connection with their perusal.

Many years ago, in a retired part of the country, a few pious people associated themselves together in a small room for religious worship, and some zealous friends from a neighbouring town were accustomed to visit them for the purpose of ministering to them the words of eternal life. The success which attended upon these services suggested the desirableness of endeavouring to build a small place of worship. All agreed as to the importance of the object, and as to the probability of obtaining sufficient pecuniary aid for its accomplishment. But after much deliberation there appeared one formidable object in their way. The only land in the neighbourhood eligible for this purpose was in the possession of a gentleman well known to be a violent opposer of all who differed from himself in religious opinions. Most of these good people, therefore, feared it would be of no use to apply to him for the sale of the land, as he was of an unbending disposition. Yet there was no other alternative, and it was suggested that they should have recourse to prayer for the removal of this difficulty. Two also out of this little company were appointed to make proposals to the owner of the land for the purchase of it. Before the time appointed for making this application, it was agreed that a whole night should be spent in prayer for the Divine blessing on the enterprise. The following morning saw the two delegates making their way to the rich man's house with anxious hearts. They found him at home, and soon disclosed the object of their visit, stating at the same time that they would cheerfully pay him the full value of the land. No sooner did he hear the proposition than with great indignation he bade them be gone, and with much incivility he turned them out of his house, sternly refusing to listen to their request.

On returning to their friends, and making known their disheartening reception, some who were strong in faith proposed that they should pass another night in prayer, and especially importune the Controller of all events that he would incline the heart of the proud landowner to yield to their request. This they did, and sent the same two delegates the next day to make another attempt to effect the purchase of the land. Again they were introduced to the prejudiced and uncourteous gentleman; but he now received them in a very different manner, apologizing for the haughtiness of his behaviour the day before, and acceding to the sale of the land, adding, "I cannot tell how it is, but I have had no sleep all last night for thinking of you and of your chapel, and I have now made up my mind to let you have the piece of land you want." It may be well conceived with what cheerful hearts and joyous steps these good men returned to their brethren, and that the whole company gave thanks to the Hearer and Answerer of prayer, for his gracious and manifest interposition on their behalf.

"When travelling on the borders of Italy," writes a Christian friend, "we arrived one evening at the town of C——, from whence we were to proceed on our journey at nine o'clock the next morning. On rising, the first thing we heard was that a young man, in the military service, having been guilty of a misdemeanour, was to suffer the penalty of death for his offence, at nine o'clock that morning. The thought rushed into my mind—How dreadful that this young man should be thus precipitated into eternity, perhaps wholly unprepared! I became greatly agitated, and I could ill control my feelings. The instant I could leave the breakfast-table, I retired to a secluded chamber, and locked myself in, and there in earnest prayer I felt compelled to plead and wrestle for the salvation of the doomed soldier. The burden of my petition was, that if he were not prepared to enter the presence of his Judge, his death might be averted, and time be given him for repentance.

"I continued upon my knees thus agonizing in prayer, till in a moment I heard the sound of a discharged volley of guns. It vibrated through my heart, my lips were closed, my prayer was stopped, and in a few minutes I was obliged, agitated as I was, to hurry down to join my friends, who were just starting to leave the town. We were quickly beyond its precincts, and heard no more of the awful catastrophe of that morning. Having been for some time past severely exercised on spiritual things, I had been led to form the resolution not to read any of the public papers that came in my way, their topics ill according with the state of my mind at that time.

"I adhered to this resolution until about two months after, when, in a distant town, I one morning almost unconsciously took up a paper, and the first thing that caught my eye was the account of an extraordinary event, which occurred at the town of C——, viz., that a young soldier having been sentenced to death, was accordingly brought out for execution in the usual manner by the hands of his comrades, twenty-four of whom were at a given signal to fire at his heart. The signal was given, the guns were discharged, but, to the amazement of all, every bullet missed its aim! The volley had been fired, but he stood unhurt, and so extraordinary and even miraculous was his escape considered, that his pardon was instantly granted, and he was permitted to live! His subsequent history remains unknown."

Some time ago the missionaries in the Feejee Islands were threatened with an attack by enraged hostile chiefs, who came forward uttering their threats and brandishing their weapons. The missionaries were unable to repel force by force, even if they had wished to do so. They shut themselves up in the mission-house, and united in earnest prayer to God, entreating his merciful and almighty protection. After they had continued in prayer for some time, it was observed that there was less of noise outside the house than there had previously been, and at length it ceased altogether. One of their number went out to ascertain the real state of things. At first he found no one; but at length he met a man, and interrogated him thus:—

"Where are the chiefs?"

"They are gone," said he; "they found you were praying to your God, and they know your God is a strong God, and they are gone."

Thus did God honour the prayers of his servants in the hour of their extremity.

" I well remember," said the son of a Christian missionary to the author of this book, "hearing my mother speak in touching terms of the narrow escapes my father had during our sojourn in Jamaica. Once we were nearly thrown, together with the horse and gig, over a steep precipice into the sea. My father endured five attacks of yellow fever, and on one occasion he suffered so much, that the medical attendants gave up all hope of his recovery. For some time he lingered in a state of insensibility hardly to be described. My mother watched and wept; friends did the same; the faithful Christian negroes also wept as they saw life fast ebbing away. Death seemed just about to seize his prey. Prayer-meetings were held, and at last some hundreds of negroes were assembled, and earnestly beseeching Almighty God with tears to spare the life of their beloved missionary. Often had he stood up before judges in their defence. Often had he been cast into prison for protecting them from their tyrannical oppressors; and now, with a warmth of affection and intensity of feeling unknown amongst Christians in England, they cried mightily to God. Hour after hour passed by; messengers were passing from the chapel to the mission-house, to obtain tidings of the sick man. At length, when his spirit appeared about to depart, and to leave all earthly scenes, the pious negroes agreed to unite *silently* in one heartfelt petition to Him 'in whose hand our breath is:' and believing that 'man doth not live by bread alone, but by every word which proceedeth out of the mouth of God,' they thus unitedly prayed. That multitude joined in one petition ascending from their inmost souls; and at that very hour the shadow of death fled at the rebuke of the Lord! A change took place, signs of health appeared, and he, for whose restoration so many supplicants prayed, was raised up from his bed of languishing; and that chapel and mission-house did indeed become filled with songs of joy, praise, and thanksgiving. 'He lives! he lives!' was the joyful exclamation that ran from one to another through that congregation, with an effect which I cannot describe, and which was greatly increased by the emotional nature of the unsophisticated negroes.

"This touching incident in the life of my father is, to my mind, a strong proof of the truth of our holy religion. Here was something of an altogether higher than human origin, in the commencement, progress, and issue. Can Infidelity or Atheism point to such effects or to such a result? It was the preaching of Jesus which led these poor despised negroes to act as they did. Their missionary was to them the messenger of Christ, and the bearer of glad tidings, and on that account they loved him. That love was from heaven,—its emotions and effects were heavenly. The missionary's love to Christ prompted him to do for the negroes what no human considerations would ever have accomplished. Missionary and people were there united with a love stronger than death."

The following letter will not unsuitably close the present chapter. It may encourage ministers of the gospel to enforce the duty of prayer on all their hearers under all circumstances of trial and temptation. Christ himself gives universal encouragement to approach the throne of grace, when he says, "Men ought always to pray and not to faint." Under such an authority all difficulties and doubts are as chaff before the wind. "It is a certain fact," observes the late Rev. John Foster, " that whenever a man prays aright, he forgets the philosophy of it, and feels as if his supplications *really would* make a difference in the determinations and conduct of the Deity."

"REV. AND DEAR SIR,
    "It has often been the wish of the writer to address you, but a sort of half notion that you would think it an intrusion, has prevented him from taking the resolution till very lately, and he does so at last with a request in his hand. 'Ah! the old story, I thought it was a begging case.' 'No! stay, dear doctor; I beg you won't condemn the paper to the flames without a hearing. Mine is *not* the *ordinary* begging case.' 'No,' I hear you say; 'every man thinks his own case more deserving of commiseration than his neighbour's.'

"To the point. A young man, living the gay life of London, as it is called, went with a friend to hear you preach three years ago. Your discourse was directed principally, if not altogether, to the young, and you dwelt on the efficacy of prayer, and particularly said, and reiterated it, 'My dear young friends, I conjure each one of you not to sleep this night without prayer. If you can't pray at length, say, *Lord Jesus, save my soul! Lord Jesus, save my soul!* Let that simple prayer be perseveringly offered, with the desire accompanying the words, and you *cannot* pray in vain,—*you cannot fail* to receive a gracious answer;—as the Bible is true, as God is true, *you shall* receive a gracious answer, and be indeed made partakers of the salvation which Christ has wrought out for all who come to him. Salvation from the power of sin here, and from its consequences hereafter, the love of God, for Christ's sake, shall be yours in this life and through eternity.'

"Such were the very words, or as near as may be, for the writer trusts to memory. (It is to himself that he alludes, as having been an auditor.) He took no notes, but the words were fastened, as nails, in a sure place. The seed was sown, and vegetated in a measure, but in a field full of tares, which completely hid, or choked, the blade. God, in the abundance of his mercy towards me, suffered affliction to come upon me,—my health gave way under not undiligent study in my profession, conjoined with that attendance on the goddess of pleasure which, though meant as relaxation, is anything but refreshment to the body or even mind. This illness lasted six months, during which time I scarce gave a thought to futurity, unless it were to despond. I was a stranger to the *free grace* of God. I said to myself, or the arch enemy of souls said to me, 'You know the kind of life you have led; you are not the character to be heard, if now, in the prospect of death, you are frightened into prayer.' This succeeded, and it was not till recovery seemed probable that I seriously inquired, 'Can I be saved?' It was during that inquiry that your discourse on prayer returned to my recollection; there I at once found that I had gained firm ground for my foot. I dwelt upon your words as the choicest I had ever heard or read; I compared them with the Bible and found them true; I compare them with my own experience, and I find them true. Since then I have had more than one opportunity of proving the sustaining power of faith in Christ when in the near prospect, as was supposed, of death.

"I saw you, my dear doctor, as chairman of the private meetings of the Congregational Union. I had not seen you since the occasion I have adverted to: your presence revived (it could not heighten) all my love and respect. Your rising to take leave was a sad blow to me, for I had intended, after the meeting and business was over, to have sought a moment's interview with you at Mrs. H——'s, at your leisure. I should have asked you to preach *that* sermon over again; or, if you cannot recollect the particular sermon, my request is that at all events you will incorporate the part I have related in another.

"God has given you, dear sir, many, many proofs of his blessing on your labours. Here is another. I mention it from a desire that you may be refreshed by it in your work; and my reason for asking you to preach that sermon again, is the desire and confidence I have that it will again be blessed to some soul, or souls, for doubtless others beside myself must have profited.

"I do not withhold my name and address, because I should thereby be shutting myself out *from the possibility* of a line from yourself. That, however, is a favour I am far from asking, as I know the multiplicity of your engagements would render any such request unreasonable.

"That the son should bless the father, seems reversing the order of things; but you, my dear father, have taught me that I may *pray* for a blessing on you, and I do so now most sincerely.

I remain, my dear sir,
Yours,
Faithfully and gratefully,
J. L. W."

LUKE.

Youthful Disciples.

"In that hour Jesus rejoiced in spirit, and said, I thank thee, O Father, Lord of heaven and earth, that thou hast hid these things from the wise and prudent, and hast revealed them unto babes : even so, Father ; for so it seemed good in thy sight."—LUKE x. 21.

THE new feature in the history of religion which had been foretold as characteristic of the Christian dispensation is here brought prominently to view. It was to be a universal religion, providing for the wants and well-being of the whole human race. While it overlooked no class of society, it poured its blessings in profusion upon those who were the most destitute. The poor and needy, whom all other religions, except the Jewish, disregarded, were especially sought out and befriended by the religion of Christ. It was among these that it found its first votaries and propagators. It sprang not from the high and mighty, thence to descend to the unlettered and despised; but began with the latter, and made its way by their means to the nobles and princes of the earth.

Who does not perceive in this fact proofs of the Divine wisdom and goodness worthy of the devoutest acknowledgment? And who would not seek, in his humble measure, to participate in the complacency of the Saviour whose spirit, in contemplation thereof, was filled with a joy that for one short hour dispersed by its radiance the clouds of sorrow in which he was enveloped.

The more seriously we reflect on the benign aspect and provisions of the gospel, the greater cause shall we find to love and adore its great Author, and the more deeply shall we feel the obligation that is laid upon us individually to fall in with his gracious designs. We shall seek to follow in the footsteps of the Master, who, when he first stood up to read in the Synagogue at Nazareth, found the place where it was written, " The Spirit of the Lord is upon me, because he hath anointed me to preach the gospel *to the poor;*" who took little children in his arms, put his hands upon them and *blessed them,* and said rebukingly to his disciples, " Forbid them not to come unto me, for of such is the kingdom of heaven." When " the chief priests and scribes saw the wonderful things that he did, and the children crying in the temple, and saying Hosanna to the Son of David, they were sore displeased, and said unto him, Hearest thou what *these* say ? And Jesus saith unto them, Yea ; have ye never read, Out of the mouths of babes and sucklings thou hast perfected praise ? " The proud Pharisees were silenced by an appeal to their own Scriptures, and to the words of David, their king; but in their hearts they hated and despised this manifestation of infant homage. Let us take heed that we despise not one of these little ones.

The power of the Holy Spirit is never more magnified than when by his gracious influences, in connection with the word of God, very young persons are made recipients and dispensers in their measure of its most precious truths, as well as possessors of the most exalted hopes and aspirations. " The promise is unto you and *to your children,*" and never, I believe, has that promise been pleaded in vain by any whose prayers have been accompanied by the diligent use of appointed instrumentality and the force of a holy example.

On one occasion, when I was called to preach in the south-eastern part of England, I stayed at the house of a respectable family, where I witnessed a touching but most encouraging illustration of the power of the gospel to sustain and cheer a youthful sufferer under great affliction, and to fit him early for the skies.

He was the eldest child of my kind hosts, who from his birth had watched over him with a love that found its highest bliss in the thought that to them God had entrusted an immortal soul to be trained for heaven. His constitution was delicate from childhood, but he had manifested a lovely disposition and great docility, especially in relation to Divine things, with which his pious parents were intimately conversant. As the powers of his mind unfolded themselves, they took the greatest delight in watching their development, and both by instruction and example surrounded him with the holiest influences. He had been thus prepared for the visitation that overtook him at an early age.

When a child at school, and while playing with his companions, he sustained an injury in the back, which at first was thought to be slight, but which, after some time, resulted in hopeless disease of the spine, rendering it necessary for him to be placed in a horizontal position, in which he continued without knowing any change of posture for the period of *nine years and six months*. Amply, now, did he repay his fond parents for their tender and unwearied care; for although no greater calamity of a bodily kind could have befallen an active youth, it was in this instance, by the state of the sufferer's mind, divested of all sorrow and gloom, not only to himself but to all who saw him. Of course, every alleviation was afforded that affection could devise and supply. His couch was so constructed that he could be drawn from one apartment to another with facility, and his attendants found all their labours made easy and delightful by the peace and tranquillity of his spirit, often rising to cheerfulness and joy. He had been so "nurtured" in Divine things that it is not presumptuous to say that the "good work" was begun in him by the Spirit of God before the corrupt nature had had time to form *habits* of evil: and that in consequence of this, no severe struggle was necessary to mark the change from "death unto life." But although the work was wrought so imperceptibly, its reality was not the less conspicuous. The *fruits* of the Spirit most clearly prove His glorious indwelling, and these abounded in the life of this dear boy. Though so early deprived of the privileges of public worship, his thoughts often reverted to the time when he was taken by his parents to the house of God, and he would quote with feeling the words of a favourite hymn:—

"I have been there, and still would go ;
'Tis like a little heaven below."

His love for the Bible was very observable, and his memory was so well stored with hymns and sacred poems that he taught his nurse more than forty, in order that she might repeat them while dressing him. So far from being engrossed with his own sufferings and privations, he was deeply interested in all that concerned his friends. It was once said to him, "You make all our troubles yours." To this he quickly replied, "I ought to do so, I have none of my own." He was often asking the all-important question, "How can I glorify God?" And when he was told, "By passively enduring your affliction," he exclaimed, "Oh, if that be glorifying Him, I hope I shall lie here as long as I live." He was, however, permitted in other ways to bring honour to his Saviour. A young woman who lived in the family first heard from his lips the glad tidings of salvation, and was led by his teaching and example to confess Christ before men.

When I was staying in the house of his parents, on the occasion alluded to, I was so much struck with his conversation that I committed portions of it to writing. The following dialogue may serve as a specimen of his habitual frame of mind and his mode of expression:—

"You have had many years of weariness and sorrow."

"I have found them pass very quickly."

"Poor fellow!—but why did I say *poor* ?"

"I was thinking so while you said it; I am very, very happy; and how beautifully I am hedged in from sinning, by my position."

"But yet temptation may find us out anywhere."

"Oh," replied he, striking his hand upon his breast, while a momentary shadow passed over his face, "I *know* it."

"Well, you will one day possess a bright and perfect body, with a pure and holy soul."

"Yes," with great earnestness, "and *for ever !*"

"Do you recollect any of the texts from which you heard Mr. S. preach while you were very young?"

"One—'Enoch walked with God.' But I remember many of Mr. T.'s. The last one of his that I heard was, 'As thy day, so shall thy strength be.' I *can* set my seal to that."

I repeated to him two verses of Southwell's poem, entitled "Content and Rich:"—

> "My wishes are but few,
>   All easy to fulfil;
> I make the limits of my power
>   The bounds unto my will.
>
> Since sails of largest size
>   The storms do soonest tear,
> I bear so low and small a sail
>   As freeth me from fear."

"Yes," he exclaimed, catching the spirit of the verses; "do not make too much of yourself."

I composed a stanza for him, which he committed to memory at the time, saying, when he had done so,—
"I have the greatest delight in the recollection of poetry."

"Oh," continued he, "what a mercy that I can glorify God by passive suffering!"

"I see," I remarked, "that you dwell upon the note '*for ever!*'"

"Is it not a grand note?"

"Yes, for one class it is the best note, for another the worst."

After the Sunday services, on my expressing my sorrow that he was entirely prevented from going to the house of God, he said with animation—"But I have read in the Bible, 'They that tarry at home shall divide the spoil.' O dear sir, pray for my entire acquiescence! What a noble-minded man was Paul, of whom you have just been reading. I love him. One cannot help it—his actions make you love him."

I then spoke of my departure, and the improbability of my return, adding, "Well, we shall meet hereafter."

"Oh, that will be joyful! joyful! joyful!" was his glad and final farewell.

I saw him no more; but I learnt afterwards that his death was "a gentle wafting to immortality," so tranquilly did he quit the world.

In the sister country, where evangelical instruction is not so common as in this land, I have met with several instances of young persons among the poor and illiterate who have been made the willing and happy recipients of Divine knowledge, when the means of imparting it to them were afforded. On all occasions, indeed, when I have visited

Ireland, I have been struck with the remarkable susceptibility of that people to good impressions in early life, and I have often commented on the incentive thus afforded to the promotion among them of universal education. Let knowledge in its elements, truth in its germs, be transfused into the youthful heart and intellect of the Irish population, and nowhere, I believe, should we find our labours more richly and rapidly rewarded. Their readiness to receive and convey impressions, and their felicitous mode of expressing their emotions, have always delighted me. They have a native genius for putting everything in a new light, often indeed fantastic and quaint, yet always displaying a smartness one cannot but relish. Once overcome their shyness and distrust, and their suspicion of your enmity and prejudice against them, arising from the difference of creeds, and you find their hearts opening to the influence of kindness, and their tongue abounding in hyperbolical expressions of gratitude for the slightest mark of your favour.

Out of numerous instances that have come under my own notice, the following may be fitly appended to the foregoing narrative as confirmatory of the previous observations.

On rising one morning during my first visit to the Irish metropolis, I saw in the highway before me a group of people gathered round some object that lay in their midst, but undiscernible by me owing to the dimness of the morning light, and the constantly changing movements of the crowd of curious spectators. On approaching the spot, I found a youth of about ten or eleven years of age lying on the ground pale and exhausted, leaning on his hand on one side, and casting a dejected and languishing look on his observers and questioners. He had been sent in the night in some rough vehicle from the town of Drogheda, for the purpose of being removed to the house of his mother, which the driver was unable to find, and had therefore turned him out in the road, and there left him. I gave him a little milk and nourishment, which I had procured from a kind-hearted neighbour, and then applied for his admission to an adjacent hospital for the reception of sufferers from accidents, where he was immediately received and attended to. The resident physician, in the most graceful manner, acknowledged my intervention, but for which, he said, the poor lad had certainly died in the street. His kinsman, it appeared, for some trifling misdemeanour had thrown him on a truckle-bed, and stamped upon him till he had broken nearly all his ribs, when fear led him to plan for his removal.

"I am taking down the boy's deposition," my informant added, "and will bring his master to justice. The lad will die; but he wishes to see *you*, sir, and to thank you for your humanity."

Day after day I visited him, and as he had no opposing prejudices in his mind to be overcome, but only a few loose notions and expressions caught up from those around him, I found him willing to receive my teaching of "the truth as in Jesus." Never shall I forget his expression of earnest intelligence with which he looked up to me from his pillow, and caught the idea suggested to him, and felt its relevance and its cheering efficacy. I could not be mistaken in believing that mind to be under a benign and gracious influence, for surely, "as a new-born babe did he desire the sincere milk of the word, and grow thereby" in knowledge, faith, and patience. When about to leave the country, I called to see him for the last time, and was informed by the physician that he had been expressing an earnest wish for my arrival, as he seemed to be breathing his last.

"Ah, your honour," he exclaimed as I approached him, I am dying; but I am happy, because I am going to Jesus the only Saviour. And if I had but two things, I would be very happy indeed."

"And what are they, my boy? They shall be accomplished if I have it in my power."

He shook his head, and replied, "Let not my kinsman be hurt. He did not mean it so; but if he had not used me as he did, I should never have met with you, nor have known the Lord."

"And what is the other?"

"Oh," said he with extreme emotion, "my mother! my mother!—could I but see her to tell her not to worship the Virgin, but to worship Jesus, I would then gladly close my eyes and die."

That day he breathed his last. A judicious friend whom I had taken with me the day before to visit him, was moved to tears of joy at the expression of the young sufferer's views and feelings.

Some years after the above incident, which to this day I remember with emotion, I again visited Ireland, and stayed for some time in one of its loveliest counties. On this occasion, I went one day with a friend to see a gentleman's mansion and grounds, which stood on the borders of a beautiful lake, embosomed in the surrounding mountains; and by the charms of the adjacent scenery, attracting visitors from all parts. As I, with my companion, approached the gate which led to a view of the lake and the exquisite scenes beyond, we saw a youth of about eleven or twelve years of age, stationed as porter at the entrance. Though but poorly and partially clad, there was about him an air of politeness and deference that at once engaged the attention, and won him favour. He was without shoes and stockings, and had no covering for his head; but his countenance was mild and cheerful, his bright blue eyes beaming with intelligence, and his flaxen hair streaming in the wind. During the intervals of his employment, he was reading a book which he held in his hand.

Knowing well the fluency of the Irish tongue, and the readiness of the peasantry to answer any questions put to them in a kind and courteous manner, I did not hesitate to put it to the proof on the present occasion. Having gained his attention, I inquired,—

"What book is that in your hand?"

"Sure," said he, making a bow, and pulling down a lock of hair on his forehead, "it is the New Testament of our Lord and Saviour Jesus Christ."

"How came you by it?"

"It was given me, your honour and your ladyship, by the gentleman of the mansion, who is a Protestant, and has caused us all to be taught the book, and has made a present of one to each of us."

"Can you read it?"

"To be sure I can."

"And do you understand what you read?"

"A little."

"Let us hear you;" and I turned his attention to the third chapter of the Gospel of John, which he seemed readily to find, and said, "Now read."

He did so, with a clear, distinct, and unembarrassed voice: "There was a man of the Pharisees, named Nicodemus, a ruler of the Jews; the same came to Jesus by night, and said unto him, Rabbi."

"What does that mean?"

"It means *Master*."—" We know that thou art a teacher come from God, for no man can do these miracles that thou doest, except God be with him."

"What is a *miracle*?"

"It is a *great wonder*."—"Jesus answered and said unto him, Verily, verily, I say unto thee."

"What does *verily* signify? ."

"It means, *indeed!*"—"Except a man be born again"—

"What is that?"

"It means," he promptly replied, "*a great change!*"—"Except a man be born again he cannot see the kingdom of God."

"And what is *that kingdom?*"

He paused, and with an expression of seriousness and devotion which I shall never forget, placing his hand on his bosom, he said,—

"*It is something here!*" and then raising his eyes, he added, "*and something up yonder!*"

He saw that we had sympathy with him, and a tear stood in his eye, which he brushed away, while he told us that the party who had preceded us, consisting of a Catholic priest and two ladies, had rudely interrogated him, and when they found what book he was reading, and who had given it to him, they scoffed, and said contemptuously, "He had better have given you a pair of shoes and stockings;" and, taking his book out of his hand, had thrown it down to the margin of the lake, "And they have soiled my beautiful book," said he, showing it to us with the most poignant regret.

My companion, to soothe him for the affront he had received, said kindly, "You shall not be reproached any more for the want of suitable clothing;" and immediately offered him money sufficient to purchase what he needed, bidding him to do so as speedily as posible. He, with an air of true, though untaught politeness, thankfully received the boon, but modestly observed, he could not appropriate it as desired, *unless* he had the consent of the *person who employed him.* Of course we commended his integrity, satisfied of its genuineness, and left him to continue the reading of *the Book* till the next party should arrive.

I cannot convey the impression made upon us by the whole demeanour of the boy. But his devout intelligence on the subjects of the discourse he had been reading from the New Testament, made us thankfully believe that in that secluded spot the great Teacher had met with this young disciple, and "revealed himself unto him as he does not unto the world."

ACTS.

Christian Boldness.

"Go, stand and speak unto the people all the words of this life."
ACTS v. 20.

MINISTERS are charged by the apostle to preach the word; to be instant in season, out of season, reproving, rebuking, exhorting with all long-suffering and doctrine; doing the work of an evangelist, making full proof of their ministry. Whenever an inviting opportunity occurs of addressing a multitude on the things belonging to their peace, they are joyfully to embrace it; not shrinking back from timidity, or refusing on the false plea of a so-called prudence; but, whether men will hear or whether they will forbear, opening their mouth boldly to make known the mystery of the gospel; "holding forth the word of life."

As good stewards of the manifold grace of God, they are to strive earnestly to be qualified for all the exigencies of their office, and to be prepared for extraordinary as well as ordinary services. To this end they must not only furnish their minds with all kinds of knowledge suitable to their calling, but must likewise *train* them to the prompt and ready use of the materials thus accumulated. They must habitually cultivate the art of speaking extemporaneously, and of abandoning themselves to the resources they are conscious of possessing. Without this, the richest stores of knowledge and experience may not be available on most important emergencies, and opportunities of usefulness may hence be lost that can never be recalled.

Wayside opportunities for scattering the seeds of truth, if wisely employed, are sometimes more productive of good results than are the more regular labours of stated times and places. The multitude, by whatever cause they may have been first attracted, are never displeased at having their attention adroitly turned to some fresh object of interest; and when once their curiosity is excited and their best feelings aroused, they are not slow to receive impressions of the most salutary nature, leading not unfrequently to permanent results. The faithful minister, therefore, will thankfully avail himself of any startling occurrence or sudden calamity, any solemn event or alarming providence, to subserve the great object for which he lives—the glory of Christ and the salvation of men. No false modesty nor fear of man will operate to deter him from the prompt discharge of this duty. In humble dependence on the Most High, he will go forward regardless of all earthly considerations. " Faith is proved to be very defective," says the late John Foster, "whenever creatures are more *dreaded* than the Sovereign Lord of all creatures is *trusted.*"

One of these extraordinary occasions for the exercise of my ministry occurred many years since when I was residing at Bristol, the record of which, as I now peruse it, reawakens in some measure within me the emotions it then inspired.

The late Reverend Robert Hall and myself were once staying together at the village of Clevedon, about ten miles from the above city, then first becoming a favourite resort for visitors from the adjacent parts. We had been associated in the service of dedicating to God a new place of worship, which had been erected chiefly by the contributions of the friends at Bristol, many of whom were present to witness the result of their efforts in a village which had been but a few years before entirely destitute of the means of religious instruction. The neighbourhood, however, for miles around was still in a state of the darkest ignorance, and as a consequence all manner of vice and impiety abounded. At the time of which I write, a gang of youths of desperate character, who by their daring crimes had become formidable in the locality, had been apprehended at a little distance from this place; and three of the ringleaders having been convicted, had been condemned to be hung on a spot as near as possible to the scene of their outrages, with the view of holding forth a salutary warning to their companions. The execution was to take place on the morrow, and an unusual excitement prevailed. It was naturally assumed that a vast concourse of people would be gathered on the occasion; and a Christian lady, full of zeal for the cause of truth, waited on Mr. Hall, with an earnest request that he would attend and address the assembled multitude. She was ignorant of his physical incapacity for such a service, but so far succeeded in impressing him with its importance that he sent for me, and entreated me to go in his stead. I felt at once that it was an opportunity not to be lost, and therefore consented without hesitation. Several friends meanwhile engaged to furnish religious tracts, to the number of several thousands, for distribution.

I started the following morning, which was Easter Monday, and reached the spot, a few miles from the village, at ten o'clock. It was a spacious common, with an area capable of containing ten or twelve thousand persons. I saw them, as I approached, crowding towards it in all directions. The rude apparatus for the execution, which had been hastily prepared during the night, rose conspicuously to view. A cross-beam had been erected, under which a temporary platform had been placed on the top of a wagon. On this stood the three youthful culprits, who, with ropes round their necks and with terror depicted on their countenances, were for a while exposed thus to the awe-struck multitude. Upon a given signal, the ropes having been properly adjusted and fastened to the beam, the wagon was drawn away, and the wretched youths remained suspended in the air amidst the groans of the vast motley throng and the tears and lamentations of mothers, many of whom were present with their own offspring as spectators of the scene.

I then requested permission of the sheriff to address the multitude, at the same time soliciting his aid to preserve order. He assented, and agreed to give me his presence after the dead bodies had remained suspended for an hour, as the law required. At the expiration of that interval, I was asked to occupy the very platform from which the criminals had been launched into eternity, and under the beam from which the ends of the fatal ropes were still vibrating in the air above me. For a moment I was appalled. The height to which I was elevated, the mass of human beings I saw thickening around me, waiting with upturned countenances and a painful curiosity to hear my words, all conspired to fill me with unwonted emotions. But no sooner did I open my lips than the liberty of my speech, the strength of my voice, and the ready occurrence to my mind of suitable thoughts and images, were such as assured me of the Divine presence and support to a degree I had never experienced before, and which to this day I devoutly acknowledge.

For one whole hour the attention of this rude and strange audience was enchained, their deep silence being interrupted only by audible sighs and exclamations of excited feeling. My spirit was stirred within me, and I was animated with new life. My voice rose to an unusual pitch, and was heard to the extremity of the crowd. After addressing them at first in the language of exhortation and warning, I was moved to that of invitation and entreaty. I spoke to them of the Crucified One, who had thus himself been made a spectacle to men and angels. I told them of the malefactor who hung by his side; and as I repeated the words of that malefactor's prayer—" Lord, remember me,"—I heard them reiterated with loud sobs by several in the crowd, while tears streamed down from eyes unused to weep. When I spoke of mercy for the guilty in the breast of Him who, for their sakes, was nailed to that cross, and when I pointed to the sky where He is now sitting in authority to show pity and pardon to the penitent, they looked up to the blue firmament as though they had seen the heavens opened, and expected his visible appearance among them.

At the close, after solemn prayer, in which all seemed to join, the sheriff publicly thanked me, and, commending my address to the consideration of the people, ordered them peaceably to disperse. They did so, but not before making a rush to the place where I stood distributing the tracts I had brought with me. " *Give I one,*" " *Give I one,*" was repeated by a thousand voices until all were supplied, and the place was again quiet.

On returning to Bristol that afternoon, with Mr. Hall, and recounting to him, as we drove along, the above particulars, we saw the villagers on every side repairing to their respective homes, reading or hearing read with evident seriousness the tracts which they had received. Mr. Hall was deeply affected. The tears stood in his eyes, as he said to me, with much emotion, "Sir, I envy you the honour God has put upon you this day. Sir, I would give all I possess to have had the privilege of delivering such an address."

Some months afterwards I had the satisfaction of knowing that two or three individuals, at least, had from that hour forsaken their evil courses and turned unto the Lord.

During my last visit to Bristol, in 1858, I went to Clevedon, and conversed with some of the old inhabitants who remembered these circumstances, and who reverted with thankfulness to the great moral change which had been wrought in the neighbouring villages since that period. I found, also, to my great joy, that in the immediate vicinity of the memorable spot where I stood on the occasion alluded to, a convenient place has been fitted up for the preaching of the gospel, where numbers regularly assemble on every Sabbath-day, and where a devoted band of Christians meet for weekly prayer and praise.

---o---

The Converted Persecutor.

"And he trembling and astonished said, Lord, what wilt thou have me to do?"—ACTS ix. 6.

THE conversion of the Apostle Paul was miraculous only in its suddenness which characterized it, and the circumstances by which it was attended. These were—the supernatural light in the heavens, the audible voice, and the glorious appearance of Christ in the air, the immediate blindness of the stricken persecutor, and his deliverance from that state by a commissioned servant of God. Divested of these extraordinary accompaniments, the conversion of Saul of Tarsus was substantially the same as that of every sinner in whom the gospel of Christ is made the

S

power of God unto salvation; and in every such instance similar effects follow to attest the Divine origin of this gracious change. In all, the scales of prejudice fall from the eyes of the understanding, which is spiritually enlightened; in all, the will is directed to objects far higher and nobler than those which had before engrossed it; in all, the tongue which had spoken contemptuously or profanely of the gospel is now employed in expressing submission to its Author, and uttering vows of grateful devotion to his cause. What though, in many instances, neither the time nor the place can be distinctly assigned when this mighty transformation was wrought, the evidences of it are as visible and indelible as those left by the lightning's burning track, and are as demonstrative, too, of its supernatural energy.

On the other hand, conversion sometimes takes place in a manner which can leave the subject of it in no doubt as to the precise point of time, and the peculiar train of circumstances with which it was intimately associated. Such a period is remembered by the individual as that momentous crisis at which the stream of his life was arrested in its course, and made to flow in an opposite direction with a force which no human power was able thenceforth to divert. This man, as Paley observes, can no more forget the moment of his conversion than another can his escape from shipwreck or his recovery from a malignant fever.

In connection with this subject I may mention an incident in my own experience, which, though not very extraordinary, is yet full of instruction.

It arose out of the holy enterprise of a pious lady, the wife of a highly respectable solicitor, in a straggling but populous village in Berkshire, where, alas! there existed at that time no faithful preaching of the gospel. This lady had long cherished a deep interest in the inhabitants, who had already manifested a willingness to avail themselves of the means of grace by attending Divine service in a building of a very humble order. This she encouraged by every means in her power, and at length, with the consent and generous sympathy of her husband, she resolved on soliciting contributions in addition to his liberal aid, for the erection of a suitable place of worship. By her address and perseverance, she not only overcame pardonable objections to this mode of obtaining funds, but she succeeded in accumulating a sufficient sum for her purpose. The chapel was forthwith commenced, but during its progress met with violent and continued opposition from the lowest and most ignorant portion of the community, countenanced, alas! by some who, though moving in a superior rank, were not superior to the unworthy expressions of bigotry and envy. The building was, nevertheless, completed in due time, and I was requested to officiate at its solemn dedication to the worship and service of the Almighty. On arriving at the residence of the zealous friends to whom I have referred, I found that the gentleman had been summoned to a distance on very important business, and could not return in time for the sacred service. This was the more to be regretted, as, apart from his deep personal interest in our public engagements, his presence and professional influence would have had considerable weight among the disorderly opponents of the undertaking. Uneasiness prevailed on the preceding evening, owing to rumours of intended opposition on the morrow. These apprehensions, however, were relieved by the orderly conduct of all present during the morning service. But towards evening, when the approaching darkness might promise impunity to evil-doers, a rabble assembled, and after parading the streets, proceeded towards the hospitable dwelling where I had taken up my abode. Before it they halted, and by their increasing clamours considerably affected my hostess, who was not without reason for fearing rude attacks upon the house and its outbuildings. As the noise and shouts of the disturbers continued and increased, she entreated me to endeavour to pacify them by a few words of reason. I knew too well from a former experience the uselessness of remonstrating with a mob to make any such attempt, but quieted my friend and her household by observing that if no resistance were offered, and no notice taken of the assailants, their excitement would probably subside.

As the time approached, however, for the evening service, we were placed in circumstances of some difficulty. I had no intention of relinquishing my post at the chapel, where I knew a congregation would be gathered, including several persons from the surrounding neighbourhood, and I therefore prepared to join them. On opening the door, and when about to step out, a fierce red glare dazzled my sight. It arose from a large haystack, the property of my host, which had been set on fire by the rabble, and was now blazing at its height. Strange to say, at the same time the bells of the village church were ringing out a triumphant peal, as if in sympathy with the proceedings. The fire, however, had one advantage for us; it attracted around it the riotous mob, and kept them from the chapel, to which we speedily repaired, without sustaining further annoyance. When we arrived at the place, we found it filled with a somewhat motley assembly, a portion of which only appeared respectable and devout. I commenced the service by reading the Scriptures slowly and solemnly, with a view of enforcing order and stillness. I then offered a prayer suitable to the occasion, and to the miscellaneous character of the ostensible worshippers. While thus engaged, I felt that I had the sympathy of many in the congregation as I entreated mercy for those who opposed the truth, and supplicated the grace of the Lord Jesus Christ to rest upon us who were thus gathered together in his name. I then proceeded to read a hymn, pausing upon those lines which seemed best calculated to win attention and to affect the heart. I commenced with the verse,—

> "How condescending and how kind
> Was God's eternal Son;
> Our misery reached his heavenly mind,
> And pity brought him down."

As I was reading the following verse towards the close,—

> "Here we receive repeated seals
> Of Jesus' dying love.
> *Hard* is the heart that never feels
> *One* soft affection move,"

I emphasized the two words in italics. At that moment a noise was heard as from the fall of some heavy weight in a pew near the door. It was not repeated, however, and perfect order now prevailed, which, as the service proceeded, deepened into the unbroken stillness of devout attention.

Upon inquiring at the close, concerning the noise which had for the moment disturbed us, an individual was pointed out to me, who came forward and confessed that it was occasioned by the sudden fall of a large stone which he had brought with him to the chapel for the express purpose of hurling it at the preacher as soon as he had taken his text. "But," said the man, "the prayer of the minister, and particularly the hymn that was read, touched my heart, and no sooner, sir, had you uttered the words—

> '*Hard* is the heart that never feels
> *One* soft affection move,'

than *down dropped the stone*." Tears then came to eyes

long unused to weep. He, the intending disturber of others, was brought to be an attentive hearer of the Word; he who had plotted mischief against the preacher became his debtor to all eternity, and stood as a penitent on the spot where he had placed himself as a persecutor.

This man was afterwards visited and conversed with, and became a regular worshipper at the village sanctuary. I believe that he not only joined the fellowship of believers there, but was occasionally engaged as a humble teacher of scriptural truth in the village and its neighbourhood.

The excellent Christian lady who had chiefly contributed to erect the chapel in which this event took place, died in peace and confidence in her Saviour, amidst the lamentations of all who knew her. But the Christian sanctuary remains, and the cause for which she laboured now flourishes. We may die, but our works will live, and appear as evidences of our character, and perhaps as adjusting at last the measure of our gracious reward : " I heard a voice from heaven, saying unto me, Write, Blessed are the dead which die in the Lord from henceforth : yea, saith the Spirit, that they may rest from their labours, and their works do follow them."

Those who have lived and laboured through more than the preceding half century can, in proportion to their age and opportunities for observation, call to mind the great and formidable hindrances to evangelical effort at those times. They were often such as those I have alluded to in the above narrative, and far worse. In most places it was extremely difficult to procure suitable sites for the erection of places of worship. The "worshippers of God in spirit and in truth" were at that time compelled to meet in to employ a familiar phrase—holes and corners; nor were they even there safe from fierce attacks and rude interruptions.

Too generally those who had it in their power to quell such a spirit either passively acquiesced or openly fostered it. Dread of religious innovation was the prevailing feeling amongst the more respectable parties, and the fear of being characterized by some vulgar nickname operated more extensively than would have been acknowledged.

Time, and the extension of a better feeling towards piety, in whatever order it may be found, have shown the folly of that course, and materially abated prejudice and bigotry;— while the largely increased education of the lower classes has made them ashamed of attempting to oppose by brute force or to drown by riot and clamour the voices of good men who approve themselves not only to their own consciences, but also to the judgment of all who are candid and enlightened. The way is thus opened, and increased facilities are thus afforded, for enlarged Christian exertion and multiplied labours to cover the land with the means and ordinances of gospel truth. Let us go forth with redoubled zeal and liberality, saying, " The Lord of hosts is with us : the God of Jacob is our refuge."

II. CORINTHIANS.

A Word in Season.

"By manifestation of the truth commending ourselves to every man's conscience in the sight of God."—2 COR. iv. 2.

IN endeavouring to enforce the sentiments of Scripture, it is of much advantage to speak from a settled confidence of their certainty. Recollecting the power of revealed truth over the consciences of men through the gracious influence of the Holy Spirit, we should be free from hesitation in asserting it. To admit, though tacitly, by our timid air, that it is capable of disproof and open to argumentative attack, is to make way for cavils and objections a thousand times vanquished, yet never slain; a thousand times silenced, as it might be hoped for ever, yet again unaccountably recovering voice, and urging their claims with undiminished assumption.

In the hearts of the apostles we see that the great truths of religion were so profoundly settled, that they inculcated them without the least show of doubt or question, and without any uncertainty of announcement even in the midst of menacing persecutors. They knew that they had truth to declare, and they felt themselves to be its witnesses, commissioned by its Divine Author to bear testimony to it according to their own knowledge and in obedience to his command. Their whole manner of utterance was assured and decisive; and their bearing was that of men who evidently felt refutation to be impossible. We frequently observe that confidence imparts weight even to plausible error; how much more important, therefore, is it that, with Divine truth as our weapon, we should not fear the strongholds of opposition! Such confidence gains for truth a hearing, and ultimately an assenting testimony in the breasts of our auditors.

I have often experienced the importance of firmness and decision of manner in asserting the truth in opposition to false sentiments or erroneous opinions. Among numerous instances that I have recorded confirmatory of this, I select one that occurred many years ago during my residence in Bristol.

The Durdham Downs at Clifton, near Bristol, are bounded at one extremity by what is called the Sea Wall, which is a low stone fence running along the summit of the rocks overhanging the river Avon. Immediately beneath these rocks the river pursues its devious course, and tarries not until it mingles its lesser volume with the broad Severn, whose bright, beaming waters are visible on sunny days from the Sea Wall, and form no unimportant element in the beauty of the distant scenery. Some lofty mountains in South Wales may often be discerned from this spot, looming like clouds in the background, and sometimes standing out in more distinct shape in the clear blue sky. Stepping over the Sea Wall, the visitor commands a nearer view before and below him. A vast chasm or rent has been produced by some convulsion of nature, between the rocky walls of which the river rolls beneath at a depth of about three hundred feet. On both sides abundant foliage clothes the once bare rocks, and several trees stand on stony prominences, as if they were sentinels in advance of their less adventurous brethren. No sound breaks the silence, except what may arise from large steam-vessels navigating the Avon, and an occasional blast in some of the large stone quarries below, causing the rocks to echo and re-echo its thunder, and to roll it from recess to recess in reverberating peals.

Near a particular breach in the wall, there was at that time a little nook with a rustic seat under the bushes, where the visitor, if he were so minded, might sit secluded from all observation, and indulge in appropriate meditation as he caught glimpses of the river and the distant scenery through openings of the foliage. This was a spot I often resorted to while I resided at Bristol, and where I often mused upon subjects connected with my pulpit ministrations. One morning when I was there and thus occupied, I heard voices in the copse below, and I knew that they must issue from some persons who were making their way up a devious pathway that ascended from the shore beneath, and by a circuitous course led up the rocks to the summit

It was by no means a facile ascent; and I was therefore a little surprised to see two travellers emerging from the thick brushwood that concealed me from their view. The younger of the two was in advance of his companion, whom he was rallying aloud for his want of agility in climbing the steep and entangled path. In a moment there stood before me a gentleman of youthful appearance, who was startled at the unexpected *rencontre*, and apologised for his unintentional intrusion on my solitude. He was now overtaken by his graver companion, who addressed him as "Captain," and joined him in extolling the beautiful scenery that here met their gaze. "Lovely spot, sir," said the captain, addressing himself to me; "I am surprised at never having heard of this view before. You must surely admire it!" I replied that, as a proof I did so, I paid a visit to it by a walk of two or three miles nearly every day; and then pointing out to him several objects which he had not noticed, I bade him observe how a sheet of thin vapour spreading itself lightly over the opposite landscape had softened its irregularities, and given to it an apparent continuity which greatly heightened its charms. He assented, and said with enthusiasm, but *with an oath,* "that it almost rivalled ·Switzerland." He inquired if I had ever seen Mont Blanc. I replied that I had not, but had just perused the surprising account of its ascent by a lady. "That," said he, "must be a mistake. It is impossible!" I referred him to my authority, in the narrative of Dr. Clarke, the popular traveller. He could then no longer deny it, but continued describing the beauties of Switzerland, interlarding his description with frequent oaths and profane exclamations to intensify his expressions of admiration; and ended by saying, "That is the place to make a man happy! It would make you, sir, happy indeed to be there!" I replied very seriously, "I perceive, sir, it has *not* made *you* happy." Though observing him to change colour at so apparently rude an assertion, I nevertheless added, "*Nothing,* sir, has ever made *you* happy!" "Do you know me?" he asked, somewhat haughtily. "I know the truth of what I have said," I rejoined. His companion looked on with amazement, while the other, with a somewhat military air, exclaimed rather indignantly, "I must know the reason, sir, of your remark." "You shall have it willingly," said I. "It is evident, sir, from the manner in which you have alluded to that Great Being, 'in whose hands our breath is, and whose are all our ways,' that you and he are not in amity. You have spoken *of* him and *to* him in a manner which proves that you have no acquaintance with him; and," added I, looking him steadfastly in the face, "how a human being, estranged from the God of the universe, the only Spring and Fountain of real bliss, *can* be happy, is a problem yet to be solved; solve it if you can!" He turned pale and seemed at a loss for a reply, when his companion stepped forward, and addressing me eagerly, asked if my name was not the one he then mentioned. I assented. "Then," said he, "this is surprising! That gentleman is Captain E——. I am the widowed husband of his sister, and came over from America to join him and his relations who reside in the adjoining city. My wife was known to you, sir, when you resided at Kensington, near the metropolis, and was brought by your instructions to a happy state of mind. She had imbibed the sentiments of Unitarians, but had never been convinced of the truth of Evangelical religion until she attended your ministry. She died in my arms, pronouncing and blessing your name! And one of the purposes which brought me to this neighbourhood, where I learnt you resided, was to see you and hear you preach."

This I believe they both did; and though I never afterwards heard of them, I could not doubt but that they left the spot, where we had so unexpectedly met, in a better state of mind than that with which they came.

On resuming my meditations, I could not but reflect on the singular coincidences by which people are brought together, and the subtle links of connection sometimes revealed, that till then were entirely unsuspected. Nor did I fail to thank God for having been prompted to discharge a duty which at the moment I felt to be imperative, and to discharge it in a manner which my conscience approved.

Let the careless tourist learn from this little incident, that a word in season, a pointed inquiry or assertion, may help to dispel the delusion that real happiness can be derived from viewing Nature in her loveliness and grandeur apart from a knowledge of the God of Nature and the excellence of his gospel; and let every Christian remember that a bold announcement of the truth, even to a stranger, may lead to untold benefits, that can never be offensive if accompanied by earnestness of manner, and a solemn sense of responsibility to the Most High.

Life in Death.

"Though our outward man perish, yet the inward man is renewed day by day."—2 COR. iv. 16.

"As dying, and, behold, we live."—2 COR. vi. 9.

THIS was literally verified in the apostles, who, by their supernatural endurance of extraordinary sufferings, were "set forth as a spectacle to angels and to men;" and in Christian martyrs in their loathsome cells, who, though doomed to inconceivable privations, were yet buoyant in spirit and rejoicing in hope. We may also witness instances of the same kind in Christians of our own day, in whose experience the increase of spiritual truth is proved to be in inverse proportion to the decay of natural vigour. They may be placed in circumstances the most unfavourable to exhilaration of soul and eagerness of expectation. The flesh may be wasted by disease, the animal spirits may sink under the pressure of grief and privation, and both the outward and inward man may seem to fail. But at this critical juncture God is often pleased to give them such a sense of his presence and favour, such an actual foretaste of future glory, as at once, like a reviving cordial, re-animates the whole being. Hope springs up afresh in their bosom, kindling a joy that is unspeakable and full of glory; and they exhibit to those around them the singular spectacle of a rejoicing spirit in a decaying body; and strength of soul to mount and soar, while the limbs cease to perform their proper office, the tongue fails to articulate words, and desire, as to this world, is no more. The ravages of disease and infirmity are surmounted, and in the last dread conflict they grasp with the hand of faith and hope the palm-branch of victory and triumph. "As dying, and, behold, we live."

And since no man can foresee the manner in which he shall quit this world—at which of the thousand doors of death he shall go out of life, or through what darksome scenes he may have to pass to the regions of pure light, it will be well for him frequently to contemplate such instances. By so doing he would gain the comfortable assurance that in the worst that can befall him, he may look for a support and consolation now hardly to be conceived of, which shall gild the dark hours with heavenly radiance, and give new pinions to the soul to wing its upward flight.

One such instance I would now record for the comfort and encouragement of Christians troubled with present pains, or with fears of future and distressing conflicts :—

Mrs. R—— was for many years a member of the Christian community over which I presided. She belonged to the respectable middle-class of society, and resided in a somewhat obscure part of London with her two daughters and a number of young women whom she employed in her own business, and had taken to reside with her, that she might watch over their morals and train them up in the nurture and admonition of the Lord. By all of these she was looked up to as a mother, and by some revered as the instrument of introducing them to a better life. She had known God from her early years, and had also been familiar with sorrow and trial. Her married life, indeed, seems to have been marked with grief, arising from the bitter pangs of bereavement. Nine beloved children had she followed in succession to the grave; the last a. promising youth of fifteen years, who had given proof of his conversion to God. At length, after years of suffering, her husband died also, and she was left, like another Naomi, with but two to call her mother.

I had early noticed her punctuality in attending on all the services of religion, her sedateness of deportment, and her reserved but resolved demeanour; and having once had occasion to consult her on some matters of importance, I was struck with the sagacity of her remarks, and her evident insight into the characters of those with whom she came in contact. From that time I observed more attentively her manner of life and mode of ordering her household, which I found to be that of one whose course having been deliberately resolved upon, was pursued with dignified consistency. Her intellect was of a superior order, and she was endowed with a quickness of apprehension and an intuitive perception of truth that often surprised me. But what I chiefly valued in her was her remarkable acquaintance with the Scriptures, the depth and yet clearness of her religious experience, and her yearning solicitude for the salvation of the souls of others. I knew not till afterwards that she was in the habit of entering in a book she kept for that purpose, the name and circumstances of every fresh member added to the church, that they might be remembered by her in prayer. I prevailed upon her, in conjunction with another of like spirit, to preside over a class of young women disposed to meet together for prayer and praise; and in this sacred duty I believe she was greatly blessed. One poor young creature, so distressed in spirit from the hard usage of the world as to be in danger of mental derangement, I placed under her wise and affectionate control, and had the satisfaction of seeing her completely restored.

Thus passed the even tenor of her life for many years. After her decease, my admiration of her character was strengthened by the perusal of a diary amounting to four quarto volumes, in which she had recorded whatever had contributed to the formation of her character and her growth in Divine knowledge and spiritual attainments. Here I found most pertinent observations on the sermons I had preached, and striking proofs of her self-application of the truths uttered, whatever might be the subject of discourse.

That her diary might not be neglected, she accustomed herself to rise every morning soon after six o'clock, for the purpose of recording in it her thoughts and feelings in connection with passing events; nor would she break through this custom even when the night had afforded her but little refreshment from sleep, and little renewed vigour for the discharge of the ordinary duties of the day. Would that other Christians whose demands upon their time and solicitude are less, or at most not more imperative than were hers, and who can scarcely surpass her in the diligence with which she attended to them, were found to imitate her in this practice. It would be directly conducive to their own benefit, and to the instruction of those who might survive them, to preserve a faithful delineation of the beginning and progress of Divine grace in their souls, under the influence and modifications of the ever-changing circumstances and appearances of the present life.

In the autumn of the year 1843, Mrs. R—— was partaking of a hasty meal, when something became fixed in the passage of the throat, which after occasioning considerable suffering, was removed by surgical aid, and no further danger was anticipated. But after the lapse of a few weeks, she experienced a difficulty in swallowing food, which alarmingly increased, and at last it became evident that a fatal stricture of the œsophagus had taken place, and that a gradual death of starvation was inevitable.

One Sunday morning I received from her the following note :—

"DEAR PASTOR,

"Mr. H—— will tell you my circumstances, for I cannot write much; but pray for me that I may have Divine consolation, and receive this cup from my heavenly Father's hand with meekness and patience, and that strength and fortitude may be given to my dear children.

"Yours in the Lord,
"E. R.

"*Sabbath, Oct.* 15*th*, 1843."

I went immediately after morning service to visit her, and found her sitting in an upper chamber, composed and even cheerful, with her Bible before her. She detailed to me the nature of her complaint, and seemed fully aware of its too probable result. After expressing her thankfulness that she could yet speak, she told me that when her illness first assumed a threatening aspect, she had closely interrogated herself thus :—" I shall soon, I am told, be unable to take food; have I, then, withheld food from the hungry? No; God is my witness, I have fed them to the extent of my ability. I shall soon lose my voice; have I then refrained from using it to make known his truth to the ignorant, and to call sinners to repentance? I have not. Then this is not a judgment, it is a wise and sovereign dispensation for good and gracious purposes, and as such I receive it from my heavenly Father." Then looking at me with great seriousness and composure, she added, "*I have no fear*, the

Lord is *good*; he is a stronghold in the day of trouble, and he knoweth them that trust in him."

I had seen death in a variety of forms, but of all his approaches, this, though free from external signs of agony, seemed to me the most terrible from its slow but irresistible advances, and the absence of ordinary alleviations, without even the temporary respites of hope! Yet, with the pro spect of so dreadful a termination of life; with the conviction that although the powers of her body and mind were in comparative vigour, the means of sustaining them would soon be cut off; with the terrors before her of a sentence so appalling to nature,—she maintained a calmness of demeanour that appeared almost superhuman, and a confidence in the promises of her God that was truly sublime. "I am to pine away," she said, "in the midst of sufficiency; yet hath he not said, 'I will preserve thee alive in famine'? Mine, indeed, is an artificial famine. I have bread enough and to spare, and yet am likely to perish with hunger. But what! Did he say this to tantalize me? Ah, no! He will preserve my *soul* alive, while my body dies of starvation. *I have no fear.*"

Meanwhile, as she became more attenuated, her patience and resignation were the more conspicuous. Her conversation with her friends was most edifying, and she delighted herself with recounting instances of the Divine goodness and faithfulness towards her, as preserved in her diary and inscribed on the tablet of memory. On my return to her, after unavoidable absence, I found her confined to her bed; weaker, of course, in her bodily frame, but as vigorous and composed in mind as when I left her. "You see, my dear pastor, how my countenance is becoming fit for the grave—do you not?" Upon observing that the alteration was not so great as I had anticipated, she rejoined—"Oh, yes it is;

and if you were to see me in the morning you would say so. It is now fit for nothing else than the grave." Then, with a smile, she looked at me significantly, and repeated these lines :—

> " Princes, this clay must be your bed,
> In spite of all your towers.
> The tall, the wise, the *reverend* head,
> Must lie as low as ours!"

"But," added she with much emphasis, "I wish, while I can speak, to bear testimony to the goodness and faithfulness of my God in sustaining me. My heart and my flesh faileth, but God is the strength of my heart and my portion for ever." She then joined with me most fervently in prayer, and remarked as I left her, "Good Mr. H—— locked me up last night with God." She alluded to one of the deacons, who sent me the following account of his interviews with Mrs. R—— at this period :—

"When I entered her chamber, I found her reclining on the bed with her Bible and another book by her side, and after some general inquiries respecting her health, I learned from her that her malady was such as precluded any hope of recovery. She expressed her surprise that, being unable to take any nourishment, she should have lasted so long.

"I then asked her how she felt in the prospect of the scene which awaited her? She told me she was ready to depart and be with Christ, adding that her only fear was that she was too impatient for the arrival of the hour, exclaiming, 'I wish to say with another of the Lord's people, *When* thou wilt, as well as *what* thou wilt, and *how* thou wilt.' I observed to her that to be entirely resigned to the will of our heavenly Father is the happiest state of mind we can be in; upon which she adverted to the faithfulness of God to his promises, as the ground of entire confidence in Him under the most trying circumstances, quoting, 'The strength of Israel will not lie,' and other similar passages of Scripture. This led me to remark to her that I was not surprised to find that the word of God was her companion in her affliction, and that its promises were suited to every condition of life. 'Yes,' she replied; 'a friend has lent me the book you see there, and I thought it might seem unkind if I did not look at it. Indeed, it was written by a favourite author of mine; but in my present situation I feel that I must go to the fountain-head itself. Nothing else will do for me now.' I observed to her, 'You remember what Dr. Leifchild said about Sir Walter Scott on his deathbed;' but as she had not heard the anecdote, I repeated it to her, upon which she exclaimed, with considerable energy, 'No; there is but one book for a dying hour.'

"In the course of conversation, I mentioned to her that I had been to see Mr. Head, and was glad to find that his experience afforded another proof of the power of the gospel to support the mind in view of death and eternity; when she remarked that it was encouraging to survivors to hear of such instances, and that she had been greatly interested in what she had heard respecting the last days of Mr. Kelly, whose funeral sermon was the last she attended, not having been to the house of God since the evening on which it was preached.

"We had some further edifying conversation, which was engaged in, on her part, with dignified composure, and after commending her to God in prayer, joined by one of her daughters, who had entered the room, I left her, thankful for this instance, in addition to many such that I have been privileged to witness, of real religion bringing true peace at the last.

"Had Mrs. R—— been a woman of excitable feelings,

she might have expressed herself in more striking language and with greater emotion; but knowing her natural good sense and cool judgment, I was gratified at the calm testimony she bore to the value of the Christian's hope.

"At a subsequent visit, a few days afterwards, I found her still in the same serene state of mind, with a smile on her countenance. I inquired how she was, and she told me that she found herself getting gradually weaker, which did not occasion regret, as it brought her nearer home. She spoke much of her enjoyments at the present time, and said she had been a happy Christian for many years. She informed me that she had been converted at the age of sixteen, and she observed, if some who were converted late in life could die rejoicing in the Lord, why should not one who had known him so long rejoice in him? She said she had experienced much of the pleasure of religion, at the same time disclaiming with great earnestness any personal merit in all this, and ascribing every good to Divine grace. 'But ought I not,' she said, 'to state the fact?' Does not David say, 'My soul shall make her boast in the Lord. The humble shall hear thereof and be glad'? and soon added, 'I am so happy, that I would not exchange situations with any one on earth.' She said the only suffering she endured arose from extreme thirst. I quoted a passage from the Apocalypse—'They shall hunger no more, neither thirst any more.' She replied, 'I shall soon drink of the pure river of the water of life.' I continued the quotation, and when I had repeated 'God shall wipe away all tears from their eyes,' she said, 'He does that for me, even *now*,' thus showing that in her experience there was 'heaven begun below.'"

And now day after day she continued to waste slowly away, gradually yielding to the hand of the spoiler that body which, as she expressed it, had been for many years the pleasant companion of her soul. The strong tormenting sense of inanition and want that had so long afflicted her now ceased, and she gratefully acknowledged the singular relief thus afforded. This circumstance is alluded to by another valued member of the Church, a woman of strong sense and ardent piety, whose letter is now before me, though she herself has long since joined the spirit of her friend in the blessed world. I subjoin her touching account of their last earthly interview :—

"When she sent to say she would be glad to see me, although I much wished to see her, I felt a timidity from the nature of her disease—fearing that I could not bear to witness her sufferings in dying literally, as it were, from starvation. But I went, and the moment I saw the sweet and holy composure of her countenance, and the serene smile of delight on seeing me, all my fears vanished, and the hours I then spent with her can never be forgotten. While in sweet converse with her, I mentioned a circumstance that had harassed me for many years. She willingly and sweetly entered into the subject, and told me how much she herself had suffered on that point. Her views altogether set my mind fully at rest. Thus in her dying moments she refreshed others, and encouraged those who had to wait patiently a little longer before they could expect such a view as she was favoured with of the haven of rest. I said on leaving her, 'I fear you have excited yourself too much.' 'No,' she replied, 'it has been an excitement of delight, and I feel I shall gain some little repose after it.'

"What an unspeakable mercy that all desire of food was removed!—In relation to her resignation and faith, who would not say, 'Oh, that my last end may be like hers!'"

Another female friend whom I had requested to furnish

me with notes of her visits to the dying chamber, writes thus :—

"About six weeks before Mrs. R.'s death, I went to see her, and was surprised and grieved to find her so much altered. She very soon gave me to understand that she did not expect to recover; but was afraid she might last a long time. The thought of dying from the want of food seemed for a few moments to distress her mind. But upon my reminding her of the support and deliverance she had often experienced in former trials, I shall never forget the alteration in her countenance as she replied, 'Oh yes, you have found it to be so as well as I;

"His love in times past forbids me to think
He'll leave me at last in trouble to sink."

But you know the body shrinks from suffering, though I bless the Lord I can say, "Let all thy will be done in me and by me." "As my afflictions abound, my consolations abound also."' She then told me with as much composure as possible, the plans she wished to be adopted with reference to her business. In fact, it appeared more as if she were going into the country, and giving directions what was to be done while she was away, than that she was to die and return no more. At another time, I read at her request the first chapter of the First Epistle of Peter, and after making some remarks, she said, 'How often has my spirit refreshed itself by reading his own precious word! Frequently when I have been cast down by the trials and vexations of life, I have read a portion of Scripture, and sought him whom my soul loved, and then I felt like a giant refreshed with new wine, or like a strong man to run a race.' At another time she said, 'I am going to my heavenly inheritance. I bless the Lord! I have known him, loved him, and served him for many years.' . . .

"'I have nearly finished my course, and I trust to do so with joy. You are comparatively only just beginning. May you be kept faithful unto the end!' Again, when speaking to her about a book which had been lent to her, she remarked, 'I recollect reading it some years ago, and I found much pleasure in it, but I want something more *now*; that was a stream, but I must go to the fountain. I feel that I am in solemn circumstances, and it becomes me to look within. I believe the truths of the Bible are able to cheer and comfort the mind under every trial, and even in death itself. I have not "followed cunningly devised fables."'"

I again visited her as her pastor on the Sunday before her death, and upon my inquiring how she felt, she faintly smiled and answered, "Sinking in body, but rising in spirit—clinging to the promises—longing to be gone.

> 'Oh! if my Lord would come and meet,
> My soul would stretch her wings in haste.'

Do you think I do wrong in wishing to leave this world? Pray for me that I may have patience to 'wait all the days of my appointed time till my change come.'"

On the morning of the day on which she died, she inquired of each person in the room if it was thought she was dying. The bystanders replied they thought she was. On seeing them weep, she clasped her hands and said, "Weep not for me. Blessed be God!" and looking at her eldest daughter, added, "Bear up; faith and patience." She told them we could have no idea of what she was suffering. "But," added she, "I have One who sympathises with me—Jesus died. He knows the pains of dying. He conquered though he fell, and so shall I." . . .

From the daughter who attended her throughout the affliction with unwearied tenderness and devotion, I received the following particulars :—

"My beloved mother, when first made aware of the nature of her complaint, said, 'What a mercy it is to feel assured that this affliction is not sent upon me as a judgment. Mine has not been a false tongue, a slanderous tongue, a mischief-making tongue; no. The Lord *knows* my tongue has been employed in instructing the ignorant, counselling the young, and in endeavouring to promote peace among brethren. It is my "glory," and I have delighted to use it to my Lord's honour. This is not boasting; oh, no! I have nothing to boast of; 'tis only by the grace of God I am what I am.' She often said with emphasis,— '*Jesus, my Lord, I know his name, and he knows me; we have been on terms of intimacy for many years; there is an understanding kept up between us, and he will not now forsake me. Oh, no; I am on the Rock! I am on the Rock!*'

"When I had finished washing and dressing her one morning, about eight days before her death, feeling herself much exhausted, she said, 'Give me the looking-glass,' and perceiving that her appearance was much altered since she had last observed herself, she fell back on the bed, and raising her hands and eyes, exclaimed, ' Blessed Jesus!—

> "I'll praise my Saviour while I've breath,
> And when my voice is lost in death,
> Praise shall employ my nobler powers."

'I'm going home, my beloved girl, don't you think I am? Oh, that this might be my last Saturday with you! I die; but the Lord will be with you, for "he knoweth them that trust in him."'

"To a friend who saw her in the afternoon, she said: 'Ah, my dear friend, I am almost at home! *I am going to my purchased inheritance. Here is his note-of-hand for it,*' laying her hand on the Bible, 'and my Lord will soon fetch me to possess it.'

"She frequently said, 'Who is there that I would exchange situations with? I know not any person. Mine is not a trembling hope. No; it is the confidence of hope.'

"The following day, Sunday, two friends came to see her, and brought their little boy, a child of four years of age, who had a great desire to see our dear parent all through her illness, but had not been permitted. She looked at him with some emotion, and said, 'Christ bless you, my dear child; I am going to Jesus. Do you know me, Willy? I am going to heaven to Jesus Christ; I have known him for many years, my dear, and I am now going to be with him! May you early learn to know and love him too.' She then turned to his parents, and exhorted them to take encouragement from her experience, saying, 'I have passed through the deep waters of affliction. Nine of my dear children and a beloved partner are in heaven, and I am soon going to join them; and that gracious Lord who has sustained me will also be your strength.'

"On the Wednesday previous to her removal from earth, a friend remarked to me that my dear mother looked worse than she had done on Monday.

"I said, 'Tell her so; she will be delighted to hear it.' Our friend did so, when she said, 'That is good news!— Blessed be God.'

"In the evening she said to the Rev. Mr. Mather, 'Mine is not the hope of the hypocrite, which shall perish. No! the Almighty *knows* I am not a hypocrite, and Satan *dares* not charge me with hypocrisy.'

"On Saturday, the 11th, her surgeon came to see her; she said to him—

"'Don't you think I'm going *now*, dear sir?'

"He answered, 'Well, you are certainly very low.'

"She immediately rejoined, 'Oh you will not give me any comfort. I thought I was near death.'

"He then beckoned me out of the room, and told me he should not be surprised if she did not survive the night. When I returned to the room, my dear mother said—

"'What did he say?'

"I replied, 'That you are not far from your journey's end.'

"'Does he say so? Oh how I long to be there!'

"In the afternoon, she said, 'I am sorry to give you so much trouble, my beloved; but I think you must move the pillows, as I want to turn again. I suppose it is the restlessness of death I feel. Oh that this night might end the strife!' She frequently said, '*Oh these poor wasting limbs;—these sunken eyes! But, by-and-by; what a glorious body!*'

'Arrayed in glorious grace
Shall this vile body shine
Sweet truth to me!
I shall arise,
And with these eyes
My Saviour see!'

"Many times during the last night and day she passed her hand over her brows, in order to discover if the cold dews of death were perceptible on them, and seemed much disappointed that such was not the case, saying, 'How long, Lord?—Come, come; do come, Lord Jesus!'

"She would put out her hand for us to tell her if her pulse was lower. About the middle of the day, on my remarking, 'Pulsation has ceased in the arm for many hours,' she said with great earnestness—

"'You will not deceive me; bring me the glass.'

"On our doing so, she expressed herself dissatisfied with her looks, saying, 'How little difference!'

"I said to her, 'Are you able to think of Jesus Christ now, my beloved?'

"She answered with intense earnestness, 'Yes!'

"I said, 'Then he is very precious to you now?'

"'Oh, yes,' was her feeble answer.

"About two o'clock she again asked for the glass, and on observing the change which had taken place in her appearance during the previous hour, she clasped her hands, and raising her eyes, said, as well as her poor stiffened tongue would allow, 'Blessed Jesus, it is almost over now.' And turning to us said, 'Weep not for me.'

"Soon after, I said, 'You will soon behold the pearly gates.'

"After a few minutes she replied, 'He is coming! He is coming!'

"She lay in an unconscious state apparently, for a few minutes, but on my whispering to a friend who stood by, she opened her eyes and looked round sweetly upon us all. That look will never be forgotten by any of us; the brightness of her eyes was superhuman; then throwing her left arm as high as she could extend it, she smiled sweetly.

"I exclaimed aloud, 'Christ Jesus, my beloved?'

"She motioned with her head to show that she heard and understood me, and immediately her happy spirit took its flight to the presence of that Saviour whom unseen she had so long loved and adored. Those who were present imagined themselves surrounded with a multitude of angels, who received with joy the departing spirit, and triumphantly conducted it into the eternal kingdom of rapture and delight, where she now, with all the holy angels and ransomed hosts, ascribes an eternal hallelujah to God and the Lamb, and in the fulness of heavenly bliss, joins in their more exalted song."

Providence and Grace conjoined.

"A night and a day I have been in the deep."—2 COR. xi. 25.

THE apostle alludes in these words to some peril by sea, the particulars of which are unknown to us; but the style of this expression seems to warrant the supposition that on one of the three occasions on which he suffered shipwreck, he spent a night and a day, or the entire twenty-four hours, in a small open boat which had escaped from the wrecked vessel, or possibly on a plank or part of a shattered ship which floated with him to the shore. It may be that the reference is to some such shipwreck as that endured by him, and described in Acts xxvii., which terminates with the illustrative words, "And the rest, some on boards, and some on broken pieces of the ship; and so it came to pass that they escaped all safe to land."

Whatever may have been the especial circumstance, we know that Paul was preserved by an overruling Providence; and we may fairly conclude that wherever he landed on that occasion, he preached the gospel of Jesus Christ to the people, who doubtless received him as one wonderfully spared by that capricious ocean on whose agitated bosom he had spent twenty-four long and anxious hours.

I had these very words in my mind when an incident of a similar character occurred in my own history. Having fulfilled and terminated an engagement to preach for several successive Sabbaths at York Street Chapel, Dublin, I prepared for my return to Kensington, near London, by a route different from that which I had taken in going to the Irish capital. To vary my course, I traversed the country, and embarked at Waterford in a packet-ship which sailed from that port to Milford Haven, and thus avoided my previous route by Holyhead. I little anticipated to what this preference would expose me.

When I arrived at Waterford, the sea was gathering itself as if in prophetic anger, and the thick black clouds were rolling overhead before a driving blast, which was evidently not then at its height, and only moaned and wailed with menacing sounds, as if to forewarn all whose business was in great waters, not to trust themselves thereupon for some hours yet to pass away. In anticipation of very foul weather, the captain of the vessel which had been announced to sail that evening, refused to put out to sea, although the cargo and some of the passengers were already aboard. I thought it better to sleep on shore, as I intended to arise betimes and be ready for the vessel, which might stand out to sea in the early morning. Only a large dilapidated and gloomy-looking hotel was at hand, and there I took up my abode and endeavoured to snatch a brief repose. In vain, however, did I court slumber, for keen bright flashes of lightning struck through the darkness of the night and my own chamber. These were followed by peals of house-shaking thunder, and the dashing against the windows of deluging rain. The wind rose to a gale, and whistled shriekingly through the long, dreary passages of the hotel, and whenever any lull took place in the moanings of the wind and the volleys of the thunder, the brief silence was disturbed by the loud, hoarse, nautical cries of the sailors below, engaged in nocturnal embarkation and naval operations. A wakeful, weary, tossing night, therefore, was my lot, but during its long and slowly dragging hours I often lifted up my thoughts in thankfulness to him who had hitherto watched over me, and had enabled me to serve him, though but feebly, at home and abroad.

The morning arrived at last, but not with joy which usually cometh with the morning. The storm was still lingering; it had not passed over, but only a part of it had gone away with the night. Still the morning was so far favourable that the captain thought we might set forth without danger; and as the cargo was now all on board, and the passengers assembling on the shore, the determination to make the voyage was announced, and we all hastened on board, where we found some who had passed the sad, stormy night there, together with the proprietor of the vessel and of its cargo, who was a member of the Society of Friends. The crew was composed of Irish and Welsh sailors, some of whom understood their duty better than each other's language.

We had not long stood out to sea before we saw and felt that we had exposed ourselves to the force and fury of an increasing storm. Instead of abating, it was momentarily gathering its strength together. As we made difficult way over the swelling waves, we seemed to be only advancing into deeper and wilder elemental confusion. The white-crested billows rolled proudly and madly on; and instead of the usual green sea, we saw far before us a heaving snow-field, as it were, of white foam, with patches of dark waters between, the whole presenting the appearance of a hilly district of the land, when thick and heavy snows have fallen upon it just where the traveller is cutting his way through the white mounds and divided heaps. The rolling and pitching of the ship were most trying to those passengers who were unaccustomed to such experiences. It was impossible for such to stand upright without clinging tenaciously to handle, or rope, or side. Even the crew seemed disturbed, and their confusion of tongues became worse confounded. I and some others turned to the captain. He said little, and was too much occupied to listen to foolish and timid inquiries from landsmen. Yet we instinctively watched his countenance, and read in its passing shades or phases of animation the incentives to our own hopes or fears.

We felt what he looked; one brief word or bright glance from him cheered us; one dark frown discouraged us beyond recovery at the moment. Strange that we should so look on the countenance of man, when no mortal power could help us to escape the fury of the elements! but such is the weakness of helpless ignorance.

The daylight, struggling and scanty as it was, and had been all day, soon began to decline, and yet we had not reached our destination, or even neared it, so far as we could determine. Indeed, we ascertained that the wind was driving us in a different direction, though in what precise direction we knew not. Towards evening we descried in the distance what appeared to be a wreck, but as we approached it we found that it was a small dismasted vessel. It was rolling about helplessly, and was driven before the wind like a mere plaything of the tempest. We now sailed close to it, and discerned two human beings lashed to the remaining stump of the broken mast, with matted hair, soaked garments, bloodless faces, and apparently completely exhausted. I joined the owner of the vessel in urgently requesting our captain that he would take instant measures for saving these two miserable creatures. It may scarcely seem credible that we were opposed by the remonstrances of some fellow-passengers, who were so absorbed in anxiety for their own safety and speedy deliverance, that they would have abandoned two helpless fellow-men to inevitable destruction. Their remonstrances amounted to open accusations, when the captain, yielding to our request, and accompanied by two of his ablest seamen, launched the ship's boat, and entered it. We were then indeed in great danger, for the bold crew of that little boat were our own chief hope; and their loss would certainly be the forerunner of ours. They endangered our lives in going to rescue others.

It was, therefore, with no small solicitude that we all fixed our eyes on that little boat as it buffeted the surging billows; as it now rose like a mere cork towards the skies, and now sank like a mere sea-weed into the trough of the enormous waves. Our skill, our guides, our safety were embodied and contained in the tenants of that frail structure. They were, indeed, but men; but they were to us the best and bravest of men; for what is the storm-driven ship without its captain and its ablest seamen? At length, to our great relief, they succeeded in reaching the dismasted vessel, and in attaching a tow-rope to it, and bringing it over swelling and menacing waves to our ship's side. A dozen strong hands were stretched out towards them, and tenderly though energetically were the two exhausted men unloosened from their lashings, and lifted up into our own ship, when they immediately received all needful attention. Here, then, were two lives saved, even though this had been done at the risk of many more. Great danger makes worldly men selfish, while it awakens the sympathies of the benevolent.

But the night was to be gone through; and the thick shadows dropped down upon us as if threatening us with increased troubles. A single gleam of red sunlight streaked the dull western horizon, but no sunbeam had gladdened us throughout the day. The last visible things were the white-crested waves, and the breaking foam; all else had rapidly withdrawn into broad, deep gloom. These lighter things also at last disappeared, and then we had neither whitening foam below nor gleaming stars above. All was impenetrable and melancholy darkness.

The morning showed us again the same troubled sea, stretching far in seething confusion. But after an hour or two we were gladdened with a distant view of the Milford coast. Like a dark line it loomed upon us, and yet eluded us, for the unfavourable winds restrained us from making the haven. No considerable abatement took place in the winds. They blew almost as violently as before, and drove us towards a lee shore or rock-bound island. On such a shore no safe landing could be effected. Rocks jutted out into the sea, and those portions of them which were visible through the dashing spray too faithfully warned us of what might be expected far beyond the visible ridges, and under the breaking surf. A certain shattering and sundering of the vessel awaited us if we were driven upon those shelving and sharp projections. Yet to these very perils we were rapidly drifting, for the steersman could not now make the ship answer to the helm. The rudder had lost its command over the vessel, and the man his mastery by means of the rudder. The sea was now our master, and the word "captain" was but an empty title. Under such mad sway as this, what could our hope be? A few more minutes might consign us to that watery grave which we had dreaded for so many hours in the night, and had hoped to escape from in the morning. If we had hope the day before, and if then we obtained occasionally a cheering word from captain or crew, now we were reduced to despair, for the anchor, which was thrown out to stop our perilous drifting, failed to bite the ground, and dragged along uselessly. The steersman foreseeing our immediate peril and imminent destruction, forsook his helm, and ran along the deck crying out in piercing tones, "O God! we are all lost—have mercy upon us!"

Though all were thus thrown into visible trepidation, I had composure enough to request that all would join me in addressing one prayer to Him whom the winds and sea obey, and who alone could now hear us and save us. The majority united with me, and while we were thus engaged, some of the crew threw out another anchor, and, as if in answer to our prayer, it now caught, of which fortunate circumstance we were all made aware by the sudden check given to the vessel.

By skilful seamanship the captain was able to avail himself of this favourable opportunity, so that the ship began to wear round, and soon gliding past the jutting rocks, once more gained the open sea. The same steersman was now at his old post; his countenance betokened his relief from anxiety, and, as he returned to his helm, he exclaimed—and with what a difference of tone!—"Thank God, we are all safe!" "Thank God!" was the repetition of many lips around me,—"Thank God!" was my own, not once only, but for many a day after I had landed.

We landed at Milford that same evening. It was the evening of a Saturday, and along the landing-place were gathered several of the townspeople who had been alarmed at our conjectured danger, and had anticipated our destruction. Though we all were strangers in person, they pressed forward to congratulate us on what they rightly called our wonderful escape from shipwreck.

It may be supposed that I rose on the next—the Sabbath morning—in a very disturbed state of mind. Every one who remembers his return to land after a long or rough sea voyage, will understand that I walked with difficulty, and still imagined myself on deck and out at sea. As well as I was able, I made my way towards the church, determining to attend the service. The clergyman, who was about to do duty, overtook me, and politely requested permission to accompany me, and to accommodate me with a convenient seat. It was, however, in vain that I tried to remain, and I was compelled to vacate my seat and seek the fresh air. While walking along I began to reflect upon my escape, and to ask myself if the Divine Being designed any special benefit for myself or others by this deliverance. I had been detained from preaching to my own congregation on that day as I had intended; and for what purpose? Thus I perambulated the town, receiving kind salutations from several of the inhabitants who recognised me as one of the rescued voyagers.

I now perceived that two persons were making their way towards me. They soon addressed me, and respectfully inquired if they were right in attributing to me my own name. I acknowledged their correctness, and expressed my surprise that they had become acquainted with my name, when they confessed that they had obtained it from an inspection of the trunks and luggage landed from the packet. They proceeded to apprise me that they had been sent by the minister of the Independent Church in the town to solicit that I would, on account of his indisposition, preach for him in the evening. I accompanied them to his abode, and explained my inability to collect and arrange my thoughts, but was, by strong persuasion and earnest appeals, induced to comply with his request, though I confess somewhat reluctantly. The minister then told me that only on the previous day he had been reading in a religious periodical the account of my ordination at Kensington, and that he was struck with surprise when he was informed that a gentleman of the same name had landed from the endangered ship.

It was speedily and widely circulated through the town that one of the escaped voyagers would preach at the chapel in the evening. Some time before the hour of service the sanctuary was crowded with worshippers, many of whom, as I was informed, had never entered it before, and some indeed who had never previously been in any place of worship. The sight of the large assembly aroused me, and

I was strengthened to overcome my weariness and indisposition by the thought that it might be the purpose of the All-wise Father to overrule my recent danger and deliverance to the spiritual advantage of one or more of my hearers. To my great surprise, when I rose in the pulpit, I saw sitting before me, in two or three long pews, evidently set apart for their use, the captain and some of the passengers and crew of the vessel in which I had been tossed. My emotion was deep and almost overpowering when I gazed upon the familiar countenances of my brethren in recent perils by sea. I had looked up to the captain in the hour of danger, he now looked up to me in the hour of deliverance. In the second pew I observed the two men who had been recovered from the little dismasted vessel. There they sat looking up to me, clothed and in their right mind. Never had they expected to look on human features again; never had they hoped to set firm foot on an unmoving surface; but there they were in the midst of friends—friends made so by compassion, and ready to join with their untutored voices in the praises of him who manages the seas, and delivers the souls of those who are in great peril.

I was so deeply moved that I could scarcely proceed with the service; nor were the congregation themselves unmoved. A solemn feeling evidently pervaded the whole assembly, and it was with manifest effort that many of them restrained themselves from open demonstrations of their feelings. I preached with fervour and feeling such as I cannot describe, and I endeavoured to turn to the best and most profitable account our recent deliverance and our present mercies. I spoke of the thankfulness to which our escape should give rise; of our recent nearness to a watery grave; of our united prayer on the wave-washed deck; of our resignation even then—at least in some instances—to apprehended death;

and of the motives which the whole circumstances should supply to increased devotion to God and his service. I referred to the wonderful power of our blessed Saviour when upon the lake of Gennesareth he rebuked the winds and the waves, and they subsided into peace and calm. I exhorted my auditors most earnestly to go to him for refuge from a worse calamity than any tempest of sea and air ; and I concluded with a fervent appeal to this effect to my fellow-voyagers in particular, and my hearers in general.

When I took my seat in the coach the next morning to proceed homewards, I was warmly thanked by a number of the townsfolks who had heard me preach, and I could not but feel that some good effect would follow from my singular introduction to a strange pulpit and a strange people.

Some years afterwards the worthy minister whom I had helped called upon me at Kensington, and informed me that my Milford Haven service had never been forgotten in that town. Several of those who had not been within the chapel doors before, had afterwards become constant attendants ; and two notoriously profane characters had been so impressed by what they heard on that evening, that a work of grace proceeded in their souls, and they were then members of his church.

I have never again set foot in that town ; but although not very far short of half a century has elapsed since I was in it, I have never forgotten the service in which I was then and there engaged. Often recently have I heard the place named in connection with great improvements, an enlarged harbour, great docks, and numerous modern buildings. But all these things have little interest for me, excepting that in the midst of the mere mention of them I seem again to behold the jutting rocks outside the harbour, the assembled people on the shore, the crowded chapel, the two pews full of captain, crew, and passengers. All these adjuncts of the former time rise up before me, and awaken emotions of heartfelt gratitude to Him who delivered my soul from the lowest deep, and lengthened out my days that they might be spent in his service, and contribute, in however small a degree, to his honour and glory.

EPHESIANS.

Filial Piety Honoured.

"Honour thy father and mother; which is the first commandment with promise; that it may be well with thee, and thou mayest live long on the earth."—EPH. vi. 2, 3.

THE parental relation is a lively image of the Divine authority and tenderness, and parents ought to be honoured by their children for the sake of that resemblance, and because, under God, they have received their existence from them. This duty is not left to depend on natural affection alone, which is precarious and often decays, but is enforced by a Divine command, and that the only one in the decalogue to which is annexed a promise of recompense.

That recompense is indeed one of temporal advantage, which may be enjoyed where the performance of the duty has not been prompted by religious principle; but where such a principle has operated yet more powerfully than even natural affection, the reward will include a spiritual benediction, "life, and the favour of the Lord."

Remembered undutifulness to parents after their decease will be a source of painful uneasiness and of fruitless remorse; but the consciousness of having piously discharged this enjoined duty to them will embalm their memory in our hearts, and surround it with undying interest. When the remembrance of a long exhibition of affection is not crossed by shadows of disaffection, the departure of those whom we have loved is submitted to as a natural event; and though time heals the wounds of bereavement, it never obliterates the impressions of early and peaceful homes, of the quiet dutifulness of manhood, and the willing tribute of filial tenderness and gentleness accorded to the feebleness of honoured age.

A verification of these remarks will be found in the following simple narrative, transmitted to me by a friend, who vouches for its truth. It contains nothing extraordinary, excepting perhaps some singular coincidences, and the devout reference made by the individual who is the subject of it, to a superintending and directing Providence at every stage. In this latter respect he is but too seldom imitated even by those who do seriously review the influence of circumstances on the formation of their characters, and on the shaping of their courses in the varied paths of life.

He was born at a little town in the north, of pious parents, who brought up a family of children (of which the subject of this narrative was the eldest) in frugal comfort, without being able, however, to make any provision for future years. When about nine or ten years old, he was apprenticed in a house of business in the neighbourhood, and had a small allowance of weekly wages. His father requested him, while on his deathbed, and in the presence of the rest of the family, to take care of his mother and his brothers and sisters, when he should be no more. Observing him to hesitate, and rightly divining the cause of his unwillingness to undertake such a weighty responsibility, he added, " Promise, lad, and God will enable thee to perform the promise !"

" Then, father," said he, " I do promise."

He was thus, at the age of less than fifteen years, entrusted with a charge which was indeed a heavy burden for one so young and of such slender means; but the promise of Divine help supported him, and made the burden light. He procured, by diligent endeavours, situations for two of his brothers, and one for a sister, in a large and flourishing town at some little distance. To its precincts he removed the rest of the family in the most economical manner, and returned to his employment, hoping that by his own scanty earnings, together with those of the other branches of the family, a decent livelihood might be obtained for them all, and particularly for his beloved mother.

Thus had he proceeded, and he might have advanced farther, had things continued favourable; but it was otherwise ordered; for one day he received a letter from his sister, apprising him of the almost utter destitution which threatened them, and stating that nothing but the fear of being afterwards blamed by him for concealment could have induced her to make this unpleasant disclosure. He hastened to comfort them, but found the state of affairs even worse than he had expected. Now all his energies were aroused, and his trust in Providence was put to the proof by the exigencies of the case. He appealed to his employer, requesting to be released from his engagement, that he might, if possible, do something for himself. His master, learning the painful state of the case, generously consented, and gave up his indentures to him with a satisfactory testimony of character.

Thus freed and furnished, he sallied forth to the neighbouring manufacturing town, walking up the street early in the morning, and directing his prayer to God to open the heart of some one to employ him. It was immediately answered in this manner:—He accosted a merchant, whom he saw at the door of his counting-house, and solicited employment. At first he was replied to rather roughly, and told that he looked like a runaway apprentice; upon which he produced his cancelled indentures and his testimonial, and stated the condition of his family. The merchant's heart was now touched, and finding him willing to undertake any employment whatever, even the lowest, he installed him in his warehouse. Here, like Joseph in Potiphar's house, he proved a blessing to the family. At the close of his first week he received, to his surprise and satisfaction, one pound for wages, the master having already perceived the service he was likely to afford him. Away with a glad heart he hastened to his loved parent, and placed the produce of his industry in her hand. It was the first sovereign he had to bestow upon her, and mother and son rejoiced together before the Lord.

It may well be imagined that things began to wear a more cheerful aspect; and as he still continued to display the same industry and tact for business, and also to ingratiate himself with his master's customers, and with the travellers who called for orders, he soon rose in general estimation. It may be remarked, that all this time he was, with the rest of his family, a diligent attendant on the ordinances of religion, keeping the Sabbath-day holy, and devoting his spare time to the visiting of the fatherless and the widow, and the outcasts of society in prisons and other places, being very intent on their reformation. God's eye was upon him for good, and his blessing rested upon him while he was thus obeying him and keeping his commandments.

And now another turn took place in his affairs, of which, under Divine direction, he was not backward to avail himself. He began to think of setting up in business for himself, and his fertile mind was exercised as to the best means of procuring capital wherewith to commence his projected course. He remembered an uncle at a distance, whom he knew to be rich, but who had hitherto treated his relatives with cold indifference and neglect. The next morning saw him on the railroad to the place of this relative's residence. On alighting at the station, he saw this very man looking over the bridge which crossed the railroad to allow of a road traffic, as if awaiting some person's arrival. He quickly reached him, when his uncle impatiently inquired what brought him thither; adding, "I have been uneasy about you all night, expecting to see or hear from you, though I know not why." He was soon informed of the young man's intentions, and a loan of money was requested with much diffidence. An unseen power having prepared the way, apart from which so unusual a thing could hardly have happened, this bold request was immediately granted, and the enterprising orphan joyfully returned to commence trading on his own account. It was a singular coincidence that his former employer failed soon afterwards, and the young tradesman was in a condition to purchase the business of the unsuccessful man on favourable terms. The Lord made him to prosper in due time, and one of his brothers is now employed by him in the same concern. The other members of the family, with their mother, are well provided for, and his business, in which not less than thirty or forty hands are constantly engaged, is one of the most flourishing in the place.

It should be added, that his zeal for the honour of God's house, and his benevolent solicitude for the highest welfare of neighbouring society, knew no abatement, but rather increased, from the time of his prosperity in the things of this life. Faithful, indeed, to his promise is God to all that obey and serve him. "Trust in the Lord and do good, so shalt thou dwell in the land, and verily thou shalt be fed."

This young man might, in some sense, excusably have declined the charge entrusted to him by his dying father, but he obeyed the one parent and supported the other; and it is fair to infer that such an honourable compliance with the calls of filial duty brought down upon him the blessing of Heaven, and that on this account "*it was well with him.*"

HEBREWS.

The Spiritual Rest.

"We which have believed do enter into rest."—HEB. iv. 3.

THE apostle is here speaking of that holy peace and serenity of mind which we obtain by believing the gospel, and which may well be called the "rest" or Sabbath of the soul. This spiritual rest was prefigured by the seventh day Sabbath instituted at the Creation of the world, and by the repose of the Israelites in Canaan after the harassing journey of the wilderness. The Christian Sabbath is also an emblem of this rest, and intended to be subservient to its attainment. There will thus be the keeping of a Sabbath, both outwardly and inwardly, to the end of time.

In discoursing on this passage one Sunday morning, I took occasion to describe the nature of this spiritual blessing, as consisting in a release from the servitude of sin, and from the apprehensions of a troubled conscience; in peace with God through our Lord Jesus Christ, and in that joy in the Holy Ghost which is at once the pledge and foretaste of the joys of an eternal Sabbath.

On conversing, a few days afterwards, with one who was among the most respectable and intelligent of my hearers, he adverted to the subject of discourse, and gave me the following account of himself, which I considered worthy of being committed to writing :—

"I was originally," said he, "a costermonger, and at that time a young man of great muscular strength, but of dissolute habits. I associated with a number of loose young men, and my habits and indulgences in their society prevented me from gaining anything beyond a slender and precarious subsistence. Being of an active and enterprising turn, I resorted to several expedients for gaining a livelihood which few persons in easy circumstances would have conceived of. In this state some of my more successful acquaintances helped and recommended me; and although I should now regard such succour as providential, I then only looked upon it as singular and opportune.

"I need not tell you, sir, by what steps I was induced to become a prize-fighter. I now as bitterly deplore this fact as I once gloried in it. My physical strength was great, and by a course of training and practice I was able to attain to a great proficiency in my adopted calling, so that at length I was known in the ring as the champion of W., and there are persons, I believe, still living who could recount to you the scenes and occasions of my pugilistic victories. I am ashamed to repeat these details, but I wish you to know how great a change Divine grace has wrought in me. At the time I am now referring to, so degraded had I become, that I could not have spoken a single sentence without an oath.

"At this period in my history, a woman in humble circumstances, who since her marriage had become truly religious, came to drink tea with my wife, whom she had formerly known. I and a companion, who had become my seconder in the ring, were preparing in an adjoining room for a convivial party. We then overheard this person say to my wife, 'I am so happy, for I know that my sins are forgiven me. God has given me many tokens of this, and I have not the least fear of death, for I know that whenever I die I shall go to him in heaven.' I wondered at what we had overheard, and felt a strong desire to see a woman who knew that her sins were forgiven, and who did not fear death, and was sure of going to heaven. Such peace and assurance appeared to me most singular and unaccountable. Yet, though I longed to hear more, I felt unsuitable for such company, and was ashamed to go into the room where they were conversing. My companion, however, had no such scruples, and as he joined them, I heard the same voice talking to him, and persuading him to accompany her to chapel, and hear the Rev. Isaac Saunders preach, he being at that time the minister of the Broadway Chapel, Westminster. She also urged him to induce his friend, meaning myself, to go also. On which my companion remarked—'I do not think I can persuade him; but I know that if he once promises to go, he will do so.' 'Yes,' rejoined she, 'I believe he will; and will you promise to bring him, and not break *your* promise?' Thus urged, and scarcely considering what he said, he replied, 'I will.'

"To keep his word, the next Sunday my companion persuaded me to proceed with him to the chapel. I thought, sir, as I was walking along,—what an unsuitable place for me to be seen at! Every one present will look at me with wonder. The first thing I saw on passing through the chapel doors was a number of charity children in clean dresses and orderly array. Ah! thought I, could I be but one of them! But it is now too late for me to think of being anything that is good. I fancied everybody in the sacred building was looking at me and my companion. We both, therefore, stood in as retired a part as possible during the whole service, and declined to accept a seat, adopting every device to avoid notice. At the close of the service we heard Mr. Saunders say—'There will be a public collection here next Sabbath to defray the expenses connected with this place of worship.' I resolved to attend at that time, and contribute something to the collection.

"On the following Sabbath I was at the chapel, but only during the evening service, as I thought I could then better escape observation. My chief concern was to contribute to the collection without being recognised. This I contrived to do by passing my arm round the back of another person as we passed out, and dropping a trifle into the plate, but all the while feeling a dread of being observed.

"When the succeeding Sabbath arrived, I repaired to a church near my dwelling, and as I was going along, the wickedness of my past life flashed upon me, and my sins came to my remembrance with appalling distinctness; in particular my sins of profanity. I was so shocked at the recollection of the fearful words I had used, that I inwardly determined never to swear another oath. Strange to say, from that moment I was able to leave off the habit, and every oath seemed to fly from me, never to return.

"When I entered the church, the clergyman was standing at the altar, and reading thus :—'God spake these words, and said.' What, communed I with myself, God, the Great God speak, and speak to us! As the commandments were delivered, I found my heart condemning me deeply, and when the clergyman exclaimed, 'Thou shalt do no murder,' I was struck to the heart with the thought that of this sin I was verily guilty. I felt that the blood of some of my own countrymen might be lying at my door. I was self-convicted and full of remorse. . On retiring from church, I spoke ot my feelings to my companion, and remonstrated with him, saying—'What have we been doing? You and I have certainly been guilty of all these things, and you know we have. What is to become of us?' I was greatly troubled, but my associate was undisturbed, and attempted to soothe me by saying—'Ah, you are minding what that woman talked about; but everybody knows she is mad. You are too much of a man to be frightened by a foolish woman.' To this I only replied, 'I wish we were only as mad as she is.'

"After this I took another companion of my former days with me, to hear Mr. Saunders preach. As we listened, I trembled at the solemn truths the minister uttered, and doubted not but that they were producing a similar effect upon my fellow-hearer. On looking at him, however, I perceived to my great surprise and displeasure, that he was utterly careless, and was gazing around as if he were enjoying the novelty of the scene. This was so repugnant to my excited feelings, that, incongruous as it seems, I felt ready at the moment to knock him down.

"I now became an altered man, and was affected with deep concern for my eternal salvation. Shortly after this a circumstance occurred which I mention to you only to show the marked change that had taken place in me and in my reputation. I was sued for a tax which I knew I could not justly be compelled to pay. On my appearing before the magistrate, and the case being stated against me, I was asked to make oath that I was not liable to the tax. I scrupled to do so, and said that I had conscientious objections to taking an oath. So remarkable was this new feature in a character once so notoriously profane, and so well known even by many present was the change that had been wrought in my life, that the magistrate accepted my bare affirmation, and acquitted me from the obligation to pay the sum.

"But although I had thus become a thoroughly changed man, I do not mean to say that all at once I found peace.

On the contrary, I was for many months in great distress of mind on account of my sins, and was at times overwhelmed by a sense of their enormity. At last I opened my mind fully to the Rev. Mr. S., who met me with great kindness, and dealt with me very wisely. It was in conversation with me at this juncture that he quoted the passage from which you have just preached :—'We which have believed do enter into rest.' From that time I was filled with joy and peace in believing, and have continued to this day walking in the fear of the Lord, and in the comfort of the Holy Ghost."

I may simply add that I found upon inquiry that this good man bore a high character for uprightness and consistency of conduct. He was not only successful as a tradesman, but deservedly respected as a member of society. While he related to me the above circumstances, as he sat by his fireside in a comfortable home, and surrounded by a well-disposed family, I could not but regard him as a remarkable instance of the truth, that "Godliness is profitable unto all things, having promise of the life that now is, and of that which is to come."

―――o―――

The Faithful Promiser.

"Let us hold fast the profession of our faith without wavering; for he is faithful that promised."—HEB. x. 23.

THE following is communicated to me by the wife of a Welsh minister, who, regretting her inability to give a due impression of the scene she witnessed, observes,—" In English it seems *cold*, compared with the burning, transporting expressions in Welsh, which I myself heard and recorded at the time."

"Mrs. T——," the individual to whom she refers, "was," she says, "a member of my husband's church when thirty-two years of age. She was the child of pious parents, and early accustomed to attend the house of God. Endowed with great liveliness of fancy and powers of memory and description, she evidently made no common impression on those around her. She was fond of relating anecdotes, chiefly on religious topics, and was particularly interested in the old Welsh Puritans, with whose quaint sayings she was familiar, and she would quote them with zest while recounting their battles with the ungodly. She knew by heart large portions of the Bible, and used to delight in hearing different preachers, whose sermons she would afterwards repeat, and imitate their voices to the life. All this made her company much sought after, and might have proved injurious to her spiritual growth; but the Lord, whom she loved, took his own method of bringing her to live near to himself, and ripening her early for glory.

"On her marriage with a seafaring man, she left her native place, and came to reside at B——, where she was comparatively among strangers. Here her health soon became delicate, and, owing to her husband's avocation, she was much alone; and yet *not alone*, as her dying testimony triumphantly proved. The sickness and death of two babes, and the general failure of her own strength, often kept her from the house of God; so that she was little known even to the members of the church; but her pastor and his wife visited her frequently, and as her weakness increased, their sympathy and prayers were her chief solace.

"The last week of her life, her husband being away at sea, she earnestly longed for his return, that she might see him once more. For some days, although the doctors had given her up, she seemed unwilling to die, and prayed that

God would let her have her desire; but the day before she died her anxiety had vanished, and she was willing and longing to depart. God, however, granted her request. Her husband arrived on the morning of her last day, and she was enabled calmly to tell him all she wished.

"Of all the scenes I ever witnessed, her dying bed was the most sacred and sublime. She seemed to have *conquered* death before it approached her. I was with her the day before she died; she took hold of me with both hands, and said, 'O dear Mrs. ——, *this* is the place where religion pays for all the abuse and obloquy the world throws at us. *He is faithful that promised.* Oh, yes! he *fulfils* his promise. Paul says, "He is able to keep that which I have committed unto him against that day."' '*That day,*' she repeated several times. 'Now is *that day* with me. *He is faithful!* He never broke a promise to his children—*never.* Oh, thanks!—oh, blessed be his dear name that he ever thought of me—ever remembered me, a poor worm!' Her weak frame was then exhausted; when revived, she said, 'The blood of Jesus Christ his Son cleanseth from all sin! Oh, thanks for the blood!—it is his *precious blood* that is my *life* to-day. Oh, he is dear to me *to-day*. I should have been to-day *poor indeed* without my blessed Saviour. His blood cleanseth, and maketh us meet for the inheritance of the saints in light. You think that it is hard to bear so much weakness; and so it is: but, oh, could you see with me the glorious light yonder—*yonder*, beyond the stream of death!'

"She at this time appeared as if communicating with unseen spirits. Then gathering all her strength, which was but little, with an angelic smile she shouted, 'Blessed is he whose transgression is forgiven—whose sin is covered!—Oh, yes, *blessed!*'

"On a friend's repeating to her the text of the *then* last

Sabbath—'If children, then heirs;' 'Yes, yes,' she said, 'that *if* is not wanted to-day : we have covenanted together long ago, and *he is faithful*, I have not a *shadow of a doubt.*'

"The morning of the day on which she died, they took to her her only child, a lovely little girl of three years old. She smiled a heavenly smile when she saw her, and said, 'I once thought that I could never bear the pang of parting with her, but the Father of the fatherless is alive ; yes, yes, he is faithful ; he fulfils his promise *to me*, and *he is sure* to do the same to my child !'

"She then gave some directions respecting her funeral, and looking at her hands, she said, 'What *old friends* the body and soul have been, but they are going to part company to-day. The grave where thou art going—the *grave*, no work nor device there !' Then she seemed to rise again from the very borders of that grave, and called out, 'Oh, the better country ! Jesus, my Redeemer and my God ! Spirits of the just ! Angels ! What glory awaits me !' At this she fainted, and her friends thought she was gone ; but she again revived, and said, 'The chariot is *long* in coming ; the ship is *long* among the breakers ; but it is pleasant to be *going* into the desired haven. I am going in *full sail.*' The joy was too great for her weak body, and that moment she expired, faintly saying, 'The blood of Jesus ——,' but did not finish the sentence."

——o——

Ennobling Examples.

"Remember them which have [had] the rule over you, who have spoken unto you the word of God : whose faith follow, considering the end of their conversation : Jesus Christ the same yesterday, and to-day and for ever."—HEB. xiii. 7, 8.

THESE words recall to me in a lively manner the venerable

theological tutor of the Hoxton Academy for Ministerial Students, the Rev. Dr. Simpson, as one of those ruling ministers, or presidents among ministers, of whom the apostle speaks. They bring before me his life and character, which deserve lasting remembrance, and which might be held up as a pattern for devout imitation. For my own sake and that of others, both those who were acquainted with him, and those who were strangers to him, I would recount some particulars concerning him which hitherto have only received a brief and little known commemoration.

The character for piety, zeal, and theological acquirements which he had sustained, pointed him out as a fit person to occupy the responsible post of president. He discharged the duties of that office most laudably for many years. Though placed at the head of the institution, he was unobtrusive and retiring, and but for the high testimony to his worth borne by a succession of students, I should not have been prepared to find in him any remarkable qualities of mind. Like one of the innumerable stars in the firmament, he was content to *be* rather than to *appear* great; and he was a striking illustration of the truth that men who are intrinsically worthy of admiration receive more of it in proportion as they seem to claim less. We willingly and liberally accord our esteem where we ourselves become the discoverers of personal worth, but we are disposed to withhold it when that worth is paraded by its possessor for our commendation.

As his habits were retiring, and the cast of his mind contemplative, the students seldom saw him, excepting when he lectured to them, or presided at their repast, or solemnly led the family devotions of the whole household. Yet while engaged in his study he was accessible to all, and was ready to afford suitable advice or encouragement, or to suggest caution, or to direct studies, just as might be necessary in each case. His comparative seclusion checked familiarity, but did not prevent the growth of confidence and esteem. Though you felt you could not trifle with him, you were equally conscious that he would not trifle with you. He spoke when you wished him to speak; and he listened carefully to all details before he offered his own counsels or cautions.

Perhaps his exaltation of mind was most manifest when he led the devotion of the household, as just mentioned. It then became apparent that he had secret and continual communion with his heavenly Master; and by the fervency of his petitions, and the scriptural propriety of his thanksgivings, he often carried his fellow-worshippers with him to the very gates of heaven. At the close of these services the students would often look at one another with evident delight, and their countenances would exhibit the traces of those emotions which he had awakened by his devout and elevating exercise.

In his religious views he was well known to be most firmly attached to what are called "the doctrines of grace." To these he always gave particular prominence in his own ministrations, and inculcated upon his pupils the propriety of doing the same. He abhorred and reprobated any timidity or time-serving policy in respect to their promulgation, while his countenance beamed with pleasure as he sat and listened to a full exposition of such principles. He confessed that when young he had been a Pharisee, and that the force and experimental truth of these doctrines had overthrown his self-complacency, and humbled him to the dust. When he had thus been brought to feel his own sinfulness, they had disclosed to him the riches of mercy and grace in the Almighty Father made known to him by

Jesus Christ, and thus had enabled him to triumph in his Saviour with great joy. It was no wonder, therefore, that he delighted to advocate such truths to every listening ear, and every heart disposed to be thrilled by the emotions which pervaded his own. Nor was it surprising that most of his students imbibed the same spirit, and were kindled into zeal by the same affections.

A distinguishing feature of his conduct was self-abnegation, and this was accompanied by nobleness of mind. Indifferent to outward appearances and to luxurious appliances, he was in like manner regardless of pecuniary advantages, and appeared indeed to be incapable of forming a just appreciation of the value of money. So conspicuous were these *traits* in his character, that it was familiarly said of him, if he saw a guinea lying before him in the streets, he would scarcely stoop to pick it up; and Thomas Wilson, Esq., the Treasurer of Highbury College (which sprung out of this institution at Hoxton), himself a pattern of liberality, said of Dr. Simpson, at a public meeting, that he had never known a more disinterested man. He fully exemplified the announcement—" A good man shall be satisfied from himself."

There must have been an inexhaustible fund of goodness and kindness in his nature, since, during the long period of twenty-five years, his urbanity was as conspicuous to the last of the students as to the first. I never met with one of them who did not revere his memory. Which of them ever voluntarily occasioned him pain? Or if involuntarily any one of them did inflict pain upon him, did not that student himself suffer a bitterer pang in his own regret? How could they feel otherwise towards him, when they knew he had their personal and ministerial welfare at heart? Nothing could exceed his solicitude for their usefulness and public success; and often have I conversed with some of them now grown aged, and others now gone to meet him in the skies, on the several proofs he gave of such solicitude. Often, too, have we recalled his strong nervous phraseology, when he spoke upon such topics to particular individuals. The very peculiarities of his sayings remain with the few who survive to the present.

It was on the ground of their ultimate and lasting success, that he steadfastly opposed the withdrawal of any of his students to settle as pastors of churches before the full period allotted to their studies had expired. I myself was once in danger of yielding to a temptation of this nature, and when his consent was earnestly requested by the parties who had invited me, his reply was in his own nervous, homely style —" If he go, it shall be over my old body, for I will lay it down in his path." I received a "charge" from his lips at my ordination over the Church at Kensington, which I can never forget, and which many others long remembered. Much of the attention I afterwards met with in that official connection, I ascribe to the affectionate manner in which he addressed me and introduced me. His judicious counsels, earnest exhortations, and faithful admonitions directed aright and wisely controlled my ministerial course and public life during the whole of this my first pastorate.

After the enjoyment for a protracted period of unusually vigorous health, to which the equanimity of his disposition and the regularity of his habits mainly contributed, he was at last overtaken by a serious disease which laid him upon a bed of suffering, and from which he never rose again. His disorder was of a kind which frequently attacks men of sedentary lives and mental abstraction in their latter days. So soon as the sad tidings of his confinement to the sick chamber reached me and some other of his former students, we repaired to his bedside, both to testify our respect and affection, and also to benefit our own souls by becoming spectators of the composure, fortitude, and even holy triumph, with which he passed through the fiery trial. His disease confined him to one recumbent posture for a lengthened period, and thus serious wounds were produced in his back, which enlarged themselves more and more. Other pains aggravated these, and it is probable that none had an adequate conception of his agony, although his constant attendants could form a more accurate opinion of its severity than occasional visitors. As soon as he was solemnly warned and knew that his death was inevitable and imminent, he summoned all his mental powers and spiritual resources to meet the last enemy with Christian boldness.

About this period, he wrote, at intervals, several letters, some of which are in print, and all of which I understand were pertinent and serviceable. One of them was directed to the managers of the institution over which he presided, and entered into the qualifications necessary in his successor. Another was addressed to the students, in reply to their affectionate epistle of condolence. The Rev. George Clayton received from him a communication, requesting him to be the preacher of his funeral sermon. I myself received a letter from him, urging me to deliver the address at his funeral over his grave. I may append the conclusion of his letter to the students, as I can thereby exhibit, in his own words, the strong affection which he bore them :—

"And now, brethren, to be parted from you, whom I deem the excellent of the earth, and whom, next to God and Christ, I count my joy, boast, and glory, will be the severest trial I have ever been called to endure. The very thoughts of parting rend my heart into a thousand pieces.

"May the Eternal God be your refuge, and underneath

you the everlasting arms to bear you up and carry you honourably through the world. May you be favoured with much of the unction which teacheth all things. May your work of faith and labour of love, in preaching the gospel, be crowned with abundant success in the conversion of sinners and edification of saints in faith and hope, is and ever shall be the prayer of

"Yours, dearly beloved in the Lord,
"ROBERT SIMPSON."

I can but glance at a few of his remarkable sayings, as they were taken down by students and friends, who, with his afflicted relatives, waited upon him. His confidence as to the safety of his spiritual state never failed him for a moment. He lamented, indeed, that his bodily sufferings engaged so much of his attention, but he exulted in anticipation of the blessed issue. "More happy," was his language, "but not more secure, the glorified spirits in heaven."

"I shall go," said he at one time, "to the gates of heaven as a poor, wretched, ruined sinner, saved by sovereign grace. But when I begin to tell my tale of his wondrous love to me, methinks all the harps of heaven will be silent, and the angels, still as statues, will listen to my ascriptions.

"I was black and deformed, and the grace which has saved me was sufficient to have rescued fallen angels, had Jehovah willed it; but here I am, expecting soon to be before the throne, while millions, not so vile as I, are cast out. Ah! if Jehovah had passed me without one glance of his kindling eye, where should I have been?"

But, it may be asked, did these his adoring thoughts of free and sovereign grace lead him to be little concerned about the interests of practical godliness or personal holiness? He abhorred the idea; and once, in dictating a prayer to be made for him by one of his friends, he said, "Mind you tell God that I want to be more holy—completely so. I am going home, but," raising his voice, "I protest I would not enter into glory till I am fully prepared and fitted for it." His prayers at times had a holy familiarity in them, resembling very much those that are recorded of Martin Luther. For many months he continued at intervals thus discoursing on heavenly things to those who came to visit him, and especially to us his beloved students. At these intervals he employed his tongue in giving expression to the strong feelings and the lively hopes which animated his heart, and he spoke like one who was in the very suburbs of the New Jerusalem. The most sublime ideas, clothed in the most forcible and appropriate language, and expressed with uncommon energy, often astonished and overwhelmed those who were standing by. The glory of free and sovereign grace, especially as displayed in his own salvation, was his constant theme—the matchless love of God in Christ Jesus, the certainty of his final triumph over death, the unbounded and glorious felicities of the heavenly world, were the topics on which he would expatiate, with an energy quite overpowering to his feeble and emaciated frame.

Once, casting his eyes upwards, he broke forth into the following spirited apostrophe—a form of speech in which he much delighted:—"O ye vaulted heavens! what are ye about? why are ye backward to praise Him? Rocks, hills, and dales, catch the sound, and reprove them for their silence!"

A large wound in his back became almost insupportable. It was in one of those moments that he said to the writer of these lines, quoting the example of Fenelon—"If the turning of a straw would alter the Divine appointment, I would not turn it." Again, he said, in a moment of excruciating pain, " My soul *disdains* to yield. O my soul, bear whatever thy Lord is pleased to lay upon thee, that God may be glorified !"

At another time,—" I am willing to die the death of a thousand martyrs, so that I might bear an honourable testimony to the truth and faithfulness of God."

One day, when several of his family were in the room, he said, " Oh that I had strength to speak what I feel ! My body, it is true, is tormented beyond measure, but the joy of my soul is transporting. Oh what must it be to dwell with Jesus in heaven, to behold his inexpressible glories, to feast on his love ? If faith can see and enjoy so much, what must be the beatific vision ? Why, the very prospect of this is compensation enough for all the pains, the groans, the dying strife of frail mortality ! Why should we refuse, and be afraid to die ? Oh yes ! blessed be his name ! I feel it, I rejoice and triumph in the thought."

Such were his prevailing sentiments and feelings, which were expressed at different times, in great variety of language, with an emphasis and energy peculiar to himself. On one occasion he broke out into the following words—" Oh, the goodness of God to the vilest of sinners ! When I climb those higher skies, I will vie with the noblest spirit around his throne in praising that grace which has redeemed my soul from the lowest hell. This shall be my song, ' Christ is all in all ; ' but, oh, eternity will be too short to sing it ! "

At another time, recovering from a paroxysm of pain, he expressed his joyful sense of ease, by saying, " Now let my soul spring forth into life, boundless life ! Yes, I shall be satisfied ; my soul, thou shalt be satisfied with seeing and enjoying."

He seemed at times as if he really saw heaven opened

with his bodily eyes; then would he speak to its glorified inhabitants, as though they would hear him and were waiting to receive him. " Here comes one," he would say, "as deserving of future torment as any of the lost, but, through the rich grace and mercy of the Almighty, having as great a right to one of your seats as any of your number."

Sometimes he was overwhelmed with a sense of his unworthiness. "What am I, a poor creature," he more than once said, "that so much concern is manifested about me?"

More than once he gave a heart-melting address to the students, charging them to preach "a *full* gospel." "Men," said he "would improve the gospel, would gild the sun; they want a *new* gospel, which is not a new one, but another. Not but what," he added, "for the savour of its truths and fulness of its discoveries, *the gospel is always new.*"

Few indeed attended his dying bed who were not the better for his counsel, exhortation, and prayers. His family in particular engaged his devout solicitude. The following prayer for them was breathed by him towards the close of his days : "O Lord! I once more pray for my posterity. Wilt thou not hear? Yes, Lord, I know thou wilt. *Bless* them! *Bless* them! *Bless* them! Fold them all in the mantle of thy covenant love. Hold them fast in thine eternal embrace—mother and children. As for me, I shall soon behold thy face in righteousness." At another time, his son-in-law, perceiving him to be in a delightful frame of mind, observed that he seemed to be favoured with a view from mount Pisgah. "Yes," replied he, " the scene begins to open upon me."

When the above relative took leave of him, on his last Saturday evening, bidding him farewell, with the expression, " Sir, you will soon enter on an eternal Sabbath." "I shall," replied the almost glorified saint, "*it dawns!*"

A few hours before his dissolution, he addressed himself to the "last enemy," in his usual strain of apostrophe, using much the same language as that of the great apostle. As though he actually saw the tyrant approaching, he cried out, with indescribable energy, "Now, have at thee, Death! Have at thee, Death! What art thou! I am not afraid of thee! Thou art a vanquished enemy by the blood of the cross. Thou art only a skeleton—a mere phantom!" and again he repeated twice, "Have at thee, Death!" Thus did he grapple in close combat with the King of Terrors, and having, like a mighty champion, defied his utmost rage, Death at last confessed him conqueror, and wreathed around his brow the garland of immortal victory.

Thus he expired, on December 21st, 1817, at the age of seventy-two, in the bosom of his family, in the scene of his labours, in the field of glory! full of days, full of honours, blessing and being blest.

Such triumphant deaths are comparatively rare in our days; but they were not rare in the days of our Puritan ancestors. Many of the ministers among them anticipated the venerable president of the Hoxton Academy in the manner of their going through life, and of their departure out of it. In a collection of the biographies and obituaries of such, in four volumes, by Walter Wilson, Esq., several such portraitures are to be found, to encourage and animate every succeeding race of believers.

I have room only to mention one of them, the closing scenes of whose life bore a strong resemblance to those of my beloved theological tutor. It is that of the Rev. Thomas Vincent, who survived the great plague of London, during the whole period of which he preached every Sabbath, at one church or other, to listening crowds, awe-struck at the surrounding devastations. He laboured afterwards at several places, the last of which was the village of Hoxton, where Dr. Simpson breathed his last. Like him, he was fearless in his struggles with the last enemy, and a more than conqueror through Him that loved him. He also apostrophised death, and chid him for his slow approach. In the same bold manner did he express his assurance of final happiness, and his ardent desire to be with his Saviour in heaven, in the presence of the holy angels.

The following are a few only of his magnanimous sayings as his days drew to an end :—" Oh, why do you keep me here from dying? Death is a conquered enemy; he has wounded my head, he hath wounded my breast (the seat of his disease and agony), but, blessed be God, he hath not wounded my conscience, and cannot touch my soul. Come on Death! where is thy bow?—where are thine arrows? Oh, come!—come! I am yet in the body—yet on earth ; but it is heaven, heaven I long to be at. Dear Jesus (he said), come and take me away. I have no business here. My work is done—my glass is run—my strength is gone ; why should I stay ? Oh come and take me to thyself. Give me the possession of that happiness which is above—the vision of thyself—perfect likeness of thyself—the full fruition of thy bliss, without intermission and without conclusion."

These were uttered at intervals, and towards the close he again broke forth, saying, " O blessed Jesus, come!—come down to me or take me up to thee! I am in thine arms!" After a pause, one observing him to be in the last conflict, inquired how he felt. Collecting all his strength, he shouted, " SAFE!—UPHELD IN THE ARMS OF A MEDIATOR!"